Two Countries

My Taiwanese American Immigrant Story

Li-pei Wu

TWO COUNTRIES: My Taiwanese American Immigrant Story

GGW Impact Publishing, Laguna Niguel, California

Author services by Pedernales Publishing, LLC.
www.pedernalespublishing.com

Cover design: Eric Labacz

Publisher's Cataloging-In-Publication Data

Names:	Wu, Li-pei, author.
Title:	Two countries : my Taiwanese American immigrant story / Li-pei Wu.
Description:	Enhanced English edition.	Laguna Niguel, California : GGW Impact Publishing, [2022]
Identifiers:	ISBN: 979-8-9860502-8-7 (paperback)	979-8-9860502-9-4 (hardcover)	979-8-9860502-7-0 (eBook)	LCCN: 2022909246
Subjects:	LCSH: Wu, Li-Pei.	Taiwanese--United States--Biography.	Immigrants--United States--Biography.	Bankers--Biography.	Taiwan--History--20th century.	Zhongguo guo min dang--Taiwan.	Taiwan--Politics and government--20th century.	Taiwan--Politics and government--21st century.	Social action--Taiwan--21st century.	Taiwan--History--Autonomy and independence movements.	Democratization--Taiwan.	LCGFT: Autobiographies.	BISAC: BIOGRAPHY & AUTOBIOGRAPHY / Cultural, Ethnic & Regional / Asian & Asian American.	BIOGRAPHY & AUTOBIOGRAPHY / Social Activists.	BIOGRAPHY & AUTOBIOGRAPHY / Political.
Classification:	LCC: DS799.82.W8 W8 2022	DDC: 951.24905/092--dc23

Printed in the United States of America

v20

CONTENTS

Two Countries

My Taiwanese American
Immigrant Story

PREFACE

The words "Taiwanese American" evoke a well of feelings deep in my core. They mean so much more than a place of origin or an ethnic identity. They represent the struggles and atrocities my family and I faced as Taiwanese living in Taiwan under Japanese and Kuomintang (KMT) rule. They represent the challenges and opportunities I embraced as a fresh immigrant in the US. When I landed in America, I changed the course of the Wu family legacy I will pass on to my two sons and their children.

I have lived a unique life. From a simple upbringing in a small village in Taiwan, to fleeing to America in 1968 to avoid repercussions from the KMT, to becoming a successful commercial banker, and finally back to Taiwan thirty-six years later in my golden years to serve as senior advisor to two of the last three presidents, it has been a fulfilling life. And how many people can say they have been Japanese, Chinese, Taiwanese, and American? I was born in Taiwan under Japanese occupation and rule. We were forced to speak Japanese, use Japanese names, and adopt Japanese customs. My family had been in Taiwan for generations, but I was forced to call myself Japanese throughout my childhood. After World War II, Taiwan was placed under the control of the Republic of China's Nationalist Party, the KMT. I was eleven when the KMT took over and the Taiwanese were forced to speak only Mandarin and call ourselves Chinese. I experienced Taiwan's White Terror period, when the KMT imprisoned or killed anybody who spoke out against the government.

It wasn't until I was thirty-three years old, when I immigrated to the US, that I experienced the taste of freedom. I learned to speak English and embrace American customs. For the first time in my life, I chose my nationality. I proudly became an American citizen, making the US my home for almost four decades. I marveled at the tremendous opportunities and freedoms my adopted country afforded but never forgot the plight and oppression of the Taiwanese people in my birth country.

When I set foot on US soil, I was fleeing persecution by the KMT, not knowing what kind of life I would have in America. But I found opportunities in the US which would never have materialized if I had stayed in Taiwan. Through hard work and perseverance, I became a successful commercial banker in Alaska, rising to the most senior management of the largest banks in the state. I then became CEO of General Bank in Los Angeles, turning it into one of the most profitable in the US, as cited by *US Banker*. Less than eight years after I joined General Bank, it was ranked number one for its return on equity among all American banks by the *Economist* in April 1990. I was honored to have been acknowledged for my work, including an invitation by President Clinton and Vice President Gore to participate in the 1995 Pacific Rim Economic Conference and being named the 1998 Ernst & Young Entrepreneur of the Year.

While I am humbled by all my successes as a banker, my greatest passion has been and continues to be advocating for an independent Taiwan. As a Taiwanese American, I've seen how the principles of freedom and democracy have impacted the US. I want that for the people in Taiwan. That is why I have spent my time and resources establishing organizations like the Taiwanese American Citizens League and the Formosa Foundation. These organizations were created to promote stronger Taiwanese identity and strengthen US–Taiwan relations. In 2004 I followed my heart and moved back to Taiwan to serve as senior advisor to President Chen Shui-bian, hoping to help the Taiwanese people in their ongoing fight for democracy.

Taiwan has set an example for the international community on how a young democracy can flourish. This road hasn't been smooth by any means, but the democratic principles that have taken shape in the last three decades are now ingrained. Yet it remains fragile because of external threats from China and internal political instability. We must do everything we can to protect Taiwan and what she stands for. I have been fortunate to have lived an American dream beyond imagination. My deepest hope is that I will one day be able to live my *Taiwanese dream* and see a truly sovereign, independent Republic of Taiwan.

My story is one of great love for both the US and Taiwan. I am grateful for the chance to tell it. Thank you to Shannon Hu and Lyn Liao for their help with translations and editing. And special thanks to my friend, Julie Lee, and my son, Gene, without whom this book wouldn't have happened. I wrote this book for my children, grandchildren, and their progeny who have known no country other than the US. I hope my book will shed light on how our family came to be Americans. I hope my love for Taiwan will live on in them as they raise their families in the US. This book is also for Taiwanese and Taiwanese Americans. I hope they will learn about and take pride in the amazing achievements of Taiwan and the people who made those achievements possible. For everyone else, I hope you find inspiration in my story—that of a Taiwanese boy of humble means who achieves success in America.

Dacheng, 1934.

On September 9, in a small town in central Taiwan, I made my appearance in the world. The town's name literally translates to "big city." Ironic, since even today there is only one main road, a little over one hundred yards long. When I was a child, it was nothing more than a pebble pathway. Sparsely populated, with about twenty or so small businesses and residences lining the street, it was clear to me even as a child that Dacheng was a backcountry village.

I never understood why my ancestors chose to settle there when they emigrated from Quanzhou, in the Fujian Province of China, in the mid-1800s. Dacheng sits in the desert area of the Shoushui River, which flows into the Taiwan Strait. Its landscape is desolate, made worse in winter when the northerly winds blow loose sand straight into the faces of hapless pedestrians. I remember the sting of that sand against my face and the grit that would fill my mouth if I forgot to close it.

I spent most of my youth roaming the farmland near my home and playing mahjong with adult relatives and neighbors. I didn't dream of opulent mansions or fancy cars. After all, I was just a poor country boy, the third son in a family of five children—four boys and one girl. I never could have imagined then that I would spend the better part of my adult life in the US, raise a family in Alaska, and become a successful businessman. Thus, the day I left Taiwan—at age thirty-three, to begin a new life as a graduate student in the Midwest—marked the beginning of an adventure that held limitless possibilities. And while I tend not to reflect too much on the past, I do believe my humble upbringing had a direct impact on how I approached life and where that life took me. This is my story.

PART I

ADVERSITY MAKES STRANGE BEDFELLOWS

Chapter One

THE RISE AND DECLINE OF THE "KINGS OF THE OIL MILL"

My great-grandfather was the one responsible for the Wu family's reputation of being very prosperous in Dacheng. We had hundreds of clansmen and owned approximately 1,700 acres of land. He created a small fortune when he saw an opportunity in farming and peanut oil production.

Although vast, much of our land was not arable because of the sandy soil and unpredictable weather. More valuable crops like rice were not sustainable, so my great-grandfather focused on peanuts, yams, corn, and sugarcane. He supplemented the income by opening a peanut oil mill, which processed not only our family's peanut crops but those of most of the adjacent farms. Despite its small size, the oil mill could process vast amounts of peanuts. Peanuts and peanut shells were heaped outside the mill like small mountains, visible from miles away. We became so well known for our peanut oil mill that we were dubbed the "Kings of the Oil Mill."

I'm sure my great-grandfather had aspirations for the Wu empire to continue thriving long after his lifetime. Unfortunately, by the time I was born only two generations later, most of the family money was gone. I was able to piece together the key reasons why our fortune evaporated so quickly from the stories that my grandfather and father told me.

My great-grandfather was a very capable and disciplined businessman. My grandfather, Wu Lian-de, inherited his father's traits and grew our resources significantly to make us one of the wealthiest families in the area. Even under Japanese rule, our family prospered during the early part of the twentieth century.

But all this changed when Japan made significant investments in the sugar industry, hoping to make Taiwan the world's largest sugar producer. Powerful Japanese sugar companies colluded with Taiwanese officials and business conglomerates to set sugarcane prices artificially low so that their sugar would be very competitive on the global market. This drop in price endangered the livelihood of the hardworking farmers in Dacheng and nearby Erlin.

Lin Ben Yuan Sugar (LBYS) was one of these conglomerates notorious for exploiting farmers through unfair crop acquisition and procurement practices. Most of my family's land was designated as harvest areas allocated to LBYS, meaning we and the tenant farmers who leased land from us were obligated to sell to LBYS. Our family lost revenue from the depreciating crop value as well as the rent collected from the tenant farmers. My great-uncle, Wu Wan-yi, the mayor of Dacheng, partnered with the mayor of Erlin and a physician, Shu Shue, to mobilize two thousand sugarcane farmers to lodge a protest against LBYS, but to no avail. From that moment, Wu Wan-yi was labeled by authorities as a dissenter and collaborator with the farmers.

On October 22, 1925, tensions boiled over after the farmers' pleas to LBYS and the other Japanese companies fell on deaf ears, even when the farmers stopped LBYS from harvesting the sugarcane in protest. Desperate because the Japanese companies had hired replacement workers and used Japanese police to protect them, the farmers pelted the police and workers with rocks and sugarcane, resulting in several injuries to the policemen.

This event, known as the Erlin Sugarcane Farmers Incident, instigated a swift and harsh crackdown against the farmers. Japanese authorities began a witch hunt to extort confessions from arrestees through inhumane interrogations. Several farmers were physically disabled, and many suffered mental distress to the point of suicide. Altogether, twenty-four were sentenced to months in prison. This incident also marked the beginning of the economic downfall of the Wu family.

In the aftermath of the Erlin Sugarcane Farmers Incident, my great-uncle was arrested for protesting against these Japanese companies. Our family did everything they could to get him released. Some even went to Japan to petition the Japanese national assembly. In the end, we were forced to sell more than half of the land that had been in the family for over two generations in order to pay for Wu Wan-yi's mounting legal expenses. This was devastating for my family, emotionally and economically.

My father told me a story about this time that I will never forget. My grandfather had to approach another prominent landowner, the Lin family in nearby Wufeng, to negotiate a sale of a plot. They had always expressed interest in our land. The Lins sent an entourage of inspectors who went over the property with a fine-toothed comb. They hemmed and hawed and, in the end, gave a quote far below the market price because they knew how desperate my family was. With no choice, my grandfather accepted the offer.

As my great-uncle's legal expenses continued to pile up, my grandfather had to invite the Lin family to inspect another parcel of land. Interestingly, the Lins had a complete change of attitude this time—there were no property inspectors and no complaints. The two sides quickly agreed on the same price as before and inked the deal.

My father, then in his teens, witnessed the transaction and was puzzled by this about-face. He asked the Lin family why, and at first, Mr. Lin was reluctant to answer. But he finally responded with a coy grin. "Simple. The first piece of land your father sold us was undoubtedly the worst of all your plots; therefore, this one must be of higher quality. At the same price, why waste time and bother with another inspection?"

This was the first business lesson I ever learned, and it also showed me how difficult those times were for my family. Misfortune continued to befall the Wus. As the eldest son, my father, Wu Yin-shi, inherited a large portion of the estate—approximately thirty acres. Traditionally, Taiwanese families relied heavily on the eldest son to manage the family business. My father, however, did not grow from the same tree as my grandfather and great-grandfather. He was a dreamer instead and showed little interest in the business. In his youth, he had hopes of attending college in Japan. But my grandfather demanded that he take on his family responsibilities.

My father did manage a daring escape to Japan once, only to be promptly escorted home by my grandfather's security guards. Having failed at fulfilling his dream of studying in Japan, he settled in Dacheng and married my mother, Hsiao Jiao-mei. But as much as he tried to be the patriarch and oversee the family business, he simply didn't have the desire or the aptitude. The land he inherited should have provided us with good rental income, but under his management, the family continued to bleed money.

Ironically, my mother was extremely shrewd, a natural business-woman, but because of Taiwan's archaic familial hierarchy at the time, she played the dutiful wife and deferred all matters to my father. Imagine what would have happened if our family fortunes had been left in the capable hands of my mother! As a quintessential scholar and dreamer, my father, instead of focusing on the practicalities of business and taking care of his family, spent most of his time on cultural pursuits. He was a patron of the local arts community and even invested in a bookstore that published poetry collections and news bulletins released by the Taiwan Cultural Association. Needless to say, he never recovered his capital from these projects.

Our family's financial situation worsened soon after I was born in 1934. WWII reached the Pacific when I was in elementary school, and the US Armed Forces launched occasional air raids against military and industrial targets in Japan-occupied Taiwan. Most sugarcane production halted, LBYS shut down, and tenant farmers dropped off unsellable crops at the back of our house as payment for their leases. The stalks of sugarcane piled up and formed a small mountain in our backyard.

The circumstances that led to the fall of the Kings of the Oil Mill and our family's continued financial loss were equal parts self-imposed, bad luck, and the unscrupulous actions of others. I sometimes wonder whether my life would have been different if I had been born with a silver spoon. Would I have accomplished what I have if I had been born into privilege? It's impossible to answer, but I do know that my childhood and family circumstances shaped the way I approached opportunities and adversity—with zeal and tenacity.

Chapter Two

THE APPLE DOESN'T FALL FAR FROM THE TREE

I grew up in a household filled with strong personalities, tracing back to my grandfather's generation. They spent years resisting the oppressive Japanese authorities, cementing the rebellious streak in the Wu family. As a child, I heard countless stories of my grandfather standing up against Japan's assimilation programs. My family also spoke proudly of my great-uncle, Wu Wan-yi, for his part in the protest against the large sugar companies. My siblings and I all inherited this rebellious nature. We had very different personalities, but we were united in our lack of regard for authority figures.

My eldest brother, Wu Wen-pei, was eight years my senior. At a very young age, he was diagnosed with bone tuberculosis, which affected his spinal growth. My parents took him everywhere to seek medical attention, but the condition wasn't treatable at that time, so the doctor tried to reduce the effects of the ailment by having Wen-pei lie in a body cast all day long. Being constrained like that was obviously difficult for a young boy, but Wen-pei never let his condition bring his spirits down. He was always involved with family events, even though he couldn't participate fully, and kept up with what was happening in Taiwan. In spite of his illness, he became a successful small business owner in Dacheng.

Wu Shu-pei, my second-oldest brother, was two years older than me. He was the most well-rounded of all my siblings. He was athletic, made friends easily, and excelled academically. He was perhaps the most intellectually curious in my family, which served him well in school but ultimately led to his tragic fate at the hands of the Kuomintang (KMT). I think of the talent he had as a young man and can't help but feel his is a story of lost opportunity and wasted potential.

My younger brother, Wu Wuo-pei, was two years younger than me. Wuo-pei was not particularly strong academically, but he had boundless energy to play sports and hang out with friends. His enthusiasm sometimes got him into trouble, especially when he was drinking, so he channeled that energy toward his favorite sport, boxing. I learned to love the sport by watching Wuo-pei in the ring.

The youngest and lone girl in the family was Wu Ji-chen (Jane), six years my junior. Although Jane was a very good and obedient daughter, she also exhibited a rebellious streak as a young adult. My father wanted my sister to move back to Dacheng after college to become a teacher, but that was not the life she wanted. She ultimately worked at a Japanese trading company in Taipei. This work opened her eyes to opportunities abroad, and she decided to emigrate to the US with her fiancé. Going against our father's will was not easy. I recognized a kindred spirit in her, though, and was able to smooth things over with our father. Jane returned the favor years later when she helped me settle into my new life as a graduate student in the US.

As for me, I didn't have quite the intellectual curiosity of Shu-pei, nor the athletic brawn of Wuo-pei. I spent much of my youth somewhat sickly from various ailments. Because of my health, my mother would give me the better portions during family meals. Sometimes Jane would complain that I was getting preferential treatment, but that didn't stop my mother from giving it or me from accepting it.

Even though my mother was partial to me during meals, when it came to punishments, it was the exact opposite. I always seemed to be the one with a target on my back when she was on a rampage. I think the reason for this was simple: sheer stubbornness on my part.

One day, my mother sent Shu-pei to the market for some tofu. Shu-pei did as he was told but lost track of time. When he returned hours later, my mother was on the warpath. She grabbed her cane, which meant she was not fooling around. Shu-pei, with his athletic skills, vanished as soon as he saw her. Wuo-pei also disappeared. With no one else around, she grabbed the nearest body—mine—and brought the cane down hard on my bottom. I yelled in between smacks, "Why are you beating me? I didn't do anything wrong!" My mother, clearly flustered, claimed it was for something I had done a few days earlier. Even at a young age, I refused to accept this and grew angrier at the unfairness. I stubbornly said, "Fine, I can take it as long as you can give it!" My mother, who was just as stubborn, carried on.

Despite these instances of unreasonableness, my mother had a profound influence on my life. Strong and decisive, she was the polar opposite of my father's sentimentality and mellowness. Her formal schooling ended when she was in first grade, but her self-motivation was astounding, and she sat in on a home school program with her two brothers to study sinology. She would read whatever she could get her hands on—poetry, novels, newspapers. Although my mother never had the opportunities of her male counterparts, through hard work and perseverance, she taught herself and her children how to be independent thinkers.

Chapter Three

REBELS WITH A CAUSE

When WWII came to an end, Japan's defeat meant it had to vacate Taiwan after fifty years of occupation. In my household, the imminent departure of the Japanese was welcome news. The last twenty years of the occupation had hit my family and others in Dacheng and surrounding areas particularly hard.

On August 15, 1945, when Emperor Hirohito was about to broadcast an announcement of the Imperial Rescript on the Termination of the War, my father rushed home from work. He and my two older brothers huddled around the radio in the living room. I ran back and forth between the living room and the kitchen with my good friend, John Cheng, to update our mothers, who were preparing lunch. Everyone erupted with joy when Hirohito officially announced Japan's "unconditional surrender."

My grandfather was nineteen when China's Qing Dynasty ceded Taiwan to Japan in 1895. He remained loyal to Qing and never acknowledged or accepted Japanese rule. In the early years of the occupation, Japanese colonists used food rations and other resources to coerce the Taiwanese people to speak Japanese and change their family names to Japanese names. My grandfather, proud and determined, never acquiesced to this. He was overjoyed when we learned that under General

Order No. 1 between the United States and Japan, Taiwan was to be placed under the control of the Republic of China's (ROC) Nationalist Party, the KMT.

Right after Hirohito's announcement, my father was so happy he scrounged up the suit and top hat he wore on his wedding day and launched into a triumphant parade up and down the lone street of Dacheng, celebrating the whole afternoon. That evening, my family had a massive feast to celebrate. My grandfather was bedridden, in the terminal stage of liver cancer, but he insisted we prop him up in his sickbed so he could join in the festivities. The disease had ravaged his body, but on this day, his gaunt and sallow face was content. He smiled and said, "I was born a Qing citizen, and I'll die a Qing citizen." He passed away a week after.

What my grandfather didn't realize was that the Qing Dynasty he remembered no longer existed. In its place were the ROC and the KMT. We celebrated this changeover naïvely, assuming things would be better with the Japanese gone.

Chen Yi, the appointed governor-general of Taiwan upon the KMT's takeover, arrived in Taiwan on October 24, 1945, to receive the departing governor-general's document of surrender. The people of Taiwan cheered Japan's departure, unaware of the rude awakening that would follow this reunion with the ancestral land.

My father had grown up under Japanese rule and seen firsthand cases of systemic discrimination against the Taiwanese. Like my grandfather, he never accepted Japan's authority, but unlike my grandfather, he had no particular allegiance to Qing. My father embraced the idea of Taiwan returning to the new ancestral land—the ROC. He envisioned China under the ROC to be this romantic and idyllic country with a rich history and boundless opportunities. Even as a young adult, he dated his letters using the Chinese dating system instead of the more common Japanese format. My father, like many of the Taiwanese of his generation, assumed the bullying and prejudice they had endured over the past fifty years would be a thing of the past.

At the same time, China was facing an existential crisis of its own, making the occupation of Taiwan a low priority. The KMT, the controlling party of China, led by Chiang Kai-shek, was on the verge of a full-blown civil war with China's opposition party, the Communist Party of China (CPC), led by Mao Zedong. Chiang's focus was on China, not Taiwan.

When the KMT soldiers arrived in Taiwan after WWII, they did not make a good first impression. Dacheng was too far out of the way to see this firsthand, but we heard about the unsophisticated soldiers who were wearing tattered clothing and straw sandals while carrying threadbare blankets and dented pots and pans. They were amazed by the running tap water installed by the Japanese during their occupation. The KMT soldiers bought similar faucets and installed them without bothering to see if their homes had piped-in water. When they turned on the faucets and saw no water coming out, they complained and even turned violent against the hardware shop owners. A far cry from the Japanese army, who, despite their defeat, were elegantly dressed and courteous during the surrender and handover presentation.

The KMT was nothing short of ruthless and corrupt—the embodiment of evil. Within months of the handover, the Taiwanese illusion of a harmonious reunion with the ancestral land quickly unraveled. There were arbitrary seizures of private property and violations of personal liberties. There was no due process or political participation of any kind for the Taiwanese. We had once again become second-class citizens in our own country.

Chapter Four

FEBRUARY 28, 1947
(228 MASSACRE)

Less than two years after the KMT took control, the tensions between the Taiwanese and the KMT reached a boiling point. On February 27, 1947, a woman was accused by KMT authorities of selling contraband cigarettes, leading authorities to harass and beat her. People witnessing this offense against one of their own began to gather and protest. A KMT officer, facing a group of angry onlookers, shot his gun into the crowd, killing one innocent bystander. This incident became a rallying cry for people throughout Taiwan.

The next day, more protestors gathered, and KMT soldiers, instead of trying to de-escalate the situation, fired upon the crowds. Taiwanese protestors took control of a radio station, broadcasting news throughout the island of the violence perpetrated against civilians. Momentum quickly grew, and people all over Taiwan, already disillusioned with the KMT, organized to protest the brutal authoritarian regime. Governor-General Chen Yi called for more military personnel to quell the uprising. The military that was supposed to protect Taiwan indiscriminately brutalized and killed innocent civilians throughout the day. All told, on February 28,

1947—perhaps the most infamous day in Taiwan's history—and in the days following, approximately thirty thousand Taiwanese lost their lives.

Since Dacheng was far removed from the more populous areas of the country, we were spared much of the horrific violence. My father and other adults listened anxiously by their radios, but there was little information available. What they did know, however, sent chills down their spines. Many of the island's elite—painters, lawyers, professors, and doctors—were among those killed. The KMT executioners seemed to target the educated, a common strategy to stamp out any future uprisings.

I will never forget my family's and community's fear and dismay. Although we didn't experience any direct violence in Dacheng, our family did have a few sleepless nights when my brother, Shu-pei, went missing. He was living and attending high school fifty miles north of Dacheng in Taichung, the largest city in central Taiwan. We tried to contact him, but communication with the city was sporadic. We knew that Taichung was one of the epicenters for the crackdown, but we didn't know the extent until my brother returned home a few days later.

When the violence first began, upperclassmen at Shu-pei's high school, Taichung First High, joined the resistance against the KMT soldiers. The school was shut down and essentially abandoned during the protests. Transportation was at a standstill—all roads in and out of the city were barricaded, so Shu-pei had no way of returning to Dacheng. He decided to hole up at the school, but he soon ran out of food. He had no choice but to find a way out of the city and walk home. He took several roundabout back roads, all the while avoiding KMT troops. The story he painted of the scene in Taichung was horrific. He saw KMT troops indiscriminately shooting Taiwanese people with bodies strewn all over the streets.

As we learned more about the 228 Massacre, our fear soon turned to rage. My father, who had such high hopes that this KMT regime would be good for Taiwan, was bitterly disappointed. He was normally a kind and gentle soul, but he was forever changed. His hatred of the KMT and Chiang Kai-shek was deep and profound, shaping and influencing my family's defiant nature for years to come.

Chapter Five

A SEVENTEEN-YEAR-OLD POLITICAL PRISONER

The aftermath of the 228 Massacre stoked two emotions among the Taiwanese—fear and rage. We now had a true glimpse of the kind of government that was overseeing our lives. The KMT was ruthless and would stop at nothing to maintain its control over Taiwan. The use of military force to murder Taiwanese citizens was something unimaginable and created an all-consuming fear in us. This was exactly what the KMT was hoping for.

As an authoritarian regime, institutional fear was the KMT's greatest weapon and highly effective in maintaining order. Those in power used whatever means at their disposal to root out any suspicious activity that threatened their authority. By 1949 the civil war in China was winding down—the CPC was on the verge of victory over the KMT, and Chiang Kai-shek and his ragtag troops had no choice but to retreat to Taiwan. Fearing another bout of internal insurrection, Chiang immediately imposed nationwide martial law in Taiwan, which would last for almost forty years. The decades following the 228 Massacre were known as the White Terror, during which the Taiwanese people lived under constant fear of persecution. Incarceration or death was common for anybody that spoke up against the party.

Like most Taiwanese, the outrage my family felt after the 228 Massacre was a deep wound that never seemed to heal. The anger was compounded by the sense of helplessness that surrounded us. *What should we do? What can we do?* These questions constantly haunted me and my family, but there were no obvious answers. We felt fortunate that Dacheng was far enough out of the way that we didn't have to endure the spectacle of KMT soldiers roaming the streets. In the early years after the 228 Massacre, we weren't directly affected by authoritative atrocities. That all changed when Shu-pei returned to Taichung and became a target of the KMT.

Shu-pei had enrolled in the prestigious Taichung First High School after he graduated from Dacheng Elementary School. At the tender age of thirteen, he would be living away from home for the first time in his life. Going away to school, even at a young age, was common in those days because educational opportunities were scarce—one simply went where the best schools were.

The 228 Massacre left an indelible impression on Shu-pei. He was a fifteen-year-old high school student, young, curious, and naïve. Being an eyewitness to the KMT's murderous brutality should have had him retreating in fear, but he became even more curious about how governments were supposed to protect the interests of their citizens. After his high school reopened, it was naturally abuzz about the horrific incident.

The student body and teachers came from diverse backgrounds, many of whom were interested, like Shu-pei, in exploring the economic, philosophical, and sociological theories of communism. Shu-pei's interest in China and communism was piqued as he listened to and participated in the discussions of his peers and lecturers. He was particularly keen to understand how Chinese communist revolutionaries, with a militia of merely two hundred to three hundred thousand, managed to best Chiang Kai-shek's army of two million. He devoured any book discussing the birth of communism in China and the strategies of the Communist Party for spreading this philosophy. It was understandable that young people like Shu-pei were attracted to this way of thinking. The theories behind communism are romantic and idealistic. It evokes an image of a utopian society where citizens and the state work together for the good of all. Nobody would be left behind; everyone would have a fair share. Why wouldn't young people, especially those who grew up poor, think this was a better option than the so-called democracy that the KMT extolled?

The Study Group and the Black Jeep

Shu-pei joined a study group in his later years in high school and dove headlong into essays and publications written by famed Chinese authors such as Shen Dehong, Ba Jin, and Lu Xun. He also read international publications such as the *Observer*, *Life*, *Time*, and *Reader's Digest*, which provided unique social commentary on wide-ranging topics. While Shu-pei displayed tremendous intellectual curiosity, he didn't have much practical life experience. He was too young and naïve to understand communist ideology beyond the theory. I don't think he truly understood the risks he and his study group were taking.

Under Japanese rule, Taiwanese citizens had a certain amount of freedom to explore different political ideologies. Two prominent political organizations that were counter to Japan's political system, the Taiwan Cultural Association and the Taiwan Communist Party, were generally left alone by the Japanese as long as no laws were broken. The KMT, on the other hand, was not nearly as forgiving.

The KMT reflected long and hard on what went wrong after its humiliating defeat at the hands of the CPC. The conclusion was that the CPC was able to heavily penetrate and influence China's population well before the civil war. The KMT believed that their defeat occurred because they hadn't taken the necessary steps to suppress this insurrection before it was too late. They would not let that happen again in Taiwan. Their solution was to systematically engage in activities, covert and overt, that would ferret out any dissent within the Taiwanese population. Shu-pei's study group and the materials they read and discussed were exactly the kind of dissenting activity the KMT wanted to quash.

Shu-pei soon learned of the risk he was taking when a handful of his study mates were arrested, including one student named Weng Chi-lin, a distant relative. We learned about Chi-lin when Shu-pei came home immediately following the arrest. He stumbled through the door, fear and shock on his face, and told us what happened. Our parents were extremely frightened. Stories of the White Terror were already prevalent throughout Taiwan, but we never imagined the KMT would begin targeting young students. The feeling of helplessness that had gripped us since the 228 Massacre reached a new level. We were all at a loss as to how we could help Chi-lin. What we didn't know at the time was that Shu-pei was also at significant risk—he never told my parents about his study group. After a couple of days in Dacheng, Shu-pei went back to school thinking that things had calmed down. My parents didn't stop him.

At that time, I was also a student at Taichung First High. I lived at an off-campus rental house only a few minutes from Shu-pei's. After Chi-lin's arrest, to be extra cautious, Shu-pei stayed at my apartment. He did his best to be watchful of unusual events and behavior, on guard against anything that might be suspicious. It was well known that the KMT had placed operatives throughout Taichung where they could monitor undesirable activities. Shu-pei even went by his house multiple times a day to make sure things were normal. After a few nights, when it appeared to be safe, he went back to his rental house on the evening of April 8, 1949.

The next day, Saturday, two strangers pounded on his front door. His housemates had left Taichung for the weekend. The landlord answered the deafening banging, and the men barged into the house. They exchanged brief words with the landlord and then proceeded to drag Shu-pei out of the house, stuff him into a black Jeep, and drive off. One of Shu-pei's friends, Lee Shi-fan, witnessed this and ran to my place to alert me.

He described in horrible detail what he had seen. It all happened so suddenly that Shu-pei didn't even have his shoes properly laced. When he crouched down to secure them, the men hovered over my brother. Shi-fan described how my brother was so scared his hands were shaking uncontrollably. Tears poured down my face as I pictured my poor brother, the fear that must have been coursing through him as he was taken away. I was in shock. I didn't know what to do next. What were they going to do with him? Would I ever see him again? What was I going to tell my parents?

Countless emotions entered my mind, but one thought was as crystal clear as the memory of that evening. I was the angriest I had ever felt in my life, and that anger was directed at one thing—the KMT. Up until then, I had never developed any deep-rooted political beliefs, but at a basic level, I believed a government was supposed to protect its people. What kind of government indiscriminately arrested citizens—teenagers, no less—and dragged them away with no explanation? This event so profoundly affected me that I vowed right then and there to do whatever I could to bring down Chiang Kai-shek and his tyrannical KMT.

From Green Island to Sindian Correctional Facility

As they had done for my great-uncle twenty-five years earlier, my family did their best to secure Shu-pei's release. This time, however, our circumstances were very different. First, we didn't even know where he was being held or what the charges were against him. We didn't know how to visit him. We didn't know his condition. We were essentially in the dark for months. Second, our family's financial situation was not good, and we had limited resources to get information or lobby on my brother's behalf. This was a very difficult time for my family, especially my father. He did his best to scrounge up whatever money he could in hopes of influencing somebody for assistance. More often than not, my unsuspecting father was cheated by con artists preying on our desperation.

Six months later, a letter from Shu-pei arrived. It was in his handwriting, but we knew the words could not be his. He wrote of his gratitude to the KMT government, thanking them for giving him a light sentence of just twelve years in prison. He explained that he was charged with a form of treason and the KMT could legally sentence him to death. Instead, they showed him leniency so that he could use his time in prison to reform his misguided ways. The letter provided some relief because we finally knew that Shu-pei was alive. But we also realized the KMT must have done something horrific to him to coerce such words.

Gradually, more information from the night of the arrest trickled in. We learned that the two strangers who had taken Shu-pei were members of the Military Intelligence Agency—plainclothes agents of the KMT. Altogether, sixty-two citizens were arrested that night, mostly students and teachers, all of whom would be spending the prime years of their lives behind bars.

Shu-pei was incarcerated on Green Island, a prison twenty miles off the east coast of Taiwan. It was the primary penal colony for political prisoners and dissidents during the martial law period and notorious for its poor treatment of prisoners. Visiting the prison was almost impossible because there was virtually no transportation to or from the island. My family was once again helpless. Shu-pei was one of thousands of prisoners at Green Island. We had no financial means, no influence, no resources of any kind that could help him. It would be years before I saw my brother again.

There were numerous stories about Chiang Kai-shek and the KMT using Green Island as a propaganda tool, touting its success at rehabilitating dissidents, particularly former soldiers of the People's Republic of China (PRC). By 1954, Chiang Ching-kuo, Chiang Kai-shek's son, was the director of the secret police and wanted to build his own reputation as a reeducator of prisoners. He was very interested in showing that intellectuals could also be converted into anticommunist propaganda props.

During a visit to Green Island by a US delegation, Chiang Ching-kuo tried to impress the visiting Americans with his reeducation techniques. The delegation, led by Major William Curtis Chase, was to be treated to a skit performed by a group of Taiwanese prisoners where they would profess their love of the KMT and hatred of the communists. The rehearsal had gone as planned, so Chiang was confident Major Chase would be duly impressed. When the curtain went up, the prisoners conveniently forgot their lines and did nothing but stand at attention. Humiliated, Chiang rooted out the six leaders of the thespian revolt and transported them back to Taiwan for punishment. Shu-pei was among the six.

A few years into his sentence, Shu-pei was transferred from Green Island to a military prison in Sindian, a small district in Taipei County. I was living in Taipei at the time, so I finally had a chance to visit him regularly. My brother was still a voracious reader, so each week I would bring books on a variety of topics. Reading was his favorite pastime in prison, making him quite a scholar even though his formal education ended before he graduated from high school. My first few times visiting, we spoke through a tiny grilled window in a cement wall. We could see each other, but it was difficult to have a real conversation. Later on, as the poor human rights record of the KMT was exposed, prisoners received somewhat better treatment, and Shu-pei was able to go outside periodically to get fresh air and exercise.

On one visit, I noticed he was limping. We never spoke of his treatment in prison because I didn't think it was my place to bring it up and I suspected Shu-pei didn't want us to worry. But this time, I asked him about the limp. My brother hesitated, looking down at his leg. Then slowly, he explained how his lower leg was broken during a particularly severe beating. His voice was calm and matter-of-fact when he recounted the horror. I tried to stay as even-keeled as he was while I listened, but the sadness and anger in me were unbearable.

During another visit, Shu-pei shared with me what took place after KMT intelligence arrested him. He had never spoken of it before. They woke him in the middle of the third night and took him to a remote mountain area. The men threw him under a huge tree and said coldly, "Tell us all you know or you die right here, right now." Shu-pei was just a kid. He didn't know anything. He truly believed his life of only seventeen years was to end at that moment. The details of his experience and the inhumanity of his captors sent chills through me. What kind of government would torture a high school student for joining a study group?

I was the only one in my family to visit Shu-pei regularly. It was too difficult for my parents to see their son this way. Upon Shu-pei's imprisonment, my father also locked himself away. Prior to the arrest, he was a very social and outgoing man. He always went out of his way to help a neighbor or the community of Dacheng. After the arrest, my father rarely left the house, and the gentle nature we loved was replaced with a bitter anger toward the government. Just as the KMT had taken my brother's freedom, it took a bit of my father's spirit.

Although Shu-pei was an impressionable teenager when he went to prison, the KMT's efforts to reeducate him did the exact opposite. Instead of reforming his misguided ways, Shu-pei delved even deeper into the philosophical, social, political, and economic ideology of the communist movement. Ironically, Chiang Kai-shek's hope to quell communist thinking did nothing more than make the movement stronger. The KMT's monstrous and evil behavior pushed left-wing supporters even further left. By the time Shu-pei was released, after twelve years of the KMT's reeducation, he was a true convert, a communist patriot in every sense of the word.

Life after Prison

Shu-pei understandably had a difficult time adjusting to life outside of prison. He was close to thirty years old when he was discharged. He had never completed high school, he didn't have practical skills for any kind of job, and his prison record would follow him for the rest of his life. With Shu-pei's smarts and work ethic, all he needed was an opportunity, but as much as my family wanted to help, we simply didn't have the resources. My eldest brother ran a small pharmacy in Dacheng, and I was an entry-level clerk at a commercial bank. Neither one of us could help in a meaningful way.

With very few options left, my father urged Shu-pei to contact our aunt—my father's younger sister—to see if she could secure a job for him. Her husband, Uncle Lin, was one of my father's best friends in high school, and it was through my father that he met my aunt. Uncle Lin became a very successful doctor and ultimately built a hospital in Fengyuan, a city a little north of Taichung. Through the hospital and other investments, Uncle Lin became extremely wealthy and well known in that area.

When I was in high school, I spent quite a bit of time with Uncle and Aunt Lin, so I accompanied my brother on his visit. As we walked up to the house and said our greetings, Uncle Lin's face tightened. He left without saying a word. Our aunt was always kind to us, but we could tell she was uncomfortable. She quietly handed Shu-pei the equivalent of $125 and asked him not to visit them again. It would have been natural for my family to be offended, but my uncle and aunt's reaction was not uncommon during the White Terror period, so we didn't hold a grudge. The fear that gripped Taiwan during that time was palpable.

Since it was difficult for political prisoners to easily reenter society, many organized to form their own support groups. Fortunately, Shu-pei found such a group to help him get back on his feet. Tsai Kun-lin, a former inmate at Green Island and a classmate of Shu-pei's at Taichung First High, decided to create a magazine called *Prince*. Tsai brought Shu-pei on board to help get the project underway. My brother was later made general director of the magazine's publishing house. *Prince* had a following, but the publishing business was very tough, and it ultimately shut down.

Shu-pei gained firsthand experience in printing from that job and was able to leverage it to build his own label-printing business. He was a one-man shop. He would scooter around to meet customers, go back to his shop to fulfill the orders, and scooter again to deliver the product. Though the work was physically exhausting, Shu-pei kept at it, and ultimately, he managed to create a nice business. He continued this work for years. Along the way, he married and had four wonderful children. He's retired now, but his children and grandchildren all live near each other, so family visits are frequent.

Shu-pei was the smartest of my siblings, yet he was dealt the hardest blow. Nevertheless, his optimism and persistence pulled him through those harrowing years. I'm proud of the way he came out of this ordeal and made a great life for himself and his family.

Ode to My Political Family

Political ideology often evokes great passion, and there was nothing my siblings liked more than a good political debate. Discussions around the dinner table were lively and entertaining but often over the top. The stubborn streak that was part of our DNA and served us well in some circumstances also created tension within the family. Shu-pei, to this day, believes that communism is the ideal political and socioeconomic system. He became so entrenched in the Communist Party that when travel opened between Taiwan and China, he made frequent visits as a VIP guest of the CPC.

Wen-pei, on the other hand, did not believe in the communist philosophy at all and couldn't understand Shu-pei's attraction to it. As for me, I was more aligned with Wen-pei, but Shu-pei's plight as a young man did make me curious about certain communist theories. Ultimately, my primary focus was advocating for an independent Taiwan. As I became better known as a proponent of Taiwanese independence, Shu-pei's involvement with the CPC raised eyebrows within certain circles. There were even wild stories that we were somehow double agents, each for the other side. Of course, none of this is true. I don't necessarily agree with Shu-pei's beliefs, but I respect him and how he has lived his life. Our political beliefs are intensely personal, and we eventually decided it was best not to discuss politics at family get-togethers.

Despite our differences, the one common thread among all my siblings was our deep, unflinching hatred of the KMT. On this topic, there was no middle ground, no compromise. The experience my family endured at the hands of Chiang Kai-shek and his band of terrorists is a wound that will never fully heal.

Chapter Six

YOUNG AND WILD

When people ask me what I was like as a child growing up in a small farming town, I find it difficult to describe. It was a simple life in many ways. My family was fairly large, so my parents rarely hovered over us. The age-old debate of nature versus nurture was not relevant in my household—nature was the default. Most of the time, my parents didn't know what kind of trouble I was getting myself into.

Dinner was the one time during the day when we all came together, and my siblings and I were expected to be on our best behavior. I look back on those dinners and marvel at how much they revealed about the family dynamic. In those days, having meat as part of the meal was always special. On those rare occasions, the meat dish would be placed in front of my grandfather. My siblings and I wouldn't dare reach for a helping until our grandfather had as much as he wanted. We would watch anxiously, mouths watering as our elder ate. After what seemed like an eternity, he would rise and leave the table. Whatever meat was left was then distributed by my mother.

Shu-pei always ate his rice first and then savored the meat last. This was a perfect example of his personality, patient and deliberate in everything he did. Wuo-pei would wolf the meat down first and then finish the rice. He was always impulsive and aggressive in whatever he did. I, on the other hand, would first examine my food carefully. After some deliberation, I would enjoy the small portion of meat. As for the rice, I left it untouched. Was this a reflection of my personality? And if so, in what way? Was I a spoiled brat? I'd like to believe my parents raised me better than that. Perhaps this was an indication that even at a young age, I appreciated quality over quantity.

Like most of the children in Dacheng, I attended the local public elementary school. School was a blur for me. Taiwan was in the throes of WWII, and since we were occupied by the Japanese, the Allies sent Americans with their fighter planes and bombers to attack Taiwan almost daily. Although Dacheng was never targeted, the air raid alarms would sound whenever the planes got too close. The town would go on lockdown and, more importantly for me, the school would close. Each morning, I would do everything in my power to delay the start of the day. I did everything slowly: getting up, putting on my clothes, eating breakfast, all with the hope of hearing the blare of the siren that meant no school. Once the alarm sounded, my muscles would magically spring into action. I'd quickly throw my backpack in the corner and be off.

On those free days, I would sometimes play on the mountain of sugarcane in our backyard with the neighborhood children. We carved tunnels into the piles to stay out of the heat. Whenever we needed a break, we'd split open a sugarcane stalk and enjoy a sweet refreshment. It was a carefree time with very little supervision.

Dacheng Elementary had a rigid and disciplined structure, which was typical of Taiwanese schools. It didn't suit me. I went through the motions when it came to schoolwork, putting in just enough effort to do well, but nothing beyond that. Although school didn't hold my interest, I did have other intellectual pursuits. I developed an intense passion for reading, especially short stories and novels. A cousin who had studied in Japan and brought back a wide assortment of books translated into Japanese gave me access to his collection, which included *Top Works in World Literature*, *Complete Works of World Philosophy*, and *Best Essays of All Time*, among others. Some of them were a bit advanced, such as *War and Peace*, but I enjoyed the challenge of trying to understand such well-known works of literature. My favorite author was Mark Twain. I was drawn to *Adventures of Huckleberry Finn* and *The Adventures of Tom Sawyer* because the young lead characters were poor children who lived in a time of great oppression.

The air raids were the reason for my sporadic school attendance, but I had nobody to blame but myself for my lack of motivation. I sulked around town, wasting days on end playing in the backyard or watching neighbors and relatives playing mahjong or some other gambling game. In spite of my laziness, I received good grades, and upon the recommendation of a teacher, I registered to take the entrance exam for the middle school at Taichung First. Up to that point, things had come easily for me academically, so I didn't take the exam seriously. When I failed to earn entrance, it was a wake-up call. I always assumed I would attend Taichung First like my father and Shu-pei.

An uncle with whom I was very close warned my father that at the rate I was going, I was fated to be nothing more than a lazy bum. That didn't sit well with anyone in my family, so my father decided I needed a change of scenery. He arranged for me to transfer to an elementary school in Taichung and stay with an older cousin. At the age of eleven, I left Dacheng and moved to the big city.

The Experiment of Youth

My new school, Datung Elementary, was considered prestigious and had a reputation for enrolling students from families of the upper class in Taichung. Needless to say, as a skinny boy from a farm town most of the rich kids had never heard of, I was an easy target for bullies. The taunting and bullying started up just as the school year began, so I knew I had to do something quickly or I would always have a bull's-eye on my back.

I hatched a simple but effective plan. On the school playground, I spotted a group of five boys around my age. I studied them carefully and found exactly what I needed—one boy fairly close to my size. This was no small feat, because I was not only skinny but short in stature and not particularly strong. I snuck up behind the unsuspecting boy, tapped him on the shoulder, and without warning, punched him in the face as he turned. The first hit was strong enough to draw blood, but I hit him two more times for good measure. The onlookers gawked in silence as the boy rolled on the ground, crying in pain. Of course I knew I would be punished, but it was worth it. Coincidentally, our test scores were posted that same morning, and I happened to get the top grade. I made my mark in two ways that day, and I was never bullied again.

As my first and only year at Datung came to an end, all my classmates were busy preparing for the middle school entrance exam. When I handed in my application, I had only one selection—Taichung First High. My teacher asked, "Are you sure that's the only school you want to apply to?" I nodded unequivocally. My confidence paid off, and I did well enough on the test to be accepted into the middle school. Many of my classmates from Datung were also admitted, including the boy I had assaulted a few months earlier. Since that incident, we had become fast friends and were looking forward to attending middle school together.

In those days, there weren't many public schools in Taiwan, and good ones were especially rare. The competition for admission from elementary to middle school to high school to the university level was progressively intense. One's entrance exam score at each level was the primary factor in gaining acceptance to a good program. I had spent most of my youth hoping, and in some ways expecting, to attend high school at Taichung First. Even though I was enrolled at the middle school, there was no assurance I would be accepted to the high school. I would have to pass the entrance exam just like any other middle school student. There was, however, a policy at Taichung First whereby if your rank was high enough at the middle school, you would automatically gain acceptance into the high school without taking the entrance exam.

I, like many of my classmates, coveted this privilege, so I strove to get my grades in order. Just because I wanted one of these spots, however, didn't mean I was prepared to put in the work. In fact, I did the opposite.

In what was far from my finest moment, I convinced a friend of mine—the son of the math teacher—to steal the math exams before they were given. I naturally aced every math exam that year, but the powers above wouldn't let me profit from my dishonesty. My class ranking was just short of what was needed to qualify for an automatic acceptance to the high school. I had to take the entrance exam, after all.

On the day of the exam, karma, fate, or whatever higher power that was looking down wasn't quite finished with me. My comeuppance was due and needed to be paid in full. Things were going smoothly at first, but when I turned to the math section, my mind went blank. The pressure, my lack of preparedness, and my unscrupulous behavior all came crashing down, and I couldn't answer a thing. After the exam, I was dejected and disgusted. I had nobody to blame but myself. I finally realized my penchant for cutting corners had caught up with me and I needed to straighten up. When the scores came out, I immediately looked at the math section, and as expected, mine was the lowest in the class. But fate apparently has a forgiving nature and was willing to give me a second chance. I did well enough on the rest of the exam to get into my dream high school. My reprieve notwithstanding, I would not forget the lesson. I didn't know what kind of high school student I would be, but I vowed never to be unprepared again.

I had a few relaxing summer weeks back in Dacheng before starting high school. Most of my break was spent reading and hanging out with old friends, but something happened at the end of the summer that enabled me to enter high school in style.

One of my favorite people in Dacheng was Wu Tian-lian, the mayor and a distant relative a couple of years younger than my father. Uncle Lian was an incorrigible character. He loved gambling more than anything, especially dice. He was also perhaps the most stubborn gambler I had ever seen. When he won, he would quit the game immediately, inciting the ire of the other players for not giving them a chance to recoup their losses. When he lost, he would keep playing until he won, pressuring the other players to participate for as long as it took. This system produced plenty of interesting moments, and for one game, I was fortunate to be on the receiving end of Uncle Lian's stubbornness.

It happened in a dice game about a week before I was to head off to high school. Uncle Lian's luck that night was not good, and he lost his stake rather quickly. True to form, he insisted the game continue and went back to his house for extra capital. By the time he returned with a fresh sack of coins, the other players had gone home. Uncle Lian grabbed my arm, sat me down, and we proceeded to play one-on-one. One hour turned into two. Two hours turned into five. The hefty sack of coins that was once in front of Uncle Lian was now in my possession. But Uncle Lian would not give up. Since he didn't have any more coins to play with, we continued with mahjong tiles as currency. Uncle Lian promised his credit was good. We played on and on, and before we knew it, the morning sun had broken through the family room window. By this time, there was a pile of coins and mahjong tiles in front of me.

I spent the next week getting ready to depart for school. A couple of days before I was to leave, I approached my father for the tuition I would need for the year. He told me to go visit Uncle Lian and get the money that was owed me. Uncle Lian, true to his word, paid me every penny I had won that night. When I reported back to my father that I had collected the money, he handed me a separate envelope and told me to use that for the tuition. The gambling winnings were for me to use as I saw fit.

I could have saved the money like a responsible young adult, but instead, I splurged like a kid in a candy store. When I first moved to Taichung for elementary school, I was enamored by the stylish clothes of the city's upper crust. My well-to-do classmates wore shiny leather shoes and pressed uniforms made from sturdy khaki material. Mine, on the other hand, were worn and full of holes. My first purchase was two pairs of leather shoes and a couple of custom-made uniforms.

My next purchase was a bit more practical, but nonetheless satisfying. In those days, locally made pencils were difficult to use because of their poor quality. The lead broke easily, and the erasers were so hard they were useless. Many of my classmates showed off their beautiful handwriting skills using pencils that were stamped "Made in the USA." I bought a dozen boxes of American-made pencils, totaling more than seven hundred, and shared my hoard with my younger sister and nieces and nephews.

The next thing on my list had no practical value at all but was perhaps the most precious. During my first years in Taichung, I noticed some of my classmates eating a snack that I had never seen before. The treat was dark and mysterious, and the look on the faces of the children as they bit into it was of pure joy. When a school friend let me try a small piece, I was overwhelmed. My taste buds had never experienced anything like it. The flavor was sweet and creamy, and the texture was smooth and silky. The name of this delicacy was as exotic and mysterious as the flavor—*chocolate*. Once I tasted it, I was hooked forever. But alas, this imported treat was well beyond the means of a poor country boy. I didn't get to taste chocolate again until I used my gambling proceeds to buy two bars of American milk chocolate, which I savored to the last square. To this day, chocolate remains a favorite, and I treat myself to one square every evening after dinner.

One of the last things I bought was an assortment of sports equipment: ping-pong paddles and balls and basketballs. I wanted to share my newfound luck with the rest of my classmates, so I brought the equipment to school. My cache, especially the basketballs, was a welcome sight to the students. I was never much of a basketball player, but I became very popular with the athletes, and I was overwhelmed with requests to borrow the balls. I asked a friend to take charge of checking out and monitoring the equipment. This was my first taste of being the big man on campus. I was generous, and the other students appreciated it. Eventually my classmates began calling me Boss Man.

I began high school with a dedication to academics I had never exhibited before. My mental collapse during the entrance exam was still fresh in my mind, so I devoted extra attention to math, but I still struggled, especially in geometry. I was too young to know my university plans, but I decided that because of my lack of aptitude in math, I would likely gravitate toward some sort of social science or liberal arts field.

I fell into a steady routine those first few months and adjusted well to Taichung First, with one exception—the food. I couldn't stand going to the cafeteria. The food had no flavor, and the colors were off-putting. No matter how hungry I was, I barely ate. I would often wander off campus and snack on street food. I would also sneak out with friends to attend late showings at the theaters. As soon as it was lights out in the dorms, my friends and I would stuff our bedcovers to resemble our forms. It wasn't particularly imaginative, but it was enough to fool school security. We would easily negotiate the campus wall and blend into Taichung's bustling nightlife. When our adventures ended, we would retrace our steps and be back in bed with none the wiser. We were having the time of our lives.

Our luck ran out one evening after attending a late showing. The movie ended well past midnight, and I had fallen asleep in the theater—as I usually did. My two bigger friends were kind enough to carry me back to campus while I slept. Just as we were crossing Taichung Park, there was a shout. "Freeze! Where do you think you're going?" My friends, being the unwaveringly loyal soldiers they were, dropped me on the spot and fled as fast as they could. I was left standing there, groggy from my deep slumber. I was processing my surroundings when I heard that familiar thundering voice. "Wu Li-pei! Don't you dare run!" It was the school disciplinary chief, Tan Chuo-min. I wish I could report that I was able to sweet-talk my way out of this, but that didn't happen. I was promptly kicked out of the dorms and forced to find an off-campus rental house with some other students.

By my junior year, my family's financial situation was beyond dire. To save money, my father suggested I move in with his sister, Aunt Lin, for my last couple of years of high school. Also, Aunt Lin's son, my cousin, was in the midst of studying for the university entrance exam, and she wanted me to help him prepare.

At first, I was against the move. My father had approached Uncle Lin, who he used to be best of friends with, a few years earlier for a loan but was denied. Uncle Lin is the same man who would later deny Shu-pei help after he got out of prison. But when my father explained our financial situation more clearly, I reluctantly agreed to move in with them. In retrospect, the move was for the best. My aunt was very generous, and I was able to save quite a bit of money in preparation for college. I was also able to help my cousin prepare for the exam, as his family had hoped.

In those days, high school students had to choose a major long before entering university. One's ranking in that major on the entrance exam would determine acceptance. Aunt Lin always wanted what was best for me and hoped I would choose medicine. The Lin family owned a large hospital, and for generations, the Lin children either became doctors or married doctors. Medicine was the family business. With my grades, there was a good chance I would be accepted into medical school at National Taiwan University (NTU), the most prestigious university in the country. But that wasn't what I wanted. I had spent so much of my free time reading books on socioeconomic and political theories that I was determined to major in economics, even though Aunt Lin didn't approve.

I had initially thought I was better suited for advanced study in political science, but a pivotal meeting with an NTU student convinced me that economics was the right path. During my senior year in high school, a good friend, Ke Yao-tang, introduced me to his older brother, Ke Yao-nan. This was during the White Terror, and many Taiwanese had gone into hiding for fear of the KMT's reprisals. Yao-nan, an economics student at NTU, was a member of the CPC and was in Taichung to stay under the KMT's radar.

When I first met Yao-nan, he asked about my college aspirations. I answered resolutely that I wanted to study political science so that I could start a revolution to rid Taiwan of its many injustices. I could tell he was impressed by my enthusiasm, but he chuckled at my youthful naïveté. He shook his head and told me that social reforms always begin with economic reforms—that is the nature of the world. He cited many instances where political and social reform only happened as a result of the depressed economic conditions for workers. Yao-nan passionately extolled the virtues of Marxist and socialist economics and insisted that the shortsightedness of capitalists would lead to economic unrest and ultimately the downfall of capitalism and the triumph of socialism.

Listening to Yao-nan's inspirational words was like a light bulb switching on in my head. After all the reading I had done and the notes I had taken just a few months earlier, the answers to all the questions I had clicked into place with Yao-nan's help. I greatly admired his philosophy and approach toward life. I wanted that same level of commitment and passion, to be a part of something larger than myself. I wanted to see the utopia Yao-nan and Marx envisioned emerge in Taiwan. Yao-nan could see the enthusiasm on my face. He was glad I had found a calling, but he also warned that the study of economics should not be mistaken for a shortcut to great wealth. It was meant to provide opportunities and better lives for all people, not just a select few. I decided right then that I wanted to follow in his footsteps and make NTU's Department of Economics my first choice.

I took the university entrance exam in 1953. To everyone's astonishment, I gained entrance into NTU's Department of Economics, ranking sixth out of the hundred students admitted. My test scores also easily exceeded the minimum points needed to gain entrance into the medical school. My aunt and uncle offered to support me financially if I opted to attend. My father, usually fairly hands off when it came to my academic choices, wrote to me asking that I consider medicine because of my family's difficult financial situation. His words, "it may be our way out," weighed heavily on me. But I had known for quite some time that there was really only one choice for me. I enrolled in NTU's Department of Economics that fall.

Chapter Seven

THE AGE OF ENLIGHTENMENT

I was about to embark on a new chapter of my life: living in Taipei, the nation's largest city, and studying economics at the nation's most prestigious university. My path up to this point had been anything but smooth, but I was excited and confident this would lead to greater things.

There were those who thought a degree in economics wasn't practical. Many—like my aunt and uncle and, to some degree, my father—thought medicine would be more valuable. I recall seeing a relative the summer before I was to leave for NTU. He congratulated me on my acceptance and inquired on my major. When he learned I would be studying economics, he turned and walked away, muttering under his breath about wasting time and smelly farts. Despite this lack of encouragement, I was resolute in my decision.

The summer before my senior year at Taichung First, I befriended twin brothers, Yang Ze-min and Yang Ze-sheng. The Yangs were from a prominent family who had high-level political connections during the Japanese occupation. Their uncle, Yang Chao-jia, was a widely respected political figure with a reputation for promoting Taiwanese democracy and sponsoring various cultural activities such as arts and literature. Through the Yang brothers, I was able to visit the famous Liu Ran Stateroom, a library that housed Yang Chao-jia's enormous collection of literature. The variety of books on economics, history, and philosophy was beyond anything I had ever seen before. The library had copies of the *Communist Manifesto*, the 1848 political document by German philosophers Karl Marx and Friedrich Engels, and *Das Kapital* by Karl Marx. I knew all too well the risks involved with immersing myself in this kind of reading. Part of me needed to satiate my curiosity about these political and economic philosophies. Part of me also wanted to understand Shu-pei's deep belief in these ideas.

Marxist theory captured my attention, much as it did my older brother's. There was something idealistic about socialism that appealed to me. Like Shu-pei, I was a young man looking toward his future, hoping to make a difference in the world. Karl Marx identified himself as a revolutionary and humanitarian, both of which were characteristics I understood and wanted to emulate. His work contained far-reaching themes of morality and justice, and his views on capitalism resonated deeply with me. I concurred with his belief that capitalist systems only benefited the property owners or the upper class at the expense of the working class and were doomed to stagnation.

I was too young and inexperienced to fully grasp the critical theories detailed in these books, but that did not stop me from enjoying the intellectual stimulus they provided. I even translated the *Communist Manifesto* into Chinese and transcribed my work in a personal journal. I found out years later, after I moved to the US, that my father, in fear of the KMT, destroyed the journal.

Life in the Dorm

As enthusiastic as I was about college life, I found myself falling into the old pattern of studying just enough to get by. Classes didn't hold my interest, and there weren't many extracurricular activities available. The one bright spot was a close-knit group of friends who provided camaraderie and intellectual stimulation that I had never experienced before. Our little clique was made up of students pursuing political science, economics, and law. Our favorite pastime was arguing over everything and anything. It didn't matter what the subject was or what position was taken—we just loved a good, heated debate. Liberalism had just taken root at that time, and the democracy movement was spreading like wildfire around the world, becoming one of our main topics for discussion. During these animated talks, I was able to hone my debating skills and develop my own political philosophy beyond the theories I had studied.

Our cadre included John Cheng, my old childhood friend, Lai Wen-hsiung (Frank), Roger Hsieh, and Chuang Ming-shan, among others. Out of all of us, Roger—a political science major—was arguably the most active, decisive, and driven. He despised the KMT, as we all did, but his passion and relentless pursuit of bringing it down and seeing a truly democratic Taiwan were an inspiration. Roger, Frank, and I would speak tirelessly of ways we could help our country. The more we spoke of the KMT's atrocities against the Taiwanese, the more our blood would boil, and the more we were determined to do something. John was always soft-spoken and introspective. I wasn't sure if he spent time with us because he was a believer or if he just enjoyed our company. But these talks apparently had some kind of osmotic effect on him. Many years later, John became the chairman of World United Formosans for Independence (WUFI), one of the largest Taiwanese independence organizations in the world.

This was the first time in my life that I had a group of friends with whom I could exchange ideas, discuss different political viewpoints, and frankly, vent about the injustices that had befallen Taiwan. I had grown up viewing the KMT as a ruthless and vile government entity, but at NTU my anger toward the Chiang regime came into sharper focus. It was all too clear that the KMT engaged in systemic oppression of the Taiwanese. The KMT may have been anticommunist, but it was anything but a democracy. Political positions within the government were reserved almost exclusively for the Chinese who had emigrated in 1949. This meant my family and the majority of the population—Taiwanese people who had been in Taiwan for generations—had no chance to participate in the governing process. Under martial law, there was no multiparty system, no ability for any citizen to exercise the right to vote or assemble in protest. My friends and I believed there could be no future for Taiwan as long as the KMT existed.

It was well known at the time that the KMT monitored student activities through its well-placed network of spies and police agents. There was no question they had infiltrated the student body and teaching staff at NTU. As young adults who fancied themselves revolutionaries, we would not be deterred. Perhaps having a close group of like-minded friends gave us additional courage—fear seemed a foreign entity when we were together. We would not stop speaking our minds. The fire in our collective bellies and our love for Taiwan eclipsed our fear of being arrested.

Disillusioned with Communism

While the countless debates I had with my good friends did much to quench my intellectual thirst, the academic program at NTU did just the opposite. I entered the university with high hopes that I would build a strong foundation of economic theory and practical application. I thought I would learn a great deal from these high-profile professors, well respected in their fields, but I was bitterly disappointed. Most seemed totally ambivalent about their job—they simply went through the motions, doing nothing more than waiting for their next paycheck. They didn't seem to care about stimulating the students. Year after year, they would use the same antiquated textbooks, the same syllabus, the same exams, even if current events or other circumstances demanded changes. Inevitably, a bored or boring teacher fosters bored students, and I found most of my classes unbearable. I thought about the irony of working so hard in high school to get into a prestigious university like NTU, when the reality was that the hardest part about NTU was the entrance exam. Once you got in, the classes did little to challenge your mind.

There were, however, a few exceptional teachers. I was lucky to have three economics professors that I still remember vividly to this day: Shih Chian-sheng, Lin Yi-hsin, and Chuan Han-sheng. Professor Shih's class on basic economic theory was instrumental in helping me understand the real-world implications for a country's populace relative to economic systems. Professors Lin and Chuan were the teachers that gave me the most insight on the contrast between socialist and capitalist economics.

Professor Lin worked as a speechwriter for Zhou Enlai, the first premier of the People's Republic of China, but later defected to the KMT. Because of his unique experience of being at one time a fervent member of the CPC and then later one of its harsher critics, he was an excellent teacher who provided easily relatable perspectives on socialism and capitalism.

Karl Marx had predicted the eventual collapse of capitalism and emergence of socialism, which emphasized fairness, justice, and resources for all. Marx believed capitalists would inevitably exploit laborers, which would lead to extreme disparity between the rich and the poor. This economic disparity would end in a working class uprising and revolution, further cementing socialism as the ideal long-term economic solution. Professor Lin felt Marx was erroneous in this thesis because capitalism had two inherent tools to remedy labor oppression: labor unions and tax policy. Labor unions would have leverage to negotiate for equitable pay and better work conditions. Along the same lines, taxation would enable the government to stimulate the economy and bridge the gap between the rich and poor.

When Professor Lin spoke of this, I, like the rest of the class, was spellbound. I had studied the theories of Marx and socialism, but I didn't have the practical know-how to see beyond theory. Professor Lin opened my eyes and made me realize that looking at something from only one perspective limited my ability to see other possibilities.

Professor Chuan Han-sheng inspired me to immerse myself in writings on the evolutionary journey of capitalist systems. In his class, I realized that socialists espoused attractive concepts guaranteeing all in society would be well fed, clothed, and otherwise cared for, but they did not account for the value of innovation and entrepreneurialism. Capitalist systems place great value on and promote individual achievement. The budding startups that compete with well-established companies, the scientist who develops a groundbreaking drug, are opportunities that thrive in capitalist economies. This inherent desire to strive for more, whether it's to build something that will last longer or invent something that will work better, seems to be lost in socialist economies.

My fascination with communism and socialism ended at NTU. As much as socialism invoked visions of fairness and equality for all, in practice the system had too many deficiencies and unrealistic assumptions. Since my university days, we have witnessed the fall of communism throughout the world, mainly because of unsustainable economics. Today only four communist countries remain. As a young man, I was enthralled with the ideology, but from a practical standpoint, it has proven to be a failed experiment. There was a quote on communism from those days that captured my thinking perfectly: "If an intellectual fails to fall under the spell of communism before turning thirty, he needs a dose of passion for the world; if he converts and remains a communist after the age of thirty, he needs a wake-up call."

In recent years, capitalism has also shown it is not immune to economic fractures. The US is plagued with political gridlock, soaring national debt, unmanageable healthcare costs, and an ever-widening wealth gap within its population. One thing is certain—the economic utopia that both systems predicted has yet to become a reality.

Rise against Oppression

Besides changing perspectives on economic theory, my time at NTU also made me think long and hard about how the Taiwanese people could prevail against the might of the KMT. Members of the KMT held the highest government positions and controlled the police, media, and military, while the Taiwanese were mainly poor farmers trying to eke out a living. As much as my NTU friends and I enjoyed condemning the KMT and debating economic and political philosophies, there was no clear or easy path for the Taiwanese. An overthrow of the KMT seemed impossible.

I realized during my last couple of years at NTU that societal change can come about in the most unexpected ways. Numerous world events during that time captured my imagination and reinforced my belief that the Taiwanese had the capacity to carve out our own destiny. The Suez Crisis and the Hungarian Revolt in 1956 were both examples of smaller, less powerful groups overcoming what seemed to be impossible odds to fight for what they believed in. In both instances, the international community pressured the more powerful to cease their oppression and aggression. It was inspirational to watch these events unfold, and I realized a couple of things: whenever the strong can take advantage of the weak, they will, and the only way for oppression to end is for the oppressed to stand up and demand change.

By the end of my college years, Taiwan's destiny had become crystal clear to me. An independent, sovereign statehood was our only path toward freedom and democracy. With a few years of college under my belt, I and my circle of freethinking friends began to champion the idea of self-determination. It was a fairly radical concept at the time, but to this day I view it as an existential imperative for the future of Taiwan.

Chapter Eight

IN YOUTH WE LEARN

I look back with mixed emotions on the times my friends and I spent at NTU talking about revolution with little action. My four years were filled with passionate debates and newfound perspectives, but upon graduation, it was time to move on to more practical pursuits, like finding a job. Most of my graduating class faced two years of mandatory military service, but I was so severely underweight that I was exempt and headed for the job market.

With a fresh diploma from a prestigious university, finding a job was not going to be a problem. There were plenty of well-paid, secure opportunities within the government sector. The only requirement was that I take an exam to become a civil servant. Passing such an exam was routine, but taking a job as a government worker, where my boss would essentially be the KMT, was something I couldn't reconcile with myself. How could I work for the corrupt and illegitimate entity that I had vowed to overthrow? As a new graduate about to start my career, it felt complicit to follow such a path. Instead, I entered what could be described as my period of self-exile. I took a teaching job in a remote, rural area in Chushan, a small township a little south of Taichung. These remote locations coveted NTU grads and didn't require civil exams. I also felt the location would do me good—the relative isolation would let me reflect on what I wanted to do with my life.

The teaching job paid $12 a month, less than what I earned when I was a part-time tutor in college. Teachers were given modest dorm rooms for free and a small stipend for food, so I was able to scrape by. My colleagues and I would sometimes visit the lone local tavern, where we could get a bowl of rice, a side dish, and a beer for $1.25. The routine was simple and straightforward. I taught, I ate, I slept.

The only breaks in my routine were the times when my old friends Roger Hsieh and Frank Lai would stop by for a visit. On those occasions, we would head to the tavern to eat, drink, and talk until the sun rose. It was as if we were transported back to our old dorm, debating the latest philosophical or social issue. Even though our situations had changed, our passion was still as strong as ever. Our problem was not lack of motivation but lack of experience. We simply didn't know what to do, so we did the next best thing—we talked about it. When there was a pause in the constant prattle, the silence hung over us, and the reality of our situation was like a blast of cold air. But we'd warm ourselves again as we raised our glasses filled with Hungluh Chiew, a liquor made from fermented rice, and toasted the demise of the KMT.

Jilted

A year into my stint in Chushan, I ran into an old NTU classmate, Yu Hsin-wang. He suggested that I move to Keelung, a city just a little northeast of Taipei, where he was teaching at Kuang Lung Vocation High School. Hsin-wang knew of an opportunity at his school where I could potentially double my current salary. Also, since Hsin-wang had extra space at his house, I would be able to save money by staying with him. It was the practical thing to do, and it was time for me to end my self-exile.

The move to Keelung worked out as expected. My income improved, and I had more of a social life. Roger and Frank appreciated the new location because it meant they wouldn't have to travel as far to visit. It also meant we had more than one tavern to choose from on their visits.

They would stop by Keelung when they had time off from their work on a graduate research project commissioned by the United Nations to study Taiwanese customs. Apparently, the UN paid well, so they were more than happy to treat. When the three of us were together, Taiwanese politics dominated the conversation, as usual. Life in Keelung fell into another routine, this time with a better-paying job and a more pleasant living environment. But then my life was upended from a direction I least expected—romance.

I was already well into my twenties, so it was natural to think about a wife and family. I didn't have much experience or interest in this area. My main focuses had been work and thinking about the demise of the KMT. Also, my humble upbringing didn't instill much confidence that I would be a strong suitor for anybody.

One of my colleagues, Lí Siew-jìn, asked if she could introduce me to a friend of hers named Mei. I didn't have high expectations, but I was amenable to the introduction. It turned out Mei and I had a lot in common. We had both studied economics at NTU and become teachers in Keelung. I viewed myself as a revolutionary and didn't think I was suited for marriage, but as I got to know Mei, my thinking began to change. Meeting the right girl, coupled with pressure from my family to settle down, led to the inevitable. Mei and I agreed that nuptials were on the horizon. I was surprised at how naturally our relationship blossomed. It felt good and exciting to plan my future with somebody.

Our next step was making sure our families agreed to our plans. Mei was the only daughter in her family. Her father had passed away years earlier, and her mother ran a small general store to provide for the family. I wanted to make a good impression on Mei's mother when it came time for us to discuss our future, so I asked an elderly aunt to accompany me when I formally asked for Mei's hand in marriage. My aunt's husband was a former bank manager and later started his own successful business.

My hope was that Mei's mother could see that I came from a good family, but things didn't turn out the way I expected.

When we met, Mei's mother was blunt. "This is the only daughter I have. How can I expect her to be financially comfortable if I allow her to marry a teacher?" I wasn't sure how to respond to this. I knew I wasn't the best-looking or richest fish in the sea, but I felt I deserved some respect. I had graduated from the top university in Taiwan, I had a good job, and I was a decent person. To be outright rejected like this was unsettling.

I then did something I never thought I would do. In order to appease Mei's mother, I took the civil exam to qualify for a job within the KMT, a thought that turned my stomach. But the heart wants what the heart wants, so upon passing the exam, I accepted an entry-level position at one of Taiwan's largest state-owned banks, Changhwa Commercial Bank (CCB). In retrospect, it may have been the best career move I could have made, but at the time, an internal battle raged within me. I was assigned to CCB's branch office in Douliu, Yunlin County, a town a little south of Taichung. Working at CCB was considered very prestigious, and I expected this gesture to make my future mother-in-law happy. I arranged a second meeting with Mei's mother to give her the good news on my career change, but this meeting was just as brief as the first. Her response to my new job? "Douliu is so far from Keelung—I'll never get to see my daughter." I left her house shaking my head.

At a Loss for Words

I told my family about the obstacles in my love life, and my father insisted on coming to my aid. He had a reputation for beautiful calligraphy, so he wrote numerous letters to Mei, asking her to convince her mother to give me a chance. When he learned Mei's mother was concerned about the distance between Keelung and Douliu, my father contacted an old friend who was able to pull some strings and get me transferred to one of CCB's offices in Taipei, less than thirty minutes from Keelung. I was getting exasperated trying to satisfy this woman, but I had come so far, so I pushed forward. I could see from my family's effort that they wanted to see me settled and happy, so I went with the plan.

Armed with a prestigious job, a better salary, and a closer location, I visited Mei's mother again. This time, the meeting lasted a bit longer because instead of just one complaint, she had many. First, I didn't own a home in Taipei. Second, she didn't think I looked particularly healthy. And last but not least, she didn't like the look of my teeth! I was speechless! After months of effort to create a better life for her daughter, to end in this kind of humiliation was infuriating. If she was never going to approve of me, why go through the pretense? Why waste everybody's time? As the anger washed over me, I rose to my feet and said to Mei before storming out of the house, "Your mother is impossible. If you think we have a future, come with me now. If not, stay here and be your mother's baby girl forever." Mei followed me, crying uncontrollably and pleading with me to stay. I told her to go home. The next day, I received an express letter from her asking if we could remain friends. I tossed the letter in the trash.

Relegated to Workplace Limbo

The three-year relationship with Mei ended abruptly and unceremoniously. My heart was broken, but I needed to move on with my life. There wasn't much solace to be found in my job working for the entity that I had grown up despising. Frank and Roger had a great laugh when they learned of my employment at the bank. They made fun of my disheveled and unkempt clothes. I lived as if I had no ambition for the future. The two of them had an ongoing bet that I wouldn't last longer than a year in the banking profession. If you had asked me then, I'm sure I wouldn't have believed that my career in banking would span four decades!

The one thing most of my friends didn't know about me was that I had a level of dedication to work that wasn't obvious. I didn't dress or act like a banker. But each morning when I entered the CCB branch, I went to my station and did my work to the best of my ability. Even though I was an entry-level clerk, I learned the ins and outs of the banking business. I didn't know how long I would stay in this field, but I realized I had an aptitude for it.

Not long into my employment at CCB, I entered the bank's annual essay competition, in which employees were asked to write their thoughts on the banking business. I spent days on my essay about the processes at CCB and ways for the bank to improve its customer service. I thought my essay was insightful and could bring about positive change in the bank's operations. After submission, I expected a heartfelt pat on the back from upper management.

A few days later, two agents from the investigation section at CCB's headquarters showed up at my desk. They asked what I wrote in my essay. I confidently and naïvely explained that I wrote about various ways CCB could improve its business. They burst out laughing and told me that I was a celebrity. "People all over the bank want to know who this Wu Li-pei guy is. They want to know who was brave or foolish enough to criticize CCB. Where did this guy come from?" Instead of paying attention to the content of my analysis, they cared more about who had written the report. In fact, senior management thought whoever was bold enough to write such a thing must have high-level connections with the KMT. Bank employees actually tiptoed around me because they thought I was spying for the government. They had no idea I fantasized every day about bringing down said government. Eventually, everybody realized I was just a clerk who had written something I hoped the bank would take seriously.

I learned a few things early on in my career at CCB. State-owned entities such as this don't think about improving their businesses. When organizations have the backing of an authoritarian government, they are caught in a bureaucratic machine that doesn't require innovation. With little competition, there was no need to strive for excellence. I also learned that corrupt governments like the KMT create an atmosphere of paranoia and suspicion. The people that do well in such environments keep their heads down and don't cause trouble. That is not who I am. I spent seven years as a clerk at CCB watching my peers get promoted while I remained in the same low-level position. Because of my essay, there was no future for me at the bank. I continued to do my job, but I waited and hoped for something to change my course.

Chapter Nine

AN UNEXPECTED SHOT AT HAPPILY EVER AFTER

After my unsuccessful courtship of Mei, I was even more convinced marriage was not in my future. I was still enamored with the idea of being a revolutionary, and the thought of dragging a spouse and children into that world didn't make sense. However, pleasant surprises happen when you least expect them. I was immersed in my work life at CCB when, out of the blue, a matchmaker changed my life forever. This matchmaker was not a colleague or family member. He was one of my best friends and had been like a brother to me since college. My matchmaker—and future brother-in-law—was none other than Frank Lai.

Frank Lai

When I first met Frank at NTU, we didn't hit it off immediately. In fact, I would say neither of us particularly cared for the other. Perhaps it was because we were both stubborn and vocal that we often butted heads. There was nothing we enjoyed more than a heated debate. But as we learned more about each other and our common feelings toward Taiwanese politics and the KMT, we became great friends. This friendship would change the trajectory of my life in ways I could not have imagined.

After completing graduate school at NTU and his mandatory military service, Frank could not bring himself to work under the KMT, so he took various odd jobs. At one point, he and some friends sold duck eggs at a farmers market to make ends meet. He had excelled as a student at NTU's Department of Political Science and eventually found work in the field as an instructor and researcher. His passion for Taiwan's self-determination and democracy was boundless, so he decided to continue his education and pursue a graduate degree in political science. His qualifications were so strong he was able to gain entrance to a top program in the US on a full scholarship. When he told our circle of friends, we were so proud of him.

The Matchmaker

A few nights before Frank left for the US, the two of us celebrated with food, drinks, and a movie. Frank was unusually quiet. He was normally boisterous and full of energy, so I assumed he was nervous about leaving Taiwan. During the movie intermission, we went outside for a smoke. I assured him that he would do great in graduate school. He shook his head—he wasn't worried about school. He was worried about his family.

From a young age, Frank had been the patriarchal figure in his family. His father was essentially an absentee parent. Mr. Lai was born into wealth and lived his life without learning responsibility. He agreed to an arranged marriage at a very young age and had two children, Frank and a daughter, Hsiu-chu (Jenny). Mr. Lai was never able to properly care for his family. He squandered away his inheritance on questionable ventures and a playboy lifestyle. Frank's mother had a difficult time raising two children on her own, so Frank and Jenny spent most of their childhood living with their grandparents. As they grew up, Frank looked after his sister as well as he could.

His primary concern about going to the US was for Jenny. This was what was on his mind when we shared a cigarette outside the movie theater. With a heavy sigh, he blew smoke into the cold night air and said, "What will happen to my sister? She's so innocent and kind, but my old man doesn't know how to take care of her, and I don't know when I'll return."

I don't remember exactly what got into me—maybe it was seeing my good friend so worried, maybe it was the celebratory mood, maybe it was the few beers I'd had, but I blurted out, "Don't worry. I'll be in charge of finding her a nice boyfriend. If I don't find anyone, I'll marry her myself!" Frank's face lit up, and we enjoyed the rest of night.

A couple of days later, Frank called me from Taichung, his hometown, and said in English, "Your proposal has been accepted!" My brain needed a moment to register what he was saying. What proposal? What was being accepted?

"The other night, you said you were going to marry my sister! My grandmother totally supports the idea. Come to my house as soon as you can to make the engagement official!" I didn't even get a word in before my impulsive, clever, future brother-in-law hung up on me.

I had really boxed myself in this time. I could easily extinguish my friend's excitement and clarify what I had actually said that night, but as I thought about it, I realized I wasn't upset. I was approaching thirty, my family was hoping I would settle down soon, and I had nobody else in my life. I knew Frank's family well. I had met Jenny only a couple of times, but my impression of her was good—she had gone to one of the best high schools in Taiwan and was very kind. She was attractive, if a bit thin. I hadn't gained any weight since I was rejected by the military for being underweight, so who was I to complain?

Neither of our families had any kind of wealth, so all in all, we were a good match. It was decided—we had a wedding to plan! I called Frank back and asked him when I should be in Taichung to formalize the engagement. His hope was to complete everything before he left for the US, so we only had a few days. The timing was tight, but once I made up my mind, I saw no reason to delay. I went home to Dacheng right away to share the good news with my parents, who were naturally ecstatic.

In those days, Taiwan had a fairly elaborate engagement ritual involving many family members and a variety of ceremonies and traditions. Since neither family had the resources to indulge in such things, we kept it simple. The Wu family was not required to provide a monetary gift to the bride's family, and the Lai family did not have to give a dowry to the new couple. My mother did, however, manage to find a gold engagement ring for me to give to my bride.

Usually a designated matchmaker helps to officiate the engagement. We didn't have one, so the day of the engagement, just before I was to get on a bus to Taichung, I stopped by Roger's place to ask him to be our matchmaker. He jumped to his feet with enthusiasm and said, "Let's go!" He was still wearing his usual pair of clogs and didn't bother to change, but I didn't mind. His attire fitted the theme of the engagement perfectly.

The celebration consisted of two tables at a simple restaurant in Taichung. It was a pleasant affair with just close family. Frank was the most excited person there. He was soon to leave Taiwan, potentially never to return. He wanted to start his new life in the US knowing that his family, especially his sister, would be well cared for. I sat next to Jenny, but we barely spoke. There would be plenty of time to get to know each other once we were married.

Jenny and I had a very short engagement period. Her brother had told her about me, and she was impressed that I was a graduate of NTU. When Frank recommended me for marriage, she readily agreed. Both of us took a leap of faith based on our trust in those closest to us. We were wed in 1963 in Taipei. As we settled into marriage, we recognized that we were very different people. Jenny, four years my junior, was very traditional. She was even-tempered, quiet, soft-spoken, and always thoughtful. I, on the other hand, was fiery, stubborn, and impatient—the polar opposite.

Our first home as a married couple was the dorm that CCB provided its staff-level employees. It was a tiny shoebox with a small living room doubling as a dining room. It had two even smaller bedrooms, the smallest of which was in the corner of the apartment, sectioned off with a curtain.

Despite the small size, our place was always bustling with relatives. We had nieces or nephews from Dacheng staying with us because the school system was better in Taipei. Frank's fiancée also lived with us for a short time after she graduated from NTU's Department of Economics. She needed a place to stay while she waited to get approval to study abroad and meet Frank in the US. We insisted our house guests take the larger room while Jenny and I slept in the curtain room. There was always someone living with us the first couple of years of our marriage, which made Jenny's life quite busy.

When our sons, George and Gene, arrived, Jenny was even busier. I would go off to work, and she would manage the cooking, cleaning, shopping, and caring for the boys. In those days, we didn't have dishwashers or washing machines, so everything was done by hand. But in all those years, Jenny never once complained.

The circumstances that led up to my "proposal" and engagement, while amusing, reflected a time when young people didn't think about marriage the way they do today. We didn't agonize over this decision. When it was time to get married, we did. In almost six decades of marriage, Jenny and I were able to create a good life for ourselves, have a family, and support each other through thick and thin. Perhaps I wasn't as poorly suited for marriage as I thought!

Chapter Ten

LIEUTENANT OF A GANG

O f all my revolutionary friends at NTU, Roger Hsieh was the one with the most passion and enthusiasm. While the rest of us engaged in theoretical discussions, Roger was out recruiting, making plans, and taking action to see our dream of overthrowing the KMT come true. Roger could somehow motivate all of us to do things that we wouldn't otherwise consider. In retrospect, many of his plans were ridiculous, but he would do whatever he could for the cause.

I recall one time he recruited Frank's cousin, a physics major, to teach him how to build an explosive device. I don't know what Roger was going to do after he learned this skill, but I'm sure he had a crazy plan. When I was working at CCB, Roger spent hours with me learning the security protocols of the bank because he wanted to rob one in order to fund his revolution. He later reconsidered this idea. Such was the life of a revolutionary. He couldn't stand by and watch the KMT continue its reign of terror against the Taiwanese. Roger needed to walk the walk. He was a true patriot.

A few years after Roger graduated from NTU, he took a teaching position at Fengshan Military Academy in Kaohsiung, a major city in the southern part of Taiwan. I was shocked that he, of all people, would choose to teach at an established KMT-sponsored institution. He explained that it was a golden opportunity to "infiltrate the enemy" by hiding in plain sight. His goal was to use his position to influence the cadets and indoctrinate them with Taiwanese independence ideology. From there, he hoped to move up the chain of command and change the mindsets of the higher-ranking officers. He thought it was poetic justice to use the resources of the KMT against itself.

King Con's Revolution Aspiration

Perhaps one of Roger's greatest skills was convincing others to join his cause. He could read any situation like a great poker player and bluff his way out of impossible positions, ultimately earning him the nickname King Con. Roger was also extremely social and adept at making friends. He recognized early on that the only way to achieve independence was to garner support from all kinds of coalitions. He had Taiwanese friends like us but also friends who were *waishengren*—Chinese immigrants who came to Taiwan in 1949.

Many of the older waishengren became high-level officials within the KMT government. Roger befriended many second-generation Chinese, such as Bao Yi-ming and Chiu Hung-ta. He realized that instead of promoting the more radical idea of independence with these younger waishengren, he could speak of general democracy for Taiwan, which ultimately resonated with their anticommunist beliefs. Roger delicately found a middle ground to merge these two ideas of independence and democracy—he made Taiwanese independence advocates like myself and second-generation Chinese democracy advocates like Bao Yi-ming recognize that the KMT was our common enemy.

Yi-ming was Roger's classmate at NTU and exhibited much of his zeal. He had a lot of energy and was always ready to participate in Roger's schemes. One idea the two cooked up was to implement a strategy whereby politics and organized crime intertwined. It was well documented that historically, Chinese political leaders often used crime syndicates to push forth their agendas. The government could pursue less reputable action through the gangsters, while the gangsters enjoyed preferential treatment from the government around their illicit activities. Roger and Yi-ming's idea was to form some kind of syndicate to enact political reform. But they didn't just want to gather a group of random people, they wanted to actually find and use real criminals to form this "gang." Yi-ming would be the point person on this particular project, and Roger somehow recruited me to be part of this clandestine plan.

On the night before Roger was to leave for Kaohsiung and his new position at Fengshan Military Academy, he came to see me. We spoke briefly about his plans at the academy, and just as he was about to leave for the train station, he yelled out, "You are in charge of Taipei!" Before I could find out what he was talking about, he was gone. I later learned Roger had boasted to Yi-ming about having a horde in Taipei ready to mobilize for his revolutionary cause—meaning me. That was how I "volunteered" to be part of Roger's criminal organization.

A Mob in the Making

The organized crime syndicates that Yi-ming tried to recruit for the cause were fairly well known to the general public and had colorful monikers such as the United Bamboo Gang, the Four Seas Gang, and the Flying Eagles. Most of these organizations were comprised of a younger generation of gangsters with no apparent allegiance to the KMT, unlike their predecessors. Yi-ming's hope was to take advantage of this and convince these criminals to join the underground effort to overthrow the KMT. His strategy was to recruit the boss of each organization and appeal to their sense of democracy. He hoped the allure of political reform would convince them. In retrospect, while full of good intentions, the plan was naïve and unrealistic. To Yi-ming's credit, though, he was able to generate interest among a handful of gangsters, enough to actually hold a meeting to organize and discuss next steps.

The initiation ceremony with Yi-ming's new gangster recruits was to be held at a hotel in Beitou Park, a district in Taipei. I was to attend as a representative of Roger's coalition. Yi-ming wanted to impress the attendees and show we had force in numbers, so he asked me to bring somebody along. The only person I could think of was Chang, an old friend from NTU who had similar political ideologies. I thought of Chang for a couple of reasons. I remembered him as a kind, reliable friend, but more importantly, he was one of the tallest and most physically imposing people I knew. If I was going to be at a dinner with a bunch of gangsters, I wanted Chang in front of me.

Chang was a middle school teacher in central Taiwan, so I needed to convince him to make a trip up to Taipei. I called him and said we needed to meet on an urgent matter, but I didn't go into specifics. As I knew he would, he agreed without asking too many questions. When I picked him up at the train station, my eyes lit up. He was still the tall, strapping young man that I remembered, exactly what I needed for the evening.

We hopped on a bus headed for Beitou, sitting in the back for privacy. Only then did I explain the plan. Upon hearing the purpose for the visit, my friend stood up, almost hitting his head on the roof of the bus. After a moment, he sat down and whispered, "After all these years of no contact, you ask me to meet you for *this*? I'm a middle school teacher, for Christ's sake, and you want me to become friends with gangsters? What's wrong with you?" I tried to calm him and explained that discussing the details over the phone would have been too risky. Then I reminded him of all the discussions we had at NTU about Taiwanese democracy. After my emotional plea, I was sure that he would help me.

"I don't want any part of this," Chang said flatly. I'm usually not prone to panic, but I was about to enter a room full of gangsters without my bodyguard. I could feel my blood pressure rising. I had told Yi-ming that I would be bringing a charismatic compatriot from Taichung. I couldn't show up alone. Since I wasn't able to appeal to Chang's sense of loyalty, I was left with only one option—begging. I pleaded with him to come this one time. He wouldn't have to say a word, just act the part. I would do all the talking and get us out of there as quickly as possible. I also promised never to involve him again. Chang could see the desperation in my eyes and reluctantly agreed. We were only a few minutes from Beitou, and I breathed a sigh of relief. Little did I know our adventure into the criminal underworld was just beginning.

Deputy Mountain Master

The meeting was held in a large conference room in the Hsin Hui Fang Hotel. The floor was covered in Japanese tatami mats, and a screen divided the room. There were about a dozen of us altogether. Yi-ming was the first to speak, introducing everybody. I gathered from the introductions that pretty much everybody there was a bona fide, hardened gangster.

I didn't know much about how these guys operated, but after a few minutes of observing, I came to understand each person's role. The hierarchy was very well defined. Each member had a specific title, role, and responsibility. The gang's big boss was Dragon Head; the second-in-command, Deputy Mountain Master; the administrator, Paper Fan; the military commander, Red Pole. Straw Sandal and 49er were foot soldiers. I couldn't keep track of who was who, but I'll never forget Dragon Head. He was called Mr. Huang, and he was the owner of some kind of saloon and perhaps the most intimidating person I had ever seen in my life. He was not a large man, but he spoke with the deep growl of somebody twice his size. When he smiled, he looked even more menacing because his teeth were stained from extensive betel nut use.

There was a formal initiation ceremony that included an animal sacrifice so that we could all take a blood oath of brotherhood. They brought out a live chicken and placed the poor animal on the altar. Dragon Head Huang pulled out a sword and *whack*! I glanced nervously at Chang, and he glared at me. When the initiation ceremony concluded, Yi-ming was given the title of Dragon Head, and I became Deputy Mountain Master.

The socializing began after that. Food and drink were brought out as we gathered around the table to celebrate our new initiative. Chang hadn't said a word all night. As we toasted and drank, my new blood brothers peppered me with questions. Eventually Dragon Head Huang pointed at Chang and asked, "Brother Wu, what's with your big friend?

He hasn't said a word all night. Can't he talk? I want to know what kind of person I'll be working with. Oi, Brother Chang, tell us about yourself. What do you think of what we're trying to do here?"

Chang looked at me, mouth hanging open. I nudged him, but he only managed to move his lips and grunt. I looked around the table. What was a boisterous, festive group just a moment earlier had become a silent pack of thugs waiting for a response from my poor friend. After an eternity, Dragon Head Huang broke the silence by slamming his fist on the table and shouting at Chang, "What do you think this place is? Anyone who walks in will be able to walk out?" To make matters worse, Chang, still unable to speak, wasn't even looking at Dragon Head Huang. I realized he was staring silently at the sword next to Huang's chair. It was still dripping with chicken blood.

Before tensions could escalate even more, I jumped in and apologized profusely for Chang's behavior. "Please excuse my friend. This is my fault. He came tonight from Taichung. I didn't think it was wise to discuss our plans on the phone, so he is just learning about our group. That's why he is nervous. He means no disrespect. I've known him for years, and I can vouch for his character." After I spoke, Chang seemed to snap out of his paralysis and apologized to Dragon Head Huang. The boss still looked dissatisfied, so I grabbed Chang and we excused ourselves to the other room.

Chang whispered, "I'm leaving right now. I think you should come with me. This is insane!" I agreed with him but said it wouldn't look good for us to exit so quickly. I begged Chang to stick with it a little longer for both our sakes. He nodded and took a couple of deep breaths before we headed back to the banquet room. Chang addressed the group in a calm, confident voice. "I apologize for my behavior earlier. I now have a better understanding of what we are trying to accomplish. This is something I've discussed with Brother Wu since college. I'm honored to share this opportunity with my brothers in this room." Dragon Head Huang stood up and shook Chang's hand to show his acceptance of the apology. The room went back to its celebratory mood as if nothing had happened. I gave an approving nod to Chang as we continued our dinner. The rest of the evening passed without incident.

As dramatic as the initiation ceremony was, nothing ever came of it. I learned later that a few of my blood brothers were arrested for various crimes unrelated to our revolutionary aspirations. With no momentum to further our cause, the group essentially disbanded. I lost touch with Yi-ming but learned years later that he left Taiwan for the US to pursue a graduate degree. He eventually moved to China to try to get into politics but didn't have much success. The last I heard, he was living in Hong Kong, working as an antiques dealer.

I honestly don't know how I found myself in such a ridiculous situation. Our passion for Taiwan was so strong that we were willing to try anything. The hopes and dreams of seeing a better Taiwan drove all of us back then and still does to this day.

Chapter Eleven

THE FORMOSAN SELF-SALVATION INITIATIVE: THE BEGINNING

In Taiwan the annual Mid-Autumn Festival or Moon Festival is a time for families to gather and enjoy good food, much like Thanksgiving in the US. The holiday always reminds me of the Moon Festival of 1964, when Dr. Peng Ming-min and two of his students, Roger Hsieh and Wei Ting-chao, were arrested for printing and attempting to distribute the Manifesto of Formosan Self-Salvation. All these years later, when the rest of my family is preparing the festival feast, I look up at the moon and think of that fateful night. I remember the cool evening air and my anxiety as I paced back and forth on the rooftop deck of my apartment, wondering what had happened to my friend Roger. I remember the optimism to spark change and inspire democracy was extinguished in the wake of the mysterious black car that took the three away.

The manifesto was Roger's brainchild. After graduation, many of us continued with our humdrum lives, even though our passion for the cause never waned. But Roger was not satisfied with simply talking or thinking about revolution—he was consumed with making it happen. All the false starts and stops, all the half-baked plans and ideas, ultimately led him to the manifesto. He truly believed this document would be

Taiwan's version of the Declaration of Independence. If the Taiwanese could unify and stand against the KMT, true democracy for Taiwan would be inevitable. This was the purpose of the manifesto. It was a rallying cry for Taiwan to separate itself from the corruption of the KMT and become an independent sovereign country. The manifesto is one of the most important documents in the history of Taiwan's independence movement.

Roger Returns from the Military Academy

Roger's passion for Taiwan was all-consuming. He inspired countless others to take up the mantle for Taiwanese independence. Unfortunately, this enthusiasm blinded him to the realities of the KMT's depravity. I don't think he understood the dangers of being so outspoken. He didn't realize that when he joined the teaching staff at the KMT-controlled Fengshan Military Academy, his "covert" activities were already attracting attention.

One of the senior instructors at the academy befriended Roger and convinced him that he was sympathetic to Taiwan's plight. Roger believed this person would be a valuable asset to the cause because of his access to high-level officials within the KMT. This instructor knew exactly how to bend Roger's ear, claiming he would influence the upper echelons of the government to press for democratic reform. He convinced Roger he would alter his curriculum so that young officers would have an affinity for the independence movement. Roger was too enthusiastic to see the red flags when the instructor asked Roger to introduce him to more Taiwanese who were involved in the independence movement.

Thinking this was a lead he should capitalize on, Roger traveled to Taipei to visit his old professor and mentor, Dr. Peng Ming-min, to discuss the opportunity. After Dr. Peng heard about this instructor who had gone out of his way to ingratiate himself with Roger, he said immediately, "You're in danger. Leave the academy right away!"

Dr. Peng was familiar with the KMT's surveillance tactics. It was likely Roger had been on the radar of the KMT's secret police for quite some time. Up to that point, Roger's efforts and activities, while enthusiastic, could be viewed as the whims of an idealistic young man. This was the first time his actions put him in real danger. He could easily have succumbed to his fear and retreated into a low-profile life, but that was not Roger's way. Frightened but undeterred, he vowed to press forward.

Roger followed Dr. Peng's advice and quit his teaching job and moved back to Taipei. The professor was able to find him work as an editor for *China Today*, a Japanese propaganda periodical. Once back in Taipei, Roger focused again on the manifesto. It was around this time that he introduced me to Dr. Peng. Although I had never studied under him, Dr. Peng's reputation as one of the top academics of his generation preceded him. He was one of the youngest tenured professors at NTU's Department of Political Science and had received numerous accolades worldwide as an expert in international air law. When Roger told me Dr. Peng would be assisting him on the manifesto, I was awestruck by how much the professor was willing to risk to help Taiwan. I didn't know it at the time we met, but Dr. Peng would become one of the most influential people in my life and one of my closest friends.

Ominous

My relationship with Roger, forged during our time at NTU, was more than just a friendship—we were like brothers. The endless hours of political and philosophical debates helped shape my own ideology and vision for Taiwan. After graduating from NTU, I lost touch with many classmates, but Roger and I always made a point to stay connected.

With Roger back in Taipei, the two of us would often get together for an after-work drink. It had been many years since we graduated from college, but no matter the time or location—the NTU dorms, the taverns at Chushan or Keelung—our conversations started up right where they'd left off. Our aspiration for an independent Taiwan continued to feed our souls. Roger was in the process of creating the first draft of the manifesto, so we would often discuss various concepts or language. I was honored that he valued my opinion and included me in this process. During these meetings, Roger spoke of his collaboration with Dr. Peng, but he never mentioned the other coauthor, Wei Ting-chao. It may have been because I didn't know Ting-chao personally and Roger preferred to limit the number of people fully involved.

We usually had our meetings at my small apartment. During these late-night sessions, Roger and I would speak in low voices in the corner of the living room. Even though Jenny didn't know what we talked about, like all Taiwanese that lived through the White Terror, she was concerned for our safety and that of our unborn child, due later that year. Despite her anxiety, she left us to our work.

Roger had borrowed $1,250 from his father and deposited it in an account at CCB under my name. As an employee, I earned higher interest rates than regular customers. Roger's plan was to use these funds to finance the manifesto.

In the early part of 1964, the manifesto was near completion. It was time to plan the printing and distribution of the document. Even though he had a full-time job, Roger still found time to edit the final document and source vendors who would help with the typing, typesetting, and final printing. Given the subject matter, Roger was limited in who he could approach. But his resourcefulness never ceased to amaze me. He ultimately found a company that was willing to typeset the manifesto, but before he approached the vendor, he replaced any reference to the KMT with the word "communists." This way, anybody working on the job would think it was an anticommunist propaganda document. Roger's plan was to then change the word back to "KMT" by hand.

Finding a vendor to print the initial run of ten thousand copies was also a challenge. Roger was ultimately able to find an unlicensed publisher of adult magazines who was willing to take on the job. The publisher, however, ferreted out the subject matter of the manifesto and refused to complete the work. We found out later that this vendor also took a sample of the document to the police. Roger didn't know it, but he, Dr. Peng, and Wei Ting-chao were under constant surveillance from that point forward. In the end, Roger found a small printing company who promised to have the completed documents delivered by the Mid-Autumn Festival.

In the early morning of September 30, 1964, the day of the festival, Roger and Ting-chao went to the printing company to supervise the final printing and then moved the documents to a nearby hotel, where Dr. Peng was waiting. They divided the copies evenly into two suitcases so they could be transported easily. The plan was for Dr. Peng and Ting-chao to take the suitcases to a friend's home on Hengyang Road in Taipei. They would meet there the next day to mail them.

Earlier that morning, Roger stopped by for a quick visit. I'll never forget the look of excitement on his face when he said, "Today is the day we change the world!" He had been working and planning this for so long, he couldn't contain his elation. As much as I wanted to share in Roger's enthusiasm, I was distracted because Jenny had experienced discomfort that morning. She was in her final trimester with our first child, and I needed to get her to the hospital. I congratulated Roger on his achievement and told him to come by later in the evening to celebrate the festival. I rushed him out the door, not knowing that would be the last time I would see him for many years.

Roger, Dr. Peng, and Ting-chao never got to carry out their mission. As they were packing away the copies of the manifesto, they heard an ominous pounding on their hotel door. Before the trio could react, the door crashed open, and several plainclothes agents stormed into the room and shouted, "Freeze!" Roger tried to flee but was beaten badly, and all three were dragged from the hotel and driven away in an unmarked black vehicle. The suitcases filled with their work were confiscated.

Vanished

When Jenny and I returned from the hospital, I was in a great mood. The check-up showed no problems, so I was finally able to relax and enjoy the holiday. Our apartment was on the top floor of the building, and the rooftop deck was perfect for celebrations. I brought up a couple of chairs and some beer to wait for my only party guest, Roger. An hour later, I began to worry. It was unlike Roger to be late without calling. With each passing hour, my stomach knotted more. When the clock struck midnight, I was in a full-blown panic, but there was nothing I could do. I couldn't go to the authorities. I didn't want to reach out to other friends lest I inadvertently get them involved. I went to bed hoping there would be news the next day.

In the morning, I scoured the newspapers, but there was no information on Roger, Dr. Peng, or Wei Ting-chao. I didn't know what to think, so my imagination ran wild. Had Roger been captured? Was he still in Taiwan, on the run? Had he fled the country? That first question churned in my mind over and over again. With each passing day, I grew more and more worried. Something was clearly wrong. Was I in danger? Roger spent so much time at my apartment—it was obvious we were close friends. The funds that were to be used for his plan sat in a bank account in my name. The potential evidence against me was undeniable. Moreover, if Roger had been captured, it was likely the authorities would question him. The KMT had no qualms about using brutal interrogation techniques to get information. Roger was a scholar, not a soldier. It seemed only be a matter of time before I was implicated. More questions raced through my mind. What would become of Jenny and our unborn child if I were arrested? How could my parents endure the downfall of another son?

I wasn't the only person worried about Roger. His brother and his parents came knocking on my door, panicked and desperate. They peppered me with the same questions I had, but I had no answers to assuage their fear.

A week after the disappearance, two Japanese newspaper reporters showed up at CCB to question me. They wanted to know if I had any information on Roger and Dr. Peng's disappearance. I could hear the blood pounding in my ears from panic, but I calmly said I didn't know anything.

My sister, Jane, was in Taipei for college and living with us at the time, so I sent her to Roger's place to see if she could find out anything. I told her that if she was questioned, she should say that she was checking up on Roger. When she arrived at his apartment, she was met by a man claiming to be the landlord. He pressed for Jane's identity and the reason for her visit. When my sister gave the rehearsed answer, the landlord smiled and gave a chilling response. "Roger went home. He is in Erlin." We knew then that Roger was in trouble.

A few more days passed. I was desperate to do something. I decided to visit Roger's apartment myself to see if I could dig up anything, but I didn't want to go alone. Once again, I enlisted the tallest person I knew—Chang, my old classmate from NTU and gangster brother. Chang picked me up at my home on his scooter and asked what had happened to Roger. I gave a vague answer. I didn't know what to expect when we reached the apartment, so I prepared a story in case we were questioned. Since Chang didn't know any details, I would do the talking, hoping this would work out better than our initiation dinner in Beitou. My plan was to say that I was an old friend and classmate of Roger's and we were supposed to celebrate the Mid-Autumn Festival together. Roger didn't show, and I wanted to make sure he was okay.

Chang and I rounded a corner and turned into the narrow alleyway where Roger's apartment was located. As we approached the dead end, a man in street clothes walked toward us and raised his hand for us to stop. He asked if we were looking for Roger. I wanted Chang to keep going and ignore him, but the alleyway was too narrow. We had no choice but to stop. The man asked again if we were looking for Roger. I noticed he was wearing black leather boots—military-issue footwear. I got off the scooter and recited the story I had rehearsed in my head. The stranger's face lit up, and he said, "I'm also a friend of Roger's. Nice to meet you."

I played along and made small talk, but in the back of my mind, I was thinking about how we could get away as quickly as possible. The man pulled out a small notebook and pen from his pants pocket and asked my name and where I was from. I mumbled something about how we were late for another appointment and that I would stop by again later. Chang got the hint and started the motor. We turned around and were on our way before the stranger could say another word. After we left the alley, Chang asked what that was all about. I swore under my breath and said Roger was in trouble, but it was best not to ask questions. We rode the rest of the way home in silence.

The next day, I phoned Roger's workplace, *China Today*, to see if I could get any information. I had called the newspaper many times before, but this time, I didn't recognize the man's voice on the other end. He asked why I was calling, and I used the same story from the day before. When he pressed me for my name, I took a deep breath and identified myself. I figured they had all the information about me, so there was no reason to lie. The man told me that Roger had taken time off from work because of his health.

On October 24, 1964, almost a month after Roger's disappearance, I noticed an article on page six of the *China Post* titled "Professor and Two of His Students Imprisoned for Sedition." The article didn't give much detail, but it confirmed our worst fears:

> Peng Ming-min, Roger Hsieh, and Wei Ting-chao were captured red-handed as they engaged in subversive and seditious activities . . . they are charged with sedition, and will be tried by a military court.

It was the Taiwan Garrison Command, a secret police/state security organization, that had arrested them. Although I had been mentally prepared to hear this news after being in limbo for so many weeks, seeing the confirmation in print was still a shock.

Their arrest made me question my future in Taiwan. I had a wife, and I was about to become a father. I needed to take care of my family, but I didn't know whether I would be implicated in the planned dissemination of the manifesto. I was worried Roger might have inadvertently put a target on me, but I learned much later that he never once said my name while in prison. My emotions swung crazily during that time. There were moments when I was so angry with the KMT I wanted nothing more than to bring it down, but I was also paranoid that I would be arrested at any second. I was consumed with rage and fear.

Chapter Twelve

ROGER HSIEH: AFTERMATH

All told, Roger spent eleven years in prison. One would think that his passion for Taiwanese independence would have been curbed with all the time he spent locked away and tortured. But Roger's love for our home country could not be suppressed.

News of the arrest reverberated internationally. Dr. Peng was a pioneer in the burgeoning field of international air law and widely respected throughout the world. I don't believe the KMT expected the intense scrutiny that followed his disappearance. It was satisfying to me to see Chiang and the KMT on the defensive for once. For a time, the KMT relaxed their grip on the populace, but once the spotlight faded, they were back to their old ways.

Roger faced unspeakable brutality while in prison, but the isolation from the rest of the world was equally devastating. He was no longer able to do what he did best, spread enthusiasm among other activists and take action against his oppressors. The KMT eventually released him in 1969, after years of pressure from the international community. We all hoped this would be a new start, but the KMT wasn't done with him. Determined to make an example of Roger, they used the guise of two unsolved bombings, one in Tainan in 1970 and another in Taipei in

1971, to interrogate Roger and eventually coerce a confession out of him. He spent another six years in prison, this time in solitary confinement.

Roger came to visit me in Alaska not long after his second release from prison. We still had lively discussions, similar to those we had as idealistic young men, but each evening, Roger needed to soak in a hot bath to relieve the pain in his broken body. I helped him apply medication to his damaged ribs, ankles chafed from the shackles, and dislocated shoulders. I saw firsthand the effects of the KMT's brutality. In spite of the obvious pain and sacrifice he'd endured, he never complained, and his trademark enthusiasm never wavered.

After Alaska, Roger spent time traveling throughout the States, visiting many of the major American cities, including Chicago, New York, Houston, Los Angeles, San Francisco, and Seattle. He even spent time in other countries, like Canada, Germany, the United Kingdom, and Sweden. He lived somewhat of a nomadic existence until he visited Frank Lai in New York. He met his life partner, Gigi, there, and they got married in December 1980. Roger's beaming smile at his wedding made me hopeful that he had found some much-deserved peace and happiness.

A couple of years later, I moved to Los Angeles to join General Bank. I had heard that Roger was having a tough time getting on his feet after settling in New York. I wanted to help in any way I could. When he told me about a very popular New York–based ice cream franchise called Carvel and his hope to open his own ice cream shop, I agreed it was a great idea. I wanted to discuss it with him in more detail.

Just as I was thinking about how to set up a Carvel location for Roger in New York, there was a knock on my door. To my shock, I saw Roger, Gigi, and their son, smiles on their faces and their car overflowing with all their possessions behind them. Apparently, right after my phone call with Roger, they'd packed up and spent the week driving across the country. Roger thought there was no better location to set up an ice cream store than sunny Los Angeles. I shouldn't have been surprised, given the antics my friend had gotten into when we were younger. I welcomed them into my home, and we spent the rest of the day discussing the first Carvel ice cream shop in Southern California.

A Failed Venture

As we worked on finding a location, finalizing the license and other documents, and learning the process of starting a Carvel franchise, I soon realized that Roger was not at all interested in running an ice cream shop. He wanted Gigi to manage the store while he continued to advocate for Taiwanese democracy and independence. With no experience whatsoever running a small business, Gigi would need help. We thought Jenny would make a good partner since we wanted to keep this venture in the family. She had a very good job at LAX, but we all agreed this was a great opportunity to do something more interesting and, hopefully, make a nice living.

Gigi and Jenny found a reasonably priced, but not premium, location a little south of Los Angeles. They attended all the Carvel training sessions together. The intent was for them to handle all the operational aspects of the business, with neither getting compensation until the store began to show a profit. I was busy with General Bank at the time, so my only involvement was paying the bills.

It didn't take long after the grand opening for us to realize we had made a big mistake. From day one, business was not good. The biggest issue was the location. The store wasn't very visible, and there was almost no foot traffic. On top of that, no one in Los Angeles had heard of Carvel except the transplants from New York, where it was a household name. We had no brand recognition to draw in customers.

After a few months of losses, Gigi abruptly announced she was quitting the ice cream business. We had signed a multiyear lease, so Jenny had no choice but to manage the ice cream store on her own. It was hard work and long hours with no profit, and it was a strain on her and our family. I'm proud of the way she weathered this difficult period. After the lease expired, we closed the shop and said goodbye to Carvel.

I learned later that the move to Los Angeles had put a great financial strain on Roger and his family. It finally dawned on me that I should have considered Roger's financial situation more carefully before entering into this venture. The priority should have been on getting Roger back on his feet, but I didn't recognize this until it was too late. Here I was, thinking I was helping Roger, but instead I was digging him into an even deeper hole. I prefer not to dwell on the past, but this is one regret that I've never been able to forget.

A Friendship Remembered

My old friend Roger passed away on September 8, 2019. Taiwan lost a true pioneer and visionary, and I lost a brother. Whenever I think of him, I can't help but reminisce about the countless nights I spent debating politics and philosophy with him. He was a brother to me in every sense of the word. I also reflect on that fateful Mid-Autumn Festival in 1964. If not for Jenny's visit to the hospital that day, I would have been with Roger and gotten arrested too.

Two weeks after his passing, I watched a tribute to Roger on the Formosa Television channel. His infectious smile flashed across the screen with the caption "Roger Hsieh—A Career Fighter." The host gave a brief overview of Roger's childhood, and then a scholarly gentleman talked about Roger's impact on Taiwanese history, namely the publication of the Manifesto of Formosan Self-Salvation authored by Roger, Wei Ting-chao, and Dr. Peng Ming-min. The segment continued with a reenactment of their arrest by the KMT's secret police the evening before they were to distribute the manifesto.

I had imagined countless times what that night must have been like for my good friend, but to see it played out on TV was surreal. If it hadn't been for Jenny's pregnancy, I would likely have been right next to Roger when he was arrested. The broadcast described in vivid and painful detail the months of torture he endured at the hands of the KMT. Back then, I didn't know that Roger never yielded. He could easily have succumbed to the pain and spared himself more suffering by implicating me, but he never did. Because of Roger, I was able to make a new life for myself and my family in the US. How does one adequately express gratitude to a friend like that?

Toward the end of the documentary, Gigi described the last few months of his life. Age and the physical abuse he suffered at the hands of the KMT had taken a toll on his body. He was treated for a myriad of problems and needed constant monitoring. The show then cut to a video segment from October 2018 when the president of Taiwan, Tsai Ing-wen, held a ceremony honoring the victims who were unjustly incarcerated during the White Terror. The president held up a piece of paper with all the names, including Roger's, and then she destroyed it, overturning the guilty verdicts. The documentary concluded with the details of Roger's passing and footage of his funeral ceremony. Tears welled in my eyes. Dr. Peng and a handful of other close friends were there, but I was not invited to the memorial service. I never had the chance to properly say goodbye to my friend.

In 2008, Taiwan's National Museum of History published an 870-page interview with three historians titled *The Manifesto of Formosan Self-Salvation: An Interview with Mr. Roger Hsieh*. In the interview, Roger recounted his life and the events leading up to the inception of the manifesto and the torment he faced after his arrest. His story, told in his own words, moved me, but I had to admit it stung that my name was only mentioned a few times. It wasn't because I felt slighted; it served as a painful reminder that the unshakeable friendship we shared early in life had waned as the years went by.

I think back on how Roger and I grew apart. During our youth in the NTU dorms, our bond was so strong I thought our friendship would endure throughout our lives. It's difficult now to say what changed for us. Was it the eleven years in prison? Was it the unsuccessful business venture? Or just that our lives took such different paths that perhaps the change was inevitable. If I had been more aware of the growing distance between us, could I have prevented some of what happened? The what-ifs are endless. One thing I do know—Roger was as loyal a friend as one could have. We didn't get to enjoy those late-night political and philosophical discussions in our later years, but his influence on my life is immeasurable. He will always be remembered for his bravery, perseverance, and love for Taiwan. I will always remember his infectious smile, unbridled enthusiasm, and unwavering loyalty.

Chapter Thirteen

SHROUD OF FEAR

"Li-pei, get your butt out of that chair. Your wife is having a baby!" I looked up from my mahjong hand, bleary-eyed. It took a moment for me to realize what my coworker, Mr. Hsiao, had just said. I had been playing mahjong and drinking for most of the evening, so my head was fuzzy. It was November 1964, a few weeks after Roger disappeared. Jenny wasn't due for a few days, so I assumed Hsiao was tricking me into giving up my seat in the game. I settled back and reviewed my tiles again.

Hsiao tapped his knuckles on the mahjong table. "I'm not kidding! You really need to head home!"

I was skeptical, but the look on Hsiao's face was sincere. I reluctantly stood and walked home. When I realized Jenny wasn't there waiting for me, I knew Hsiao was not playing a joke. I splashed some cold water on my face and rushed to the hospital.

Jane greeted me at the National Taiwan University Hospital's maternity ward. She gave me a stern look and shook her head but didn't say a word. My sister was the one who had tried to track me down when Jenny went into labor. She looked for me at my usual drinking spots but didn't know I was playing mahjong that evening. During her search, she ran into Hsiao, who assured her he would find me and relay the message.

When I stumbled into the maternity ward, Jane didn't bother to scold me. She led me to Jenny's room, where my newborn son, George, was lying in a small bassinette. It brought me joy to pick him up, but I was also awash with guilt and shame that I hadn't been there with Jenny for the birth of our first child.

The shame was unbearable. It had been a few weeks since the arrest of Roger, Dr. Peng, and Wei Ting-chao, and I was not handling the news well. Every morning I woke up fearing it would be my last day as a free man. I would spend my day going through the motions at work but always on the lookout for an unmarked black Jeep pulling up in front of the branch office. When the day passed with no incident, I would head to the nearest pub, hoping to numb myself to the constant paranoia. This had become my routine—living in fear. Part of me had hoped the authorities would take me away to end this misery, but when I looked down at my newborn son, I knew I needed to find a way out of this mess.

Yu Hsin-wang's Proposition

With a new baby in the house and the ever-present fear of KMT secret agents showing up at my door, it took an old friend to help shake me from my malaise. Yu Hsin-wang, the classmate who had helped me move from Chushan to Keelung years earlier, came to see me because he needed help dealing with the bank. He had recently given up teaching to follow in his father's footsteps in business and eventually found his calling in international trade. The people he worked with were so impressed with his business acumen that they partnered with him to create a new business venture. I was able to help my old friend obtain a loan from CCB in the amount of $2,500, quite a large sum at the time. Hsin-wang used the new capital to grow his company significantly in a very short period of time. Since I was part of the team that provided his company with the loan, I got frequent updates on how well he was doing.

I was happy for Hsin-wang. His success was well earned, so I was surprised when he told me that his company was having cash flow problems. While the growth of his company was impressive, the timing of the receipts from his sales was causing a cash strain. He often had to pay out expenses well before he received any of the corresponding income. This working capital constraint was hindering him from pursuing other business opportunities, thus adversely affecting the company. He approached me because he had heard that bank clerks, such as myself, sometimes provided personal short-term loans to banking clients. I explained that I could barely feed my family with my salary, so I wasn't in a position to lend out any money myself, but I would ask my colleagues.

I learned from my coworkers that this type of lending was fairly common. They told me they were willing to loan money to Hsin-wang as long as I vouched for him by personally guaranteeing the payback of these loans. I knew Hsin-wang was a man of integrity and he came from a wealthy family, so I didn't worry much about the financial risk.

Hsin-wang's company was a brokerage for companies based in Japan and the US interested in winning construction and equipment contracts offered by Taiwan's state-owned businesses. These were typically large contracts in petroleum, raw chemical materials, railway services, and utilities. As I learned more, I was convinced that the startup had potential, so I became more heavily involved as the go-between for Hsin-wang and my colleagues who provided working capital loans. The business continued to grow, and Hsin-wang's need for short-term loans increased. At one point, I facilitated over $12,500 in loans, all of which I personally guaranteed.

In hindsight it wasn't wise of me to extend myself like that. I had heard stories about former colleagues who provided personal guarantees on loans and lost everything. There were even instances where guarantors faced prison time. This was not the type of business one should engage in unless the guarantor had the wherewithal to handle the potential loss. In my case, I had no wherewithal whatsoever! But Hsin-wang's business continued to do well, so I didn't worry.

But then one day, Hsin-wang approached me and explained that he didn't trust the people working for him to handle the day-to-day operations. He was busy adding clients and growing the company, so he didn't have time to focus on other aspects of the business. He was afraid the weakness in operations was catching up with him and the company would go belly up without better management.

When he said the words "belly up," the magnitude of the situation finally hit me over the head like a brick. While helping Hsin-wang, I had been distracted from the constant fear of discovery by the KMT authorities. Now it was possible that I would be going to jail anyway because of bad loans! My knees buckled at the thought of having to tell my colleagues they had been foolish for trusting me. Hsin-wang, ever the salesman, caught me at just the right moment. He proposed that I leave the bank and work with him full-time as the operations manager of the company. He would focus on marketing, and I would handle all the other aspects of the business. "We will be unstoppable!" he cheerfully exclaimed.

Switching Gears

Hsin-wang's offer made me take a long, hard look at myself and my career. For much of my life, I had floated along, rarely planning anything, letting the wind decide my fate. But now fate had put me at a crossroads. Professionally, I wasn't particularly fulfilled at the bank. I had been working at CCB for seven years, watching others get promoted over me. It was a steady job, but I had no passion for it, and I knew there would be no new challenges or upward mobility in the future. I felt fortunate to have a stable and happy family life, but the unsatisfying professional life and the stress-induced paranoia I was constantly under were wearing me out. I needed to change things up, and perhaps Hsin-wang's company was the perfect remedy. Also, given the financial exposure I carried because of the company's borrowing activity, I had a vested interest in seeing that the business did well.

In January 1967, I tendered my resignation to CCB and joined Hsin-wang's company. Very few people leave secure, desirable banking jobs voluntarily, so my colleagues were caught off guard by my announcement.

Hsin-wang appointed me as the office manager overseeing day-to-day operations. My monthly salary at the time I resigned from CCB was $75. Hsin-wang wanted to show his appreciation and provided me with $113 plus a 15-percent interest in the company. When my colleagues learned that I would be working for Hsin-wang, they assumed his company must be doing extremely well. They expressed interest in lending even more working capital. With me on board, the company was able to manage the debt load more easily.

Blackness

For much of my life, I've found the adage "no such thing as a free lunch" to hold true, and it described my new job to a T. I was getting paid more, but I didn't realize how much extra work and responsibility came with the job. At CCB I would clock in and clock out at the same time every day. There was no overtime or work on weekends. With the new job, unpredictability was the norm. During the day, I was responsible for office management, which included overseeing the employees, dealing with various vendors and proposals, and making sure our finances were in order. During the evenings, I would often attend networking events to meet prospective clients. I didn't mind the extra responsibility, but there was very little work–life balance. Jenny had just had our second child, and I was missing a great deal of what was happening in my family.

Hsin-wang's company was involved with the procurement of heavy machinery, equipment, and supplies for government-owned enterprises in Taiwan. Most of the vendors were Japanese or American companies. We would help them with the bidding process, for which we earned commissions. Not long after I joined, I realized I was contributing to the corruption of the KMT by manipulating the bidding price with some under-the-table payouts. I always preferred to have up-front communication when it came to business, so this practice didn't sit well with me.

The Americans we worked with had trouble understanding this practice also, since they would generally submit their bidding price based on their cost-and-profit analysis. They gained my respect when most resisted upon learning they would essentially need to bribe officials. But integrity would not score points with the Taiwanese buyers. I had to let the Americans know this was how the game was played, as distasteful as it was.

It wasn't long into my stint with Hsin-wang that I knew I wouldn't last in this business. Watching the corrupt behavior of Taiwanese politicians was unbearable. These "civil servants" were KMT representatives who took advantage of their position to get wealthy. They didn't care about their fiduciary responsibility or public duty to the Taiwanese people, nor did they care about being good international partners with overseas companies. They only cared about one thing—lining their own pockets. I had spent most of my life thinking of ways to bring down the KMT, and here I was, doing a job that essentially paid off corrupt KMT politicians.

The other aspect of the work that I could not stomach was the constant schmoozing and entertaining of clients and government officials. Hsin-wang was supposed to be the primary client manager, but there were many evenings where I had to be his backup because he was drunk within the first hour. Often there would be two or even three client engagements in the same evening. There were many nights when I got home after a late night of entertaining only to get a call from some government officials to meet them at a local hostess bar. They would ask me to join them, but that was their way of telling me to come down and pay the bill.

I'm ashamed to say these nights of entertainment often included extra services provided by the hostesses. I would be the one to dole out the cash as each official picked out a hostess for the evening. Each time I placed a bill in the outstretched hand of a young woman, I would avert my eyes in shame—it felt like selling a piece of my soul. The level of emotional, mental, and physical exhaustion from this new job was eating at me. I wanted to leave, but Hsin-wang's company was in no position to pay back the loans to my former colleagues at CCB. I had no choice—I had to hold on for the time being.

Caution from an Investigator

The government officials with whom we had business dealings were often from the Ministry of Justice Investigation Bureau (MJIB), an intelligence and surveillance arm of the KMT. We entertained them on many occasions. One evening, I took a Mr. Wang, chief of the MJIB's Taipei office and a native Taiwanese, to dinner. I didn't know Wang particularly well, but we had socialized before, so we were more than acquaintances. On this particular evening, the drinks were flowing especially fast, and alcohol has a tendency to loosen the tongue, even on hardened KMT officials.

The whiskey bottle I had ordered was more than half empty when Wang raised his glass and opened his mouth as if to say something, but thought better of it. I assumed he was going to give me an inside tip on a pending government open bid, so I made a point of topping off his glass. A few minutes later, he surveyed the room to make sure no one was nearby. He leaned in and said in a low voice, "Li-pei, I've known about you for a while. My agency has had a tail on you for years."

I sat up, all my fears of being arrested rushing back. He raised his glass to his lips and took a long, slow drink. The dramatic pause felt like an eternity. He lowered his glass and said in a soft whisper, "You should leave the country as soon as you can."

Chapter Fourteen

FLIGHT

Mr. Wang's terrifying words of warning shook me to my core. I had almost forgotten the intense paranoia I'd felt two years earlier after Roger's arrest. After so much time had gone by, I had convinced myself that the fear was unwarranted. Now I knew my persecution complex was not delusional. The KMT was indeed watching me.

I needed to leave Taiwan. Martial law was still in effect, so there were only two realistic options for traveling abroad: a business trip or studying overseas. Traveling on business was not a long-term solution, and I did not want to cause any trouble for Hsin-wang. Thus, the only realistic option was studying abroad. But I was thirty-three years old, out of university for ten years, and I had a wife and two small children. The thought of preparing for the Test of English as a Foreign Language (TOEFL) and graduate school applications was daunting, but I knew it was necessary.

Meant to Be

Even though I had not studied for an exam in years, I was able to pass the TOEFL without a problem. One hurdle down. I now needed to get accepted into a school in the US. I focused on business programs that met two criteria: low tuition and proximity to St. Louis, Missouri, where Jane attended Washington University. Always extremely kind and helpful, my sister helped me complete the applications despite her heavy student workload. From that labor of love, a lone school, Fort Hays State University in Kansas, accepted me into its business program. The tuition was only $250 a semester, and it was less than an eight-hour drive to St. Louis. The school didn't have a big brand name, but I learned later that the academic training was more than sufficient to arm me for the challenges in my future career.

I'll forever be grateful for what Jane did for me. It was only with her assistance that I was able to come to the United States. Her journey to the US years earlier helped pave the way for me.

Getting My Ducks in a Row

With the acceptance letter in hand, things were falling into place on the US side, but there was still much to be done in Taiwan. Even though I had chosen an affordable graduate program, I still needed to manage my finances to the last penny. During my tenure at CCB, my salary had been just enough to cover expenses for my family, and I had virtually no savings. Once I started with Hsin-wang, my financial situation improved, mainly because of my ownership interest in the company. Even though I had worked at Hsin-wang's company for less than a year, the revenue and profits had increased significantly. The profit for that year would be approximately $150,000. After my acceptance to Fort Hays, I notified Hsin-wang of my plans. He tried to dissuade me from leaving, but I told him I had to go.

My 15-percent share of the profits would be $22,500, which was more than enough to cover my expenses in the US. I was told by the university that it would cost approximately $2,500 for school, including tuition and living expenses. I wanted to be fair to Hsin-wang. He had always been a good friend, and I felt bad about leaving the company. I suggested he give me $2,500 plus my airfare to the US. He could then share whatever else was owed me with the rest of the employees.

Hsin-wang insisted on paying me my full share. He agreed to the up-front payment but promised to keep the balance in a separate account until I returned from the US. If I didn't return, he would give it to the staff as bonuses. Hsin-wang was a true and honorable friend. He kept his word and took care of the employees years later when it was clear I wouldn't be returning to Taiwan in the foreseeable future.

Once my financial situation was settled, I felt like there was light at the end of the tunnel. The US was within reach. But an unexpected bump in the road threatened to derail my plans. Because I was underweight, I had been exempt from compulsory military duty after graduating from NTU. I thought the military was far in my rearview mirror, but then I received a notice from the Ministry of Education that I was required to undergo "military training for students to study abroad." I was forced to enroll in a three-month training camp in Beitou.

I realized that the camp had very little to do with military training. We only spent one session on the firing range. The rest of the time was used for "political ideologies training," otherwise known as KMT propaganda bullshit. The program was intended to make sure we were not unduly affected by foreign influences and that we adhered to KMT philosophy while abroad. The spew that came out of the mouths of the KMT-loyal scholars was insufferable, but I knew I needed to keep up appearances. I was most likely still being monitored by the MJIB.

I thought of a way to avoid suspicion and have a little fun at the expense of my KMT compatriots—I would play the role of the perfect KMT recruit. Part of the training program included daily assignments and journals that were reviewed by our instructors. I knew we were constantly being monitored, so in addition to the assignments, I kept a journal in my best handwriting, using various KMT mantras such as: "My gratitude to the government runs deep and wide. I pledge that I'll pay it forward to my countrymen as soon as I finish my education overseas." I deliberately left my journal on my desk in the classroom.

I thought the journal was a nice touch to fool my superiors, but the last thing I wanted was to bring undue attention. I guess my writing worked too well, because one day, almost at the end of the training camp, a colonel—a dedicated old-school KMT official—approached me and said, "Mr. Wu. I'm impressed with your dedication and loyalty to the country. You'll continue to be an asset for the KMT after you move abroad, I'm sure." He launched into a long speech about the virtues of the KMT and how I should think about joining the party. I mumbled a halfhearted thank you while I searched my brain. How would a loyal KMT pawn respond?

The colonel asked me what I thought about joining the KMT. I was fumbling for an answer when an idea suddenly popped into my head. I asked the colonel whether I needed somebody to sponsor me in order to join the KMT.

"Of course," he responded. "And I have somebody in mind for you."

"Thank you, Colonel. My father is very close friends with Hsieh Tung-min, the secretary of Taiwan Province. I once spoke with Secretary Hsieh about joining the KMT, and he mentioned that I would need a sponsor."

Hsieh was a prominent figure within the KMT ranks. My name-dropping clearly impressed the colonel, because his eyes lit up and his jaw dropped.

I continued, "I spent quite a bit of time at Uncle Hsieh's home when I was at NTU, and we would talk for hours about the KMT. Of course, I wouldn't want to be disrespectful to Uncle Hsieh, so I think I should ask him to be my sponsor. Don't you?"

The colonel, speechless, simply nodded and gave me a stack of application forms for KMT membership. I turned, smirked, and walked back to the barracks.

My story about Uncle Hsieh was so convincing because it was based in truth. My father did go to high school with Hsieh, and I did visit him numerous times while I was at NTU. Obviously, our politics didn't overlap, but he had been friendly to me and provided a much-needed hot meal from time to time. His star continued to rise within the KMT, and at one point, he was one of the highest-ranking Taiwanese members in the party, ultimately becoming vice president under Chiang Ching-kuo.

The rest of my time at the military camp passed without incident, and I was another step closer to setting foot in the US.

Getting a Passport

Despite the steady progress I made, the final and biggest challenge loomed before me—getting a passport. Under martial law, obtaining a passport meant going through many checkpoints, one of which was getting clearance from the Taiwan Garrison Command, the same secret police unit that had captured Roger, Dr. Peng, and Wei Ting-chao. I knew I was being monitored but had no idea what kind of evidence they had or how close they were to arresting me. One of my NTU classmates, Liu Jia-shun, was arrested the evening before he was to leave for the US and sentenced to three years in prison.

I had come so far—to be denied at this point would have been unbearable. I needed a plan to make sure this last step was successful so that I could board my flight to the US. I decided it was best to wait until the very last moment to apply for a passport. This way, the various government departments and agencies would have less time to scrutinize my application. I hoped the left hand wouldn't know what the right hand was doing.

A couple of weeks before my scheduled departure—just enough time for a passport to be processed—I walked into the Ministry of Foreign Affairs (MOFA), the agency that would initially review my passport application. The office building that housed MOFA also included the Taiwan Garrison Command and the Ministry of Education, the other agencies from which I would need approval. After I dropped off the necessary application forms at MOFA, there was nothing left to do but wait. The review process usually took a week.

Waiting for others to decide my fate was hard for me. I felt my chances of success would improve if I found a way to expedite my application. I had come to understand the bureaucratic nature of the KMT in my time working with Hsin-wang. KMT officials always appeared stiff and uncompromising, but if you knew how to push the right buttons, they usually wanted to ingratiate themselves to you. During my three-month military training, I met an instructor, Wu Zu-yu (no relation), who was a former ambassador to the US and had a senior position at MOFA. Mr. Wu spent hours during his lectures extolling the virtues of the KMT and our responsibilities as overseas students. He also asked us to contact him directly if we had any questions or problems. He said, "My door is always open." The last thing I wanted was to ever see that guy again, but I was happy to use his name to my advantage.

I went back to MOFA that afternoon. The official behind the service counter was Mr. Tsai. I politely began my well-rehearsed story. "I just dropped off my application this morning. I'm scheduled to leave for the US in about two weeks, but my school, Fort Hays State University, is requiring me to arrive earlier than scheduled so that I have time to take some English classes." I paused for only a moment to catch my breath so Tsai wouldn't have an opportunity to interject. "I just spoke to Wu Zu-yu about the situation, and he suggested I come to see you. Uncle Wu said that this office would take care of everything." As I had hoped, Mr. Wu's name impressed Tsai. He immediately found my application at the bottom of a deep pile and applied an official stamp of approval from MOFA. Tsai then escorted me to the office of the Garrison Command, where he whispered something to the attending officers. They eyed me for a moment and then promptly stamped the application. My escort then took me to the Ministry of Education. The thumping sound from the final approval stamp was music to my ears. Tsai turned to me with a smile and told me to come by the next day to pick up the passport. Altogether, I was able to get the paperwork taken care of in less than thirty minutes. To this day, I wonder how Tsai didn't hear my thundering heartbeat as he was leading me to the various offices. I kept expecting Wu Zu-yu to burst in surrounded by an army of agents, but everything went as well as I could have hoped.

The next morning, I walked into MOFA's office with clammy hands and as calm a face as I could summon. Fortunately, there was no wait at the service counter. Two minutes later, I walked out with a shiny new Taiwanese passport and a goofy grin on my face.

Saying Goodbye to My Family

I was only a few days from boarding my flight to the US. I had miraculously cleared all the major hurdles in order to begin my new life as a graduate student. The only thing remaining was to make sure my family was taken care of. When I returned home with the new passport, the reality of my impending departure finally set in. Jenny had seen firsthand the emotional toll I had suffered during the past few years. She knew my move to the US was best for me and our family. But now that I was only days away from leaving, my wife felt a fresh wave of uncertainty about our future. The challenges for her would be significant. She would be responsible for our two boys while I was away, and it was unclear when or how our family would be reunited. She didn't complain, but I heard her weeping in the middle of the night.

We decided the best arrangement would be for Jenny and the boys to move to Dacheng with my parents. We sold our apartment unit and netted $1,000, so Jenny could cover the expenses while I was away. I discovered later that she loaned this money to her father and never saw its return. She had to borrow money from my elder brother to buy our children's winter clothes. On my last night in Taiwan, as I was packing away a few personal items, I felt a nervous energy that I had never experienced before. I was excited and optimistic about this new journey, but I was also riddled with angst and guilt about leaving my family. Jenny, my two boys, and I had a quiet family dinner that evening. My children were too young to fully comprehend the situation. They simply nodded their heads when I told them to be good boys and mind their mother. The innocent looks on their faces almost made me rip up my airplane ticket.

PART II

SURVIVAL IN THE LAND
OF THE FREE

Chapter Fifteen

WELCOME TO
THE UNITED STATES

On January 19, 1968, I left for America. As the plane took off, the Songshan International Airport and Taiwan's familiar luscious greenery faded from view. This was the first time in all my life that I had stepped foot off of Taiwan. I was bound for a country that I knew only through magazines and books. I settled into my seat for the long flight and closed my eyes, but I couldn't get the images from the last couple of hours out of my head. I was flooded with sadness and uncertainty. Jenny and my two young boys had come to the airport to see me off, as well as my parents. My father rarely left the house in those days, so the sight of him almost knocked me to my knees. I exchanged few words with my family. There wasn't much to be said, as my parents understood why I had to leave. I turned one last time at the gate and saw my father holding my oldest boy's hand as they both waved goodbye.

I felt a sense of relief to be finally out of the KMT's reach, but I was now faced with a new kind of uncertainty. What would my life be like in the US? When would I see my family again?

Excitement and determination overtook me as I landed at Sea-Tac International Airport. I passed immigration and saw a large banner that said, "Welcome to the United States." I walked outside and breathed in the cool, fresh Pacific Northwest air. It was the taste of freedom.

Chapter Sixteen

I HAVE A FEELING WE'RE
NOT IN TAIWAN ANYMORE

From Seattle I flew to Los Angeles so I could spend a few days with my old friend and brother-in-law, Frank Lai, before heading to Kansas. Seeing him waiting for me at LAX almost brought tears to my eyes. Frank had already been in the US for a few years, so he was able to give me a primer on American culture. He was also active in the Taiwanese independence movement and immediately began recruiting me for the cause. He encouraged me to forget about graduate school and dedicate myself to independence activities. I was more than willing to help where I could, but I had other responsibilities. I promised Frank he could count on my support, but my priority for the short term was completing graduate school and finding a job so I could take care of my family.

A few days later, I left sunny Los Angeles for the cold of Kansas. My one-year graduate business program at Fort Hays State University started in late January, a difficult time of year to acclimate to. Whenever I opened the door, I was greeted by a blast of Kansas winter air that almost knocked me back into the house. I bundled up, but not nearly enough to withstand the freezing cold.

Those first few days in Kansas were challenging, but overall, my impression of my new home was positive—except for the weather. I had never been so cold in my life. I couldn't understand how anybody could survive in that weather. I quickly realized the answer was very simple— wear the proper clothes! I saw my classmates bundled in layers with heavy gloves, scarves, knit caps, galoshes, and down parkas so that every part of the body was covered. It was clear my father's old overcoat had no chance against a midwestern winter. My first order of business was a stop at the local department store.

Once I was adequately dressed, it was time for me to buckle down in my new life as a graduate student. It had been almost eleven years since I'd attended formal classes, so I was nervous. I looked around the lecture hall at the faces of my classmates, wondering if I had ever looked that young. But the apprehension I felt because of my age was nothing compared to the distress I experienced during the lectures. I had passed the TOEFL exam to get into graduate school, but practically speaking, I was not fluent in conversational English at all. Those first few weeks of classes were the most challenging of my life. Each day after school, I would go home dejected and worried I was in over my head. But I would not let this challenge deter me. There was only one solution—work harder. Every day, I would scour textbooks and other reference materials until I knew exactly what the previous lecture was about. Then I would preview the material of the next lecture in preparation for the class. Gradually, with each lecture, I would understand more and more without having to do too much additional research.

Overall, my grades showed vast improvement after only a couple of months. The courses where I did particularly well were ones that relied heavily on textbooks as source material. If the course didn't adhere to the formal reference material, then I had a *big* problem. For example, in a marketing class, the professor asked us to give an analysis of Oscar Mayer's marketing slogan, "I wish I were an Oscar Mayer wiener." When I raised my hand and asked the professor, "What is a wiener?" the class burst out laughing.

That embarrassment, however, was not the worst I experienced in school. That honor goes to Professor Thomas's class in financial management. Professor Thomas was a fantastic teacher. He was truly passionate, an expert in his field, and knew how to engage his students. I had never experienced a class where students participated with such enthusiasm. The laughter that inevitably emanated from his lectures was exhilarating. Professor Thomas was a master at diverging from the textbook to interject real-world situations, giving the students practical applications beyond the theory. Yet, even with all this lively energy, I dreaded walking into Professor Thomas's lectures. His fondness for going off script was exactly where I had difficulty because of my English. I watched with envy as my classmates would break off into their study groups. I never received an invitation to join, which made me feel even more isolated.

The worst part of the class was the pop quizzes Professor Thomas administered every other week. Since I was having difficulty following the class material, the questions on each quiz were nothing but gibberish to me. I had no choice but to leave everything blank. The professor would typically hand back the graded quizzes in front of the entire class from best grade to worst. Waiting to hear "Li-pei Wu!" after all the other names had been called and then taking the walk of shame to the front of the class to collect my paper was torture.

I had to find a way to turn the situation around. A couple of weeks later, I followed the two best students in the class to the library and introduced myself. I told them my dilemma and asked if I could borrow their notes after each lecture. Even though they barely knew me, they handed over their notebooks without hesitation. I was touched by their generosity and determined not to let it go to waste. I pored over their notes like my life depended on it. A week later, another round of graded pop quizzes was handed back to the class. The first name that was called out was Li-pei Wu! My ears perked up in surprise. As I walked to the front of the class, I could feel the shock reverberate through the room.

Professor Thomas handed the paper to me and gave me a thoughtful stare. I expected him to compliment me on the vast improvement, but he didn't say a word.

Professor Thomas

He called me to his office after class. I had no idea what he wanted. When he began asking numerous questions on how I made a turnaround in so short a time, it finally dawned on me that he was questioning my integrity. He couldn't believe it was possible for me to accomplish what I had without cheating. I stammered and explained as best I could that I had worked hard to catch up. I was nervous because I couldn't articulate as well as I would have liked, but I was not going to let my character be maligned without putting up a fight. I could tell my words alone would not persuade him, so I suggested that he test me right then and there. He pulled out a quiz that he was planning to use the following class. I immediately began working on it right in front of him. When he reviewed my completed work, the look on his face told me all I needed to know. He stood, apologized, and congratulated me on a job well done. I could tell he was impressed with my perseverance and the effort I had put into his class.

The professor recognized my hard work and decided to take me under his wing as a protégé. I became a frequent guest in his home. He was then in his sixties, and his adult children had all moved away. I became like an adopted son to him. We spent countless hours discussing many subjects, not only financial management. I chose "Comparison between the New York Stock Exchange and Taiwan Stock Exchange" as the subject of my master's thesis, and he was my thesis advisor. He wrote a glowing recommendation letter for my job applications. Professor Thomas was a father figure, mentor, and friend at a time when I needed those the most, and I will forever be grateful.

Good Samaritans

When I first arrived in Hays, I rented a room from an elderly Russian lady for $26 a month. The lady was very kind. She noticed how skinny I was, so she gave me homemade pies from time to time. With my heavy academic workload, I didn't have time to cook. I'd rarely stepped foot in the kitchen in Taiwan, but here, if I wanted to eat, I'd need to try. My first week, I made a meal by dumping boiled eggs, pork ribs, and any other meat that was on sale into a big pot with soy sauce, MSG, and sugar. At first taste, it wasn't bad. After five days of eating my "stew," my body rebelled. It wouldn't allow me to take another bite. I resorted to eating nothing but peanut-butter-and-jelly sandwiches. I drank quite a bit of whole milk for nutrition, but the unfortunate side effects of my lactose intolerance quashed that plan. My weight loss precipitated to the point where people around me were worried about my health.

One day I ran into Jennifer, the university counselor who was in charge of the school's international students. When she saw how emaciated I was, her jaw dropped. "What happened to you, Li-pei? I barely recognize you!" I could tell Jennifer was sincerely worried about me.

Around this time, Jenny and I spoke often about when she and the boys would be able to come to the US. I wasn't sure how we were going to make that happen. My immediate focus was to complete graduate school, but beyond that, I had no concrete plan. When Jennifer noticed my weight loss, I thought maybe I could use my health to appeal to the Taiwanese authorities. I told Jennifer about my family health history and how my older brother suffered from spinal tuberculosis. I told her, "My health issues seem to be getting worse. I don't know how much longer I can go on. If only I could have my family nearby." Jennifer immediately made an appointment with the university physician. She explained my family history to the doctor and even prodded him into making a diagnosis of tuberculosis. The doctor hesitated to do so without further tests but did certify in my health report that I had a high likelihood of bone cancer. I was fortunate and grateful that Jennifer took an interest in my case.

Another kind soul who helped me get my family to America was an English major named Barbara who tutored foreign students. I'd worked hard on my reading and writing skills, but I knew I needed to practice my speaking and listening comprehension. Barbara helped me improve my pronunciation and taught me colloquial American phrases. One day after a tutoring session, she asked me what Taiwan was like. I, of course, took the opportunity to tell Barbara about Taiwan's rich culture and friendly people. I also described all the atrocities committed by the KMT. I told her about the White Terror and the oppression the Taiwanese people had faced for so many decades. I explained that the political climate was the reason my family was unable to join me in the US.

Barbara was so moved by my story that she wanted to help. She said she had a family friend who was a US congressman—perhaps he could help. The thought of a high-profile American politician helping me reunite with my family was unimaginable, but Barbara was true to her word. A few days later, I received a letter from a congressman representing Kansas. It was addressed to the Taiwanese government and mentioned my deteriorating health and humbly requested that the KMT grant Jenny and my sons permission to leave Taiwan.

I sent the letter and my medical report to Jenny right away so she could begin the process of obtaining passports. Upon receiving the documents, Jenny visited the Ministry of Education in Taipei, the governing body that granted these types of permits. For two months straight, she argued her case in front of countless officials but was rejected each time. I realized playing nice with these KMT officials wasn't getting us anywhere—they needed the proper motivation to assist us. I told Jenny to explain that if they didn't grant the permits, we had more American congressmen prepared to lodge formal protests against the Taiwanese government.

As I had expected, the KMT officials caved under pressure. They did stipulate, however, that they would grant permission for Jenny only—not the children. Jenny responded, "My children are one and three years old. You want me to leave them by themselves?" The officials suggested the boys stay with my mother and father in Dacheng. This suggestion didn't go over well with my wife. "They are in their seventies. They need somebody to watch over *them*. How can they take care of two babies?" Eventually the bureaucrats relented and granted my entire family permission to leave Taiwan.

This was a load off my mind. Our plan was for me to finish school in a few months and meet them in Los Angeles. Things were looking up for me. I was adjusting to life in Kansas, my grades were steadily improving, my English had gotten much better, and I was making good friends. The only thing that was still difficult was keeping up my weight. Then, out of nowhere, an angel appeared to solve my nutritional problems.

My angel, Ms. Kung, had joined the graduate program at Fort Hays State University after finishing college in Taiwan. Since I was thirteen years older, she endearingly called me "Senior Mr. Wu." There weren't too many Taiwanese at the university, so we naturally became friends. When she saw how skinny I was, she made me a great offer. "Senior Mr. Wu, if you do the dishes, I'll do the cooking. Deal?" I couldn't believe it! Home-cooked Taiwanese food! I almost burst into tears of gratitude and accepted the proposal on the spot. Ms. Kung was a fabulous cook, and soon we were joined by other Taiwanese students who were scattered across the campus. A Japanese student from the business school joined us as well.

I don't think I would have made it through graduate school without Ms. Kung's help. Years later, she stopped by Alaska to visit me with her boyfriend. We had a great time reminiscing about our time at Hays. Six months after the visit, I was saddened to learn that she had passed away from breast cancer.

Chapter Seventeen

ALASKA CALLING

Graduation was quickly approaching. I had focused so much energy on completing school that I had neglected the job search. I wasn't sure what kind of opportunities there were for a Taiwanese immigrant in his mid-thirties. A few weeks before graduation, my old friend Yu Hsin-wang traveled all the way from Taiwan to visit me. His company had just finished its best year ever, generating more than $2 million in profit. He offered to share 15 percent with me if I rejoined his company. This bonus of $300,000 was an unimaginable fortune, but I told Hsin-wang that I wouldn't be able to return to Taiwan for some time and suggested he distribute the money to his employees. Hsin-wang did exactly that when he returned to Taiwan. We stayed in touch for years. Under his leadership, his company did extremely well, but the excessive work, late nights, and client engagements eventually caught up with him. He passed away at the young age of forty-nine. He was a great friend and somebody that changed the trajectory of my life in ways I couldn't have imagined. I miss him dearly.

Dream Job

Fort Hays held career fairs four or five months before graduation so recruiters could scope out the new prospects and vice versa. Considering the small size of the university, I was pleased with the number of high-quality companies that attended. In many instances, if a prospect impressed a recruiter, formal one-on-one interviews could be scheduled on the spot.

The one advantage of graduating at my age was that I had significantly more experience than most of the other candidates. My roles and responsibilities with CCB and Hsin-wang's company made me a standout among my peers. Along with Professor Thomas's recommendation and my strong academic record, I got a number of one-on-one interviews. But in spite of all my hard work, English remained my Achilles' heel. Nothing came from any of the interviews. I don't know if it was my English or if these companies were not quite ready to add Asians to their workforce. Regardless, the end result was bitter disappointment and fresh worries about my post-graduation plans.

Although dejected, I continued to visit the Fort Hays career office regularly. I scoured the job listings every day to see if there was a good fit. Just when I was about to give up, I noticed an obscure listing with the heading "National Bank of Alaska—Japanese-speaking communications clerk."

My heart practically skipped a beat. Was it possible? A commercial bank looking for a Japanese-speaking banker? There had to be a catch. I took a closer look at the particulars. The job required the candidate to be fluent in Japanese and have banking operations and international trade experience. This job description matched my profile so exactly that it was almost too good to be true. I express-mailed my résumé and waited with bated breath. Fortunately, I didn't have to wait long. Upon receipt of my résumé, the recruiting officer from National Bank of Alaska (NBoA) flew to Hays to meet me.

During the interview, my English wasn't an issue because the recruiter only cared that I spoke fluent Japanese. The fact that I also spoke Taiwanese and Mandarin and had relevant experience all worked in my favor. It was as if fate had guided NBoA to me. The bank was willing to accommodate my schedule, allowing me to meet my family in Los Angeles before heading up to Alaska. Within a week, I had an official offer letter. I stared down at the piece of paper and felt a rush of satisfaction. All the time and energy I'd spent moving to the US and obtaining my graduate degree had been worth it.

Once I had the offer in hand, I was able to think about my next home—the great state of Alaska. After spending the coldest winter of my life in Hays, Kansas, I was now about to embark on a journey to the northernmost and coldest state in the US. Was I a glutton for punishment? It would have been easy to moan and groan about Alaska's long and cold winters, but I honestly didn't worry too much about this drastic change in geography. I viewed this as an opportunity to explore another part of the US, America's last frontier.

It was an exciting time for Alaska. The largest oilfield in North America had just been discovered in Prudhoe Bay, one of the northernmost points in the state. This was one of the reasons NBoA was recruiting Japanese speakers. The forty-ninth state expected to export oil to developed Asian countries in need of natural resources, like Japan, and the bank hoped to take advantage of these transpacific business relationships.

Reunited at Last

I sent Jenny a letter simply stating, "Pack up the kids! We're moving to Alaska, where ice and snow reign!" Word soon spread within my circle of friends and family in Taiwan. Most didn't believe it. For people in Taiwan, Alaska conjured up images of year-round snow, polar bears, and igloos. Jenny didn't know anything about the state, but like me, she understood it was a fresh start for our family.

It was early 1969 in the middle of another bitter Hays winter. Jenny and our two sons arrived in the US and stayed with Frank Lai in LA. Since I had finished all the classes for my master's program, I decided to join my family and work on my thesis there. The weight on my heart finally lifted when I saw Jenny and the boys for the first time in more than a year. Jenny's eyes immediately moistened at the sight of me. George and

Gene, my two boys, were shy at first but soon circled around my legs. It was the most complete I had felt in a long time.

Getting ready for our move to Alaska went smoothly enough, but we had to manage our finances carefully. I had taken out loans from various friends totaling $6,000 to take care of all the preparations. The offer from NBoA was $1,150 per month, and I was very concerned about when I would be able to pay back these loans. There was, however, a $15,000 allowance for moving expenses, which I would be able to use at my discretion. This amount was more than enough to cover our move. A friend suggested I would be able to save money by purchasing a car in LA and shipping it to Alaska. This was all well and good, but I was facing a cash deficiency. The moving allowance was not paid up front—I would only receive it as reimbursement after I arrived in Alaska. The money I had borrowed was almost exhausted.

Obtaining a loan from a bank was out of the question because I was so new to the US and had no credit record. My old friend John Cheng had a younger brother, Cheng Shao-chou, who had been living in LA for quite some time. He was doing very well and making such a good living that he was able to purchase a home and a car. Shao-chou was very conservative when it came to financial matters. He refused to incur any debt, paying for everything in cash. With his stellar financial history, I thought he would be the perfect person to cosign a bank loan on my behalf.

To our surprise, Shao-chou did not qualify. The reason was that he had never borrowed money in the past. There was no record of his creditworthiness because he had never used a credit card before. Nothing we said to the loan officer about Shao-chou's net worth or job situation made a difference. The bank simply didn't know how to evaluate somebody like him.

When I learned of this bank policy, I realized the exact person I needed was right in front of me—my brother-in-law Frank. We went to the same bank, and this time, with Frank as the cosigner, the loan officer only had one question—how much did I want to borrow? All the loan officer needed to see to approve a loan was the fact that Frank had quite a bit of debt outstanding and he made payments on time. I couldn't believe it! Shao-chou was extremely responsible financially. He had a good job with plenty of assets, yet he couldn't borrow from a bank. Frank was up to his eyeballs in debt. He had no assets to speak of, yet the bank was willing to continue to lend to him. With Frank as guarantor, I was able to take out a loan for $2,600. I learned two things that day—the US economy is credit-driven, and the US banking system does not know how to lend to new immigrants.

With the loan, I purchased my first car, a red-and-black 1968 Dodge Dart. As I drove out of the dealership, I thought to myself, *I'm living the American Dream!* The only person who was more excited than me about the new car was Frank. He had the ingenious idea to celebrate the purchase with a road trip to Las Vegas, only a four-hour drive from Los Angeles. I had never been, but I had always been curious about the gambling capital of the world. I thought I deserved a vacation. I had worked hard in graduate school, I had a good job offer in the States, and I would be able to take care of my family. I needed to get Jenny's blessing, but she could never say no to her older brother, so we hit the road. The evening desert drive was fairly uneventful, but as we approached our destination, the glow from the neon lights was like a mirage on the horizon.

I had been familiar with gambling since childhood. Mahjong, dice, and cards were a way of life in Dacheng. But nothing I'd experienced before really compared to Las Vegas. The sights, the buzz in the air, the different games, and the boisterous crowds made for the ultimate adult playground. And I did what adults do in an adult playground—I played. Only a few hours later, I left the blackjack table down $500. This was supposed to be money for my family to get settled in Alaska! I was not looking forward to the drive back to Los Angeles.

Jenny, as expected, was livid and didn't speak to me for two months. We now had no funds to even pay for airline tickets. I had to find yet another source from which to borrow. This time, I approached my friend Dr. Chai Trong-rong, whom I'd met through Frank in LA. Trong-rong moved from Taiwan to the US in 1960 as a graduate student and eventually obtained his master's and doctorate degrees. He remained in the US and became a well-respected professor of political science at the City University of New York. While his achievements in academia were impressive, he found his true calling as a fervent advocate for Taiwanese independence. His passion for Taiwan was infectious. When he set his mind to something, nothing would get in his way.

His wife, Li-rong, was kind enough to pay for the airline tickets using her credit card. As soon as I began work at NBoA and got my moving allowance, I paid her back. For years afterward, Trong-rong would always joke that if it hadn't been for him, I never would have made it to Alaska to become a successful banker. I always had to gently remind him that all the credit should go to his wife.

In February 1969, my family moved to Anchorage, Alaska. It had been an eventful first year in the US for me, but I had a strong feeling this next step would be full of surprises as well. My family was finally together, and we would have some stability for the foreseeable future. As we stepped out of the arrival terminal at the Anchorage airport, we were greeted by the sight of a gigantic mounted grizzly bear standing on its hind legs in a glass case. At the bottom of the case was Alaska's state motto: "North to the Future."

Chapter Eighteen

A NEW CHAPTER

I helped myself to a serving of the stir-fried vegetable dish on the lazy Susan and took a bite. I was having dinner in a restaurant for the first time in more than two years with Jenny and our sons. This was a special occasion, and we all had big smiles on our faces. After thirty months of scrimping and saving every penny we had, we'd managed to finally pay back all of the outstanding debt we incurred when we first moved to Alaska. This was truly a family effort, so we celebrated in style at one of the few Chinese restaurants in Anchorage, How-How. It didn't matter that the food was so westernized I hardly recognized it—it was one of the most satisfying meals of my life.

When I first started at NBoA, we were a few thousand dollars in debt. With my salary, I was hopeful that we would be able to cover our living expenses and pay back the loans in due time. But I underestimated the unusually high cost of living in Alaska. My after-tax monthly salary of $800 wasn't getting us very far. Every month, after rent, utilities, and car payments, I would send $100 to my parents and $110 to WUFI—at the time, the largest Taiwanese independence organization in the world. The math was painfully clear—we weren't making ends meet.

Jenny could tell I was worried about our finances. She went out to find work wherever she could. She didn't speak English well but was able to earn money as a babysitter. Then she found a full-time job as a cleaning lady at a local hotel. Luckily, because she could speak Japanese, she eventually landed a permanent job at the duty-free store in the airport.

In those first couple of years in Alaska, our family had no extravagances. I knew our friends would wait patiently to be paid back, but I felt the financial burden with every fiber of my being. There would be no rest until all obligations were settled in full. As a family, we did what was required and watched every penny. We shopped only when necessary, and only at thrift stores.

The road to financial freedom had its bumps along the way. When I first joined the international division at NBoA, the hope was that the bank would have extensive business relationships with countries in Asia as a result of oil exports from Alaska. My division head was a Japanese American who was impressed with my proficiency in Japanese and assured me the bank would put me to good use. I was excited about the prospects, but within the first month of my employment, I knew the international division was in jeopardy.

The expected glut of oil exports was in limbo because of various regulatory, environmental, and political complications. Suffice it to say, the project to drill oil from Prudhoe Bay was put on hold indefinitely, along with my usefulness. Since I was one of the newest employees, I expected to get my termination papers any day. My family's financial situation was already tenuous—this setback could be the final straw. Would I be able to find work elsewhere? Should we move back to Los Angeles? I was facing an existential crisis, and I didn't have any answers. Then fate stepped in just when I needed it the most.

Reprieve

The bank's management approached me and said they didn't have anything to keep me busy in Anchorage but there was an opportunity in another branch located in Sitka. That area had quite a few Japanese in logging and fishing, and they thought it would be a good opportunity to establish banking relationships. I jumped at the offer. I didn't know anything about Sitka, but maintaining employment was the priority. I learned that Sitka was a small town along the southeastern panhandle of Alaska, bordering Canada. Most people aren't aware of the geographic enormity of Alaska. Flying time from Anchorage to Sitka was more than three hours, or about two days by car. What would I do with my family? They had just settled into life in Anchorage. Another move would cause too much upheaval, especially since I didn't know how long I would be in Sitka. We decided it would be best for me to go on my own first, and then we would decide if my family should follow.

A phone call from a senior manager at the bank, however, changed the course of my career. I never got on that flight to Sitka. I was told to postpone my move because the accounting department in Anchorage was shorthanded. Somehow, somebody in human resources had noticed that I had accounting experience on my résumé and thought I would be well suited to fill a two-week role in that department. I happily agreed but neglected to tell them that my "experience" in accounting was a basic course at NTU. I had no practical accounting skills whatsoever.

The day I reported to the job, I was nervous because of my lack of qualifications, but my worry was for naught. The controller, a recent hire from the lower forty-eight (a term Alaskans use for the contiguous United States), needed a leave of absence because he couldn't handle the Alaskan winter. There was nobody to oversee me at all. I could have enjoyed a two-week respite, but instead, I viewed this as an opportunity to finally show what I could do. I took on as many projects as I could. As soon as one assignment was completed, I moved on to the next. Gradually, so many people dropped off additional work for me that I had stacks of reports and memos drowning my desk. The two weeks flew by, and I waited with bated breath, expecting to get a tap on the shoulder about relocating to Sitka, but that didn't happen. After a month, I never heard about the move again.

Not long after my move to the accounting department, I was assigned to handle a review of all the operating plans for NBoA's twenty-plus locations throughout Alaska. As I was going through the reports submitted from each branch, I noticed multiple inconsistencies regarding their growth plans and expected operating budgets. This type of analysis was exactly what I used to discuss and research with my mentor, Professor Thomas. I pored over every report and number. The scope of my analysis was well beyond my assignment, so I did the additional work during my personal time. I wanted to be as thorough as possible.

As challenging as this work was, perhaps an even bigger challenge was preparing the report in English. It was the norm for my colleagues to dictate their reports to the word processing pool to be typed up. But my English made it hard for the typists to understand me, so, frustrated and embarrassed, I decided to type it myself. I worked for weeks, long into the night after my wife and sons were in bed, to prepare the report, but when questioned, I told my colleagues it had only taken me half an hour.

I was proud of the completed product. I made recommendations and suggestions for how the bank could stay current with the changing business environment. I was confident my analysis would stand up to scrutiny.

"You Do Know Everything, Don't You?"

Unknown to me, my report wound up in the hands of the bank's chief financial officer because two of the managers in the department resigned due to illness. From there, the CFO handed the report to the man at the top, Elmer Rasmuson, chairman, chief executive officer, and president of NBoA.

Rasmuson was a legend within the banking community in Alaska. He was a Harvard graduate, former partner at Arthur Andersen—one of the big eight accounting firms—and named president of the bank at age thirty-six. It wasn't until Rasmuson took over that NBoA established itself as the premier banking institution of Alaska. His aggressive and disciplined style was well known to the employees. There were numerous stories of Rasmuson throwing reports and presentations at executives when he didn't like what he saw. These episodes, known as "Rasmuson rage," only added to his legendary persona. When he walked the halls of the bank, you could feel the fear emanating from his employees. I was so new and junior that I had never officially met him.

After two weeks with no word about my report, I was resigned to the fact that the document was probably stuck under a pile of papers on some bean counter's desk. Then one day, a hush fell over the office floor. A man I didn't know grabbed a nearby chair, sat directly across from me, and waved a report in my face.

"Are you Li Wu?" he asked. Based on the expressions on my colleagues' faces, I knew this had to be the infamous Elmer Rasmuson.

He began questioning me as if I were a suspect in a police investigation. I did my best to quell my nerves and answer each question. There was no hiding my accent, however, and Rasmuson appeared puzzled by some of my responses. When needed, I grabbed a notebook and wrote down my answers, and to my relief, the boss nodded in approval. I answered as best I could and referred to the report numerous times.

After an hour, Rasmuson stood to leave. I stood as well. He took one step, turned around, looked me in the eye and said, "Li, you do know everything, don't you?" With that, he was off. Loud cheers erupted in the office. I looked around and realized all my coworkers had been glued to our exchange. They said it was the first compliment they'd ever heard the boss utter. After that day, my new nickname in the office was Man Who Knows All.

Chapter Nineteen

A QUICK LOOK BACK

Shortly after Rasmuson's visit, I was promoted to staff accountant, then assistant controller, my responsibilities growing with each promotion. But with the new duties, I felt I needed formal training more specific to banking. I found a two-month continuing education program called the Commercial Banking Executive Program at Columbia University's Graduate School of Business. NBoA considered this internal training, so the bank paid for it.

This program was exactly what I needed. I had spent so much of my day-to-day activities focused on various business statistics or other banking details that I'd neglected to pay attention to the high-level strategic and global aspects of business. During those two months, I also networked with a number of banking professionals with whom I still have relationships. I realized in order to succeed in business, one needed multifaceted skills: business analysis, strategic vision, and relationship management.

On my fifth anniversary at the bank, I was named vice president and controller. By the end of my seventh year, I had been promoted to senior vice president and chief financial officer. By contrast, my seven years of employment at CCB had yielded not one promotion. At NBoA, my hard work paid off, and I was recognized by upper management. It was the type of meritocracy that I understood and appreciated.

My promotion to CFO at NBoA in 1976 was profiled in various local newspapers and TV programs. Perhaps the underdog storyline was made more compelling because of my immigrant background. That same year, my family became naturalized US citizens. We were able to obtain visitor visas to Taiwan without a problem and took a family trip back home to see my parents and my brothers.

Full Circle

I'm often asked, as an Asian American in a predominantly Caucasian business, if I ever faced discrimination. The answer is yes, every day. At times, I may not have even known it was happening. Other times, it was blatant. There was one particular incident at NBoA that stood out

When I was an assistant vice president in charge of the bank's operating budget, I interacted with other departments. The vice president in charge of investments, Jason Bulwark, always complained that he didn't understand my English and often hung up on me in midsentence. If I showed up at his office, he would still complain about my English, and we would wind up in a shouting match. Some of the acrimony was due to our differing philosophies regarding the bank's investment strategy. Bulwark was aggressive in his approach, while I preferred a more conservative, analytical approach. I was often proven correct, which I'm sure added to his ire. His constant complaining about my accent was meant to demean and humiliate me. I had no problem communicating with other colleagues. Why was there a problem with him?

At NBoA, there was an award given to commemorate an employee's fifth year with the bank. When my time approached, the bank held a nice ceremony to celebrate. To everyone's surprise, Rasmuson showed up to hand me the award personally. He rarely attended these functions, so I was touched that he would go out of his way for me. But he had more than a simple gesture in mind.

Before he handed me the award, he spoke a few words. "I know that you all find what Li says difficult to understand at times. To be honest, I felt the same way. But then, hours after our conversation, I would understand perfectly what Li had been saying. I've come to the conclusion that rather than a language barrier, an intellectual and knowledge barrier is what exists between Li and the rest of us. His words come from his analytical mind, and we need time to internalize to truly understand his meaning."

After I was given such a compliment, I was, ironically, speechless. I truly appreciated what Rasmuson did for me. His message to the troops was received loud and clear. Nobody complained about my English from that day forward.

Two years later, I was promoted to senior vice president and chief financial officer. Bulwark was still a vice president, so I now outranked him. One day, when he was in my office, I said to him very politely, "I know we have had our problems in the past. I know I speak with an accent and you have a difficult time understanding me. I will do my best to speak slowly and clearly. I'll even write a memo, if you prefer. When we had difficulty communicating in the past, that was my problem. From now on, it will be *your* problem."

Chapter Twenty

TIME TO MOVE ON

My professional star was on the rise. My role within NBoA was growing with each passing year. I had good relationships with my colleagues, and I had established myself within Alaska's banking community. But most importantly, I was finally providing my family with the financial security we had never known. The future looked bright.

Prudhoe Bay began finally to pump oil from its reserves through the Trans-Alaska Pipeline System (TAPS) in 1977. TAPS, which ran south from Prudhoe Bay and ended in south-central Alaska in Valdez, made oil production and exportation economically feasible for the state. The Land of the Midnight Sun was about to become one of the wealthiest states in the nation.

NBoA, like most businesses in the state, did extremely well during this time. As CFO, one of my responsibilities was overseeing the operating projections for the bank. For most of my tenure with NBoA, the bank grew at an impressive rate. My lofty projections were on target, and everybody, including Rasmuson, was happy. By the late 1970s, my economic outlook took a turn. I was not optimistic the growth Alaska had enjoyed in previous years would continue. If crude prices dropped as I anticipated, Alaska would experience significant contraction in its state revenues. And other factors concerned me. The need for temporary workers in the oil industry would plateau, and inflation and the resulting interest rates would adversely affect economic growth. It was my responsibility to incorporate these findings into my projections and present them to the bank's executive team. My recommendation was for NBoA to slow its aggressive operating plans for the next few years. The day after I submitted my report, I was summoned to Rasmuson's office.

Before I could take a seat, the infamous "Rasmuson rage" reared its ugly head. "I've been in this business for more than thirty years. I've seen it all! If other banks have a tough time growing, that's their problem. That will not happen with *my* bank! Our mindset should be that any asset or opportunity left behind by other banks means more for us. I thought you understood that. What's wrong with you?"

I stared at him, speechless. As admirable as his business ambition was, I couldn't, in good conscience, concede his points. My analysis was based on facts and supportable assumptions. It was clear Rasmuson had not bothered to read my report beyond the conclusion. He continued his tirade. I thought that after he cooled down, we could discuss it reasonably. But his yelling didn't slow. He ended his ranting with, "Don't you understand you're one of my guard dogs? One of the best I have."

Fury and humiliation swelled within me and threatened to explode. Even though I came from humble beginnings, I had never been spoken to and demeaned like that. I hadn't felt the urge to hit another human being since I was in grade school, but that day I came close. Rasmuson was quite a few years my senior, so out of respect, I held my tongue and suppressed my anger. Our discussion was interrupted when Rasmuson's assistant came to say the governor was on the phone. Rasmuson's snarl disappeared, and he was jovial with the governor on the phone. I was stunned at the sudden reversal. Rasmuson continued his conversation with the governor as if I wasn't even there. His comment earlier about me being a dog was exactly how I felt at that moment. I was invisible—nothing to him. I went back to my office to think.

I had spent nine years at NBoA. In that time, Rasmuson had generally been very good to me. He recognized the quality of my work and promoted me quickly. He was patient and supportive in spite of the language barrier. But after what had just happened, I realized that I didn't know the man as well as I thought.

What happened that day confirmed a feeling that had nagged at me but I never acknowledged. Even though I was the third-ranked member of the executive team, I was never asked to interact with banking clients. When Rasmuson had social gatherings for Alaskan VIPs at his home, I was never invited, even though I knew bank business was conducted at these events. The only conclusion I could draw was that I was nothing more than an Asian tool for Rasmuson.

As I sat mulling over these thoughts in my office, Edward Rasmuson, president of the bank and the son of the chairman, rushed into my office. He had heard about the incident with his father. Edward was being groomed by the senior Rasmuson to one day take the mantle of the bank. He was nothing like his father. He was friendly, soft-spoken, and avoided confrontations. He and I had worked closely in recent years as his father became less involved in day-to-day bank operations, and I enjoyed his company. When my parents visited from Taiwan, he made a point of hosting my entire family at his home.

Edward, ashen-faced, paced my office, unable to find the appropriate words. When he finally spoke, he said, "He shouldn't have insulted you like that. Just ignore him."

I knew Edward was trying to de-escalate the situation, but he could tell I wasn't placated. I left the office early to contemplate my future at the bank. I will never forget the humiliation I felt that day.

The next morning, I arrived early and tendered my resignation to human resources. I had no problem reaching this decision. By staying, I would be tacitly saying it was okay for Rasmuson to treat me that way. I couldn't let that happen. I was still the primary breadwinner for the family, so the financial aspect was a concern, but in life, there are more important things than financial security. I deserved to be treated with the respect I had worked hard to earn. If Rasmuson didn't understand or recognize that, then I could no longer work with him.

Edward made a beeline for my office as soon as he heard about my resignation. Again, he apologized for his father's behavior and pleaded with me to give him one week to fix the situation. I was in no mood to hear more excuses, but I had spent nine years working side by side with Edward and so many others. I reluctantly agreed to give him the week. The senior Rasmuson, an avid sailor, had taken his yacht down to Palm Springs, California, for a pleasure cruise that day. Edward's plan was to meet his father in Palm Springs to discuss the situation and fly back to Alaska.

Before he left for California, he said to me, "Don't worry, I'll take care of everything. My father will be back in a week to apologize for his behavior."

When Edward returned, he had a big smile on his face and said everything was resolved. "Li, things will be different from now on. My dad is going to be back in the office tomorrow. How about you stop by to say hello and apologize so we can move on?"

I couldn't believe my ears. I had waited an extra week for this? Hadn't Edward assured me Rasmuson would be apologizing to *me*? Edward had once told me that with his father getting older, he and I would be the ones in charge of the bank. As much as I liked Edward, it was clear that he was incapable of standing up to his father. For him to suggest that I apologize for doing my job and allowing another person to insult me to my face was too much. All the anger and humiliation I had felt from a few days earlier came rushing back. There was no way I would apologize. "I appreciate what you are trying to do, Edward. But I'll be in tomorrow to clear out my things."

The next day, the elder Rasmuson had no choice but to come to my office. "You're sure you want to leave? Is there nothing we can do to work this out?" he asked.

I answered quickly and definitively. Yes, I was sure, and no, there was nothing to be done. Later in the day, Rasmuson came back to my office to confirm once again that I was leaving. My answer didn't change.

He sighed and said, "Very well, I'll let everybody know." I had worked with this man for many years, and I respected him in many ways. I often wonder what I would have done if he had simply apologized to me. I may have stayed at the bank for many more years. But that was not Elmer Rasmuson. The brashness and fiery demeanor that served him well under certain circumstances would not allow him to admit he was wrong. The next day, news of my resignation appeared in the local newspapers.

Final Correspondence

By 1980, a year after I left NBoA, the economic conditions I had predicted came to fruition. The growth Alaska had enjoyed for several years abated and eventually contracted. Total revenue of commercial banks throughout Alaska, including NBoA, declined dramatically. NBoA's expansion plans were put on hold, and even the great Rasmuson had to modify his strategy in a more conservative direction.

I was not in touch with Elmer Rasmuson for a long time after leaving NBoA. But thirteen years later, the November 1991 issue of *American Banker* ranked General Bank, where I was CEO, as the top-performing commercial bank of its size in the US. Coincidently, NBoA was also the top-ranked commercial bank within its size category. I wrote to Rasmuson to congratulate him on the bank's achievement and thank him for being an important part of my banking career. Rasmuson responded promptly and said that he was impressed with General Bank's turnaround with me at the helm. It felt good to reconnect after all that time. It brought me a much-needed sense of closure and vindication. Although my tenure at NBoA ended abruptly, my time there was invaluable for my career. Rasmuson, despite his hardline personality, did provide me with opportunities I may not have had at another company. For that I will always be grateful.

Chapter Twenty-One

NEW CAREER CHALLENGE

After nine years of being consumed by bank operations and financial reports, I now had no place to go when I woke up. Fortunately, when news of my departure from NBoA became public, three banks reached out and expressed interest in hiring me.

Indecision

Being wanted by prospective employers was a nice feeling, but I needed to take some time to figure out what I wanted to do next. I knew what these banks were offering. I would be an employee trying to move up the corporate ladder like I had done at NBoA. Ther e was nothing wrong with that, but I had gained a tremendous amount of experience and confidence in the last few years. During this period of reflection, I spent one month in Los Angeles exploring the possibility of opening and running my own bank catering to Taiwanese immigrants, but I wasn't able to raise enough capital to see this venture to fruition.

I returned to Anchorage and let it be known to the banking community that I was available and ready to join another bank. One of the institutions that reached out to me was Alaska National Bank of the North (ANBN). The chief executive officer was Frank Murkowski, a man I had met in passing a couple of times before. Frank was extremely aggressive in pursuing my services. During our first meeting, he impressed me right away. He was personable and optimistic about everything, a natural marketer.

Frank had served as head of ANBN since 1971. In just a few short years, ANBN went from a small community bank to one of the largest in Alaska, second only to NBoA. The branch network grew, and the bank operations became so complex that Frank recognized he needed additional depth in management. He was extremely open with me when we discussed my responsibilities at the bank. He was looking for somebody to completely oversee operations while he focused on expanding the bank's client base. Frank also had political aspirations. He had run unsuccessfully for Alaska's lone seat in the US House of Representatives years earlier, but he hoped to be successful the next time. All these factors made this job particularly attractive. I knew Frank and I would get along and I would have virtually unfettered authority.

As far as compensation, Frank impressed me with how smoothly he could handle a sensitive issue. My annual salary at NBoA just before I left was approximately $50,000. Frank, without hesitation, offered $65,000. He wanted to make sure I knew how valuable I was, and I appreciated it. He reminded me a lot of my dear old friend Yu Hsin-wang. It was such a contrast to what I had experienced only a few weeks earlier in my last encounter with Rasmuson.

I was ready to accept the offer, except for one point. ANBN was headquartered in Fairbanks, the second-largest city in Alaska, more than 350 miles north of Anchorage. Fairbanks' climate was severe, even by Alaskan standards. The winters could get as low as minus sixty degrees Fahrenheit and the summers over one hundred degrees. This was a big change from Anchorage, where my family had been comfortable for almost ten years. We had just moved to a new home near the ocean and were hoping to enjoy it as a family. I would do what was necessary for a job, but I hoped to avoid the harsh climate of Fairbanks.

I suggested to Frank that they relocate the headquarters to Anchorage for two reasons. First, Anchorage was Alaska's business hub and had approximately half of the state's population, and second, for ANBN to continue to compete aggressively, it would need talent, most of which resided in Anchorage. Frank agreed and said if I came on board, we would discuss the relocation seriously. In the meantime, he had read my mind and said my family could stay in Anchorage and the bank's corporate jet would take me to Fairbanks each day. I would even have an apartment at my disposal there. Frank topped off his pitch by arranging the jet to fly my entire family to his estate in Fairbanks, where we had a great time swimming, barbecuing, and getting to know each other. Frank's professional and personal gestures made a great impression on me. I formally accepted the offer and joined ANBN on May 5, 1978.

New Challenges

My first day on the job, I arrived at the local airfield, where ANBN's corporate jet was waiting. When I saw the entire flight staff there to serve me, the only passenger, I hesitated. I was not used to so much attention and extravagance. The flight attendant showed me to my seat and stowed my overcoat. Then the pilot asked if I was ready to take off. I nodded, trying not to look awestruck. It was a one-hour flight to Fairbanks, not much longer than the average commute, but what a way to travel! During the flight, I was able to study various financial reports and other bank information so that I would be well prepared for my first day. This became my routine. I tried to be home each night to spend time with my family. If I needed to work late, I would stay overnight in the Fairbanks apartment.

Many people who had worked with Frank in the past told me that his style was to delegate. As soon as I joined ANBN, Frank created an executive committee that was the final authority on all bank operations. I was made chairman of that committee. These challenges and responsibilities were exactly what I was looking for in a new job. But there were daunting challenges ahead. The growth Frank had overseen at ANBN came with pitfalls that I wasn't aware of until after I joined. Furthermore, the economic challenge I had feared would befall Alaska would also take its toll on my new employer.

Chapter Twenty-Two

TURNING THE TIDE

When Frank Murkowski recruited me, I wasn't aware of the myriad problems ANBN was facing. On the outside, the bank appeared to be healthy, expanding its branch network and adding personnel. As soon as I arrived, I realized this wasn't the case. The bank was a financial disaster waiting to happen. It was bleeding cash, and without drastic measures, it would not survive much longer.

Two of the bank's biggest problems were the deposit base and its loan portfolio. For a bank, deposits are the lifeblood of the institution. All of ANBN's deposits from oil companies and other customers during the heyday of the mid- to late 1970s were evaporating at an astonishing rate. And during the boom times, the bank made many loans to migrant workers who were in Alaska because they wanted to make quick money from the oil rush. As soon as the rush was over, these workers left, leaving ANBN holding the bag.

The bank's hiring practices were also in disarray. It continued hiring despite the slump in the economy. In sum, the bank was a mess because it was not able to balance its operations with the rapid economic downturn.

Doing What Needs to Be Done

What had I gotten myself into? I had no idea the situation was so dire. But that feeling faded quickly. Frank had given me discretion on all operational matters. This was the responsibility I had wanted. I rolled up my sleeves and got to work, focusing on the highest priority—capital preservation. This meant the operational expenses that were dragging the bank down needed to be addressed. I evaluated the organizational structure and made massive layoffs, reducing operating expenses by 25 percent.

Next, I focused my attention on the loan portfolios. The bank had been very aggressive in making loans to TAPS workers for mobile homes during the oil rush. Everyone was focused on taking advantage of what was right in front of them, not what would happen after the rush was over. ANBN fell prey to this mentality just like everyone else. The mobile home loans they provided were structured as five- to six-year mortgages so they could close quickly. But the pipeline construction was completed in three years, about halfway through the term of these loans. The workers had made their fast money and were perfectly willing to default on their loan obligations and move on. The bank had no choice but to repossess the underlying security on these loans: the mobile homes.

I was a banker by trade, and figuring out how to dispose of thousands of abandoned mobile homes in areas covered by snow was not in my wheelhouse. But I, along with Frank and the bank's chief credit officer, came up with a solution. There was a market for these mobile homes, and we were able to have them transported for sale. When the last of these homes were sold, ANBN was back on track.

I also suggested that we do away with the corporate jet. The crew and maintenance cost the bank more than a million dollars per year. As much as I enjoyed the convenience, the expense was completely unjustified. When I broke the news to Frank, he agreed.

The last step was to relocate ANBN's core service departments and staff from Fairbanks to Anchorage. I had discovered that Alaskan law prohibited a bank from moving its headquarters more than sixty miles a year, which would have taken us six years. So instead, I decided to relocate only the core service departments to Anchorage. I laid out a plan to identify the areas in which we needed new people and helped the various departments recruit the best and the brightest.

The bank's operations and financial health made a turn for the better a little over a year after I joined. My initiatives helped pull the bank out of the red, and I took great comfort in seeing the steady improvement reflected in ANBN's financial reports. Frank was thrilled with the quick turnaround. The board of directors was equally elated. They made me one of the directors of the board, raised my salary, and offered me stock options. Frank remained president and CEO, but it was clear that I would be handling most of the operating decisions.

Trouble Looming

While I was proud of all that I accomplished, I still never felt fully accepted. Frank was the only one who ever treated me as a colleague and a friend. That was why I was so surprised when the bank's chairman of the board visited me one day out of the blue and said the board wanted to make me president of the bank. All I could ask was, "What about Frank?"

The chairman's response paved the way for what would eventually be an even more tumultuous year than the previous one. "We're going to ask him to leave."

Chapter Twenty-Three

SHOWDOWN

I kept my face blank when the chairman made his proclamation. I needed time to digest what I had just heard. My head swirled with a million thoughts, but one thing was crystal clear—I was beholden to Frank Murkowski. He gave me a tremendous opportunity that very few bankers in his position would have even considered. Besides the professional relationship, Frank was a friend. He was absolutely right when he said a year earlier that he and I would make an unbeatable team. I had nothing but respect and gratitude for the man that the board was asking me to replace. The chairman was aware of my friendship with Frank, yet he and the other board members thought the promise of a promotion would outweigh my loyalty. The board expected me to be flattered and simply step over my friend.

I was insulted. I thought of all my friends like Yu Hsin-wang, Roger Hsieh, and Dr. Peng who would never sell out their integrity for personal gain. I calmly replied to the chairman, "Let me think about it."

Frank's Game Plan

For the next couple of days, it was difficult to concentrate at work. Even though I hadn't responded to the board's offer, by keeping this information to myself, I felt as if I had already betrayed Frank. I needed to come clean, so I arranged to meet him for lunch at a restaurant.

I arrived on time, nervous and concerned about how Frank would take the news. I had rehearsed a speech, but with each passing minute, I grew more agitated by Frank's tardiness. When he finally showed up thirty minutes late, acting like his usual cheerful self, I was about to explode. After a couple of drinks, I took a deep breath and explained in detail what the chairman had relayed. I ended with, "We don't need this place. Let's quit together."

I waited for some kind of outburst of surprise or anger, but none came. Instead, Frank was not at all surprised by the board's maneuver. He said we'd get through it, but as was typical, Frank didn't have specifics on how we were going to do that.

We left our meeting somewhat tipsy but united. I expected Frank to give me more details on our plan to thwart the board, but none came. I never heard another word from Frank or any board member regarding his dismissal. To this day I don't know how my friend did it, but his political acumen has always amazed me.

Choices

In March 1980, Frank and I attended a business conference in South Carolina. We shared a two-bedroom townhouse, and one morning, Frank came out of the shower in nothing but a towel around his waist. He said he had an urgent matter he needed to discuss. He plopped down on the couch next to me, and I moved away to place more space between us, wondering what he wanted to talk about.

"How would you like to be the next president of Alaska National Bank of the North?" he asked. He explained that he'd been laying the groundwork to run for the US Senate. His plan was to leave the bank in May to focus on the campaign. He had complete faith that I was the right person to lead ANBN.

I was surprised and touched. I had known of his political ambitions but hadn't realized he would be leaving so soon. The opportunity to take over as bank president was a dream come true. Only twelve years earlier, I was a foreign student in graduate school hoping to find a job to support my family. The thought of becoming president of a US commercial bank was unimaginable, yet here I was. I told Frank how much I appreciated everything he had done and I would make sure his confidence in me was not misplaced.

I wasn't sure how the board would react, though. Only a few months earlier, I had gone behind their back because of loyalty to Frank. Had I already tainted my relationship with them? Would they have confidence in me? Frank soothed my worries by using his favorite phrase: "Don't worry, I'll take care of everything."

The Board's Intentions

As planned, Frank stepped down in May 1980. Before his departure, the board met to discuss his successor. I recused myself from this meeting so they could speak freely. The only conclusion they reached was that I would be named interim president. Based on Frank's feedback, the announcement to officially appoint me president would happen quickly.

In the June meeting, there was still no mention of removing the "interim" from my title, but the bank was doing well, so I wasn't worried. By the time the July board meeting came and went, with no word on my status, I sensed something was not right. I approached Frank, and he put me at ease with another, "Don't worry, I'll take care of everything." I learned later that he had been lobbying on my behalf for months with each member of the board, without much progress. These people freely admitted to him they were uncomfortable having a person of Asian descent leading the bank.

When the August board meeting was scheduled, I was asked to address the board regarding the promotion. When I entered the boardroom, I could see the skeptical looks on the faces of every board member. The chairman said, "Frank thinks we should name you as his successor. Tell me, what makes you think you should be president?" I shook with anger. For more than two years, these people had witnessed firsthand how I had kept the bank from going under and improved its financial performance. The chairman had even told me they wanted me to become president when they tried to oust Frank months earlier. Now this same group was asking me to list my qualifications?

The disrespect and condescension were too much to bear. All I said was, "My track record speaks for itself." I turned and left the room without another word.

Li-pei Wu's Worth

Following the meeting, the board established a three-person committee to spearhead the search for a new president. There was still a chance I would be selected as president, but I was so offended that I wasn't sure I wanted it anymore. It didn't matter what I had accomplished for the bank—I would always be viewed as an outsider. As much as I wanted to lash out, I needed to keep my wits about me. I couldn't let these board members push me aside as if I were nothing, but it was not the time to do anything rash.

There was no last-minute reconciliation with the board. The search committee quickly hired a Caucasian banker from San Francisco in his late sixties. As much as Frank had tried to convince the board that I was the right person to lead the bank, they clearly couldn't see past my Asian face. Just like at NBoA, they didn't view me as an asset to the bank, only as a tool, an object for them to wield as they saw fit.

I was angry and disappointed at the turn of events. I wanted to fight back, but I wasn't sure how. Instead, I took a leave of absence to regroup and evaluate my options. The board didn't appreciate my work, so why not let them worry about the day-to-day operations without me? ANBN was no longer a small community bank. The board was about to get an up-close look at the complexity of the operations and the scope of the financial products and services offered.

During my absence, I asked my assistant to leak word that I was considering leaving the bank. News of my possible departure caused ANBN's stock price to drop. At least someone out there recognized my worth. Frank saw the drop in price as a strong argument to convince the board of my value, even though that would put them in an awkward situation since they had already offered the position to someone else.

Frank proposed a dual-leadership structure: a president and a vice chairman. The board offered me the position of vice chairman. I declined, stating I would only stay on as president. The board came back and agreed because the drop in stock price convinced them that the shareholders were behind me. But they had the temerity to explain that they originally offered me the vice chairman position because they were concerned that having an Asian as president would alienate customers. It was a clear case of discrimination.

I can't say for sure why I accepted. In retrospect, it was one of the worst decisions of my professional career and only prolonged my inevitable departure. Having two leaders dilutes communication and confuses the employees. In this case, the problems were more pronounced because I did not have a good working relationship with the vice chairman. He was supposed to focus on a small group of branches near Fairbanks while I continued to focus on overall bank operations. The vice chairman ignored all the operating guidelines I set. It was clear this arrangement was a disaster waiting to happen.

Turnabout

The end came fairly quickly. In June 1981, the Consulate General of Korea invited me to visit major coal companies in Korea. During the trip, I learned that the board had fired two of my closest associates without my consent. Despite all the board's assurances and sweet talk that they wanted me to be part of this dual-leadership structure, they had undermined my authority at the earliest opportunity. It was clear they had no interest in making this president–vice chairman structure work. They were simply buying time to appease nervous shareholders.

As painful as it was to be treated this way, I felt worse for my two colleagues. They were never part of this war. They worked hard for the bank and were key members of the turnaround team. When I returned from Asia, I also learned that my colleagues were fired over the phone. The board didn't even have the courage or courtesy to meet them in person.

I immediately flew up to Fairbanks to confront the chairman of the board. His explanation was that my associates were incompetent and the vice chairman agreed with the decision to fire them. I yelled, "You've been undermining me from the beginning, haven't you?"

His insolent response was, "Isn't it obvious?"

There was only thing left for me to say. "I'll see you in court."

Concluding My Banking Career in Alaska

When I returned to Anchorage, I received a call from Frank. He apologized and assured me he hadn't known the board's plans. He felt horrible for what had happened. I knew Frank had tried his best. Unfortunately, he was the only one in my corner. The main problem was that from day one, the board had never respected me. For them, regardless of my performance, I would never be good enough to take a leadership role. If I stood up for myself, I would be labeled too aggressive. If I didn't speak up, I would be passed over without a thought. This was the impossible conundrum that I faced.

In the end, when the dust settled, another board member approached me to convince me to resign. I adamantly refused and said if they wanted me gone, they would need to fire me. I was looking forward to resolving this in court. The board, realizing they couldn't intimidate me, softened its stance and asked what I wanted.

I had very little leverage other than the threat of litigation and bad publicity, but I knew it would be virtually impossible to prove the board's discrimination in a court of law. I was still in my forties, with more challenges and opportunities ahead. It was time for me to move on. I reached a settlement with the board. I would continue as president in name only for six more months. During that time, the bank would continue to pay my salary and provide access to my office and secretary. In return, I promised not to disclose the nature of my departure.

In early 1982, I closed the chapter of my banking career in Alaska.

Chapter Twenty-Four

TWICE BLACKLISTED

While I was closing my banking career at ANBN, I was also dealing with the KMT. I'd been lulled into thinking I was no longer on their radar because I'd been able to visit Taiwan twice without trouble. First in 1976, with my family, and again in 1978, when I was selected to represent Alaska at the US–ROC Economic Cooperation Conference, an annual event promoting bilateral economic cooperation between the US and Taiwan. But when I was denied a Taiwanese visa for the 1980 US–ROC economic conference, and I knew the KMT was back in the picture.

Visa Application Denied

One of the objectives of the US–ROC economic conference was for Taiwan to deepen its relationship with the US, so it seemed odd that I, an American representative for the conference, would be denied a visa, especially since I had been granted one only two years earlier. I asked Frank, who was still president of ANBN at the time, to see if he could find somebody to intervene on my behalf. Frank reached out to various members of Congress to inquire directly with the top officials of the Taipei Economic and Cultural Office, and the response was short and to the point. "We cannot issue a visa to Mr. Wu because of political considerations."

What I had feared was confirmed—my name had been added to the KMT's infamous blacklist, a roster of pro-independence activists who were banned from entering Taiwan. It was an outrage that such a thing existed. A country that professed to be a democracy but banned those opposing the KMT was no democracy at all. I had been allowed to visit Taiwan multiple times over the previous few years. Why was the KMT denying my visa now?

Protest

With this denial, I decided it was time to make my case public and shine a spotlight on the KMT's actions. I asked the Alaskan state government to intervene on my behalf since I was part of the delegation representing Alaska at the US–ROC conference, but to my disappointment, my home state did nothing.

I held a press conference to openly criticize the KMT and the Alaskan state government. I addressed the governor of Alaska: "I am a US citizen and resident of Alaska attending a conference where I would be representing Alaska to further Alaskan economic interests. Why isn't the state government standing with me to protest this treatment of one of its residents?"

Governor Jay Hammond was forced to respond. His weak answer only added fuel to the fire. "We can't get involved in Taiwan's internal matters." Now that I had the public's attention, I wouldn't let it go to waste. I arranged another press conference and again posed a simple question. "I am an American citizen. The Taiwanese government is using political motivation to deny my visa. This has become an international dispute between Taiwan and the US, yet Governor Hammond, you claim this is an internal matter for Taiwan. Do you recognize me as an American citizen, or do you view me as just another Taiwanese?"

It frustrated and saddened me that even though I was a US citizen, neither the Alaska state government nor the governor considered me to be

American. Eventually, Governor Hammond issued a public apology, and I felt somewhat vindicated. Despite the additional public pressure, the KMT did not relent and continued to deny my visa. The haunting legacy of Chiang Kai-shek was alive and well within the Taiwanese government.

Disappointed that I was not able to attend the 1980 US–ROC conference, I wondered when I would have the opportunity to visit Taiwan. Since I had shone a public spotlight on the KMT, I assumed it would be quite some time before I would be allowed to step foot in my home country. But once again, fate intervened. Frank, after being elected as a US senator representing Alaska, was appointed chair of the Foreign Relations Subcommittee on East Asia and Pacific Affairs. The position meant he would have frequent interaction with the Taiwanese government. On countless occasions over the years, I'd told Frank about the history of Taiwan, the plight of the Taiwanese people, and the true nature of the KMT, so I knew he would help me.

When I joined General Bank in Los Angeles in 1982, I applied for a multiple-entry visa because most of the founding investors of General Bank were Taiwanese American and I anticipated many trips to Taiwan. When I was approved for a five-year multiple-entry visa, I was ecstatic. Six months after I received the visa, I scheduled a trip to Taiwan. This would be my first trip since becoming CEO of General Bank. In the eleventh hour, however, I found out the Taiwanese government had revoked my visa. There was little warning and no explanation whatsoever. I had been blacklisted again.

I reached out to Frank and suggested that the best way to cut through the bureaucracy was to speak directly with Chiang Ching-kuo, Chiang-Kai-shek's son and current president of Taiwan. I knew that KMT officials only moved quickly when there was adequate pressure from above to do so.

During Frank's next visit to Taiwan, the KMT put on its typical fanfare to impress him. He and President Chiang had a private meeting to discuss various topics, and Frank raised the subject of my visa problems. President Chiang wanted to do whatever it took to remain on friendly terms, so he assured Frank that the matter would be handled. As expected, things moved a bit quicker when the president of Taiwan and head of the KMT got involved. I was finally granted permission to enter Taiwan.

The Ghost of the White Terror

With the newly issued visa, I made a trip to Taiwan in August 1983. I had hoped that the hassles with the KMT were behind me, but I realized as soon as I stepped off the plane that the ghost of the White Terror continued to haunt Taiwan.

When I entered the airport's immigration area, I was made to wait at the checkpoint for more than an hour. The immigration officer looked over my passport from front to back, back to front, reviewing each page carefully without saying a word. He then got on the phone and had a lengthy conversation. All the while, I watched as passenger after passenger departed immigration until I was the only one left.

As I stood at the counter waiting, an old classmate of mine appeared out of the blue. I hadn't seen Wang since Taichung First High, more than thirty years earlier. He had an ID badge pinned to his shirt, so I knew he was an official at the airport. He rushed over to me, and before I could even greet him, asked in a hushed tone, "What do you think you're doing?"

I was taken aback. He explained that he was assigned to the airport as part of the Taiwan Garrison Command, the intelligence and secret surveillance arm of the KMT. "I have a file on you that's a few inches thick. We know you're a prominent, pro-independence activist and you meet regularly with other dissidents like Peng Ming-min and Roger Hsieh."

I had suspected I was still under surveillance, but to hear it directly was still a shock. Wang eventually let me go, after insinuating that it was only because of his interference. I'd originally planned to meet my family at their home after I landed, but I didn't want to bring undue attention to them, so I checked into a hotel on the outskirts of Taipei. From there,

I called my younger brother, Wuo-pei, to let him know I had landed. His response left me speechless. "We already know. The authorities were just here."

Apparently the Taiwan Garrison Command, the MJIB, and the Taipei City Police Department had all paid a visit to my brother. He didn't know what to think when the full force of three separate police agencies showed up at his doorstep. He naturally thought something terrible had happened to me. Our parents had also been calling him nonstop, sick with worry, asking if he had heard from me. I immediately called my parents and oldest brother, Wen-pei, in Dacheng. When Wen-pei answered the phone and heard my voice, he let out a sigh of relief and relayed that the same scare tactic had been used at my parents' home. I felt sick to my stomach. My parents had already gone through so much when Shu-pei was imprisoned—the last thing they needed was to hear that another son was being pursued by the KMT.

I had only been in Taiwan for a few hours, and this trip was already turning into a nightmare. I refused to be intimated by these thugs, so I decided to visit Wuo-pei. When I opened the door to my hotel room, there were two agents standing in the hallway. They didn't even bother to hide their intention. The message was clear—wherever you go, we go. They followed me, never more than a few feet behind. If I stopped someplace, they stopped. If I spoke to anybody, they approached that person and asked what we talked about. The brazen intimidation technique infuriated me, but it was having its intended effect.

As much as I tried not be fearful of these goons, I couldn't help but think of an incident that had occurred only two years earlier. Dr. Chen Wen-cheng, a Taiwanese assistant professor at Carnegie Mellon University, traveled back to Taiwan in 1981, his first visit since he left in 1975. Just as he was about to return to the US, the Taiwan Garrison Command apprehended him and interrogated him for twelve hours. The next day, his body was found on the campus of NTU. The cause of death was officially listed as trauma from an accidental fall, but everyone knew it was another example of the KMT's use of the White Terror to suppress any opposition to the government.

Last Resort

After a few hours of leading my escorts aimlessly around Taipei, I returned to my hotel room around midnight. It was noon in Washington, D.C. I contacted Frank and asked him to gather a few congressional colleagues so I could explain in detail the harassment I was experiencing. I wanted them to hear directly from me that my family and I were being terrorized. I asked them to reach out to the KMT to express their outrage.

Early the next morning, I received a phone call from Chen Chien-jen, the minister of foreign affairs. He apologized for the misunderstanding. He made some pathetic excuse about miscommunications with the Garrison Command and assured me there would be no further problems. Obviously, my call to D.C. had the effect I had hoped. Chen could sense my anger and explained that the agents had simply gone overboard. I didn't want to waste any more time with him, so I hung up the phone.

I'd spent more than twelve years in the States and grown accustomed to the freedoms of being a US citizen. I prayed for a day when Taiwanese people would also be free from the ongoing threat from this authoritarian government.

PART III

TWO DECADES
AT GENERAL BANK

Chapter Twenty-Five

TURNAROUNDS

Although my time at ANBN ended abruptly, the experience I gained and the network of friends I made were invaluable. After my departure, I spent a few months working for Western Airlines in Los Angeles, one of the largest carriers in the western US. With some timely financial maneuvers and drastic cost cutting, we were able to bring the airline back from the brink of bankruptcy. I was even profiled by the *Wall Street Journal* as the "Chinaman who saved Western Airlines." The racist overtone and the term "Chinaman" made my Taiwanese blood boil, but within the close-knit community of Taiwanese Americans, I had earned a reputation as a turnaround specialist.

I was a banker at heart, though, so when I was approached in 1982 to run General Bank in Los Angeles, I took on the challenge. The twenty years I spent there encompassed some of the most fulfilling professional times of my life, but there were numerous obstacles to overcome.

A Failing Taiwanese-Owned Bank

I was first introduced to General Bank when a board member, Julian Wu (no relation), approached me. He explained that a group of Taiwanese business people, including him and his family, had pooled approximately $7 million in 1980 to form a commercial bank called General Bank of

Commerce—the name was later shortened to General Bank. The bank hired a Caucasian president, and it had already lost about $2 million since its inception and was estimated to lose another $4 million in 1982.

I was surprised that the type of bank I had dreamed of starting years earlier and researched for a month in Los Angeles was already in existence. I still thought the idea for such a bank was promising, so I was interested. But the board members wanted to hire me as a vice president to watch over the current leadership and report back to the board.

I rejected their proposal. I didn't feel it was ethical and proper for a subordinate to essentially spy on the existing president. If the board was dissatisfied with the management, they should make the necessary changes. I've always felt an organization is most productive when there is full transparency. The only way to avoid missteps would be if I had complete authority of the bank operations. Julian said he would discuss this with the board.

Aspirations

Only a few weeks after my meeting with Julian, General Bank made me a formal offer to become president and CEO. I told them I would consider the offer, but I needed to see if General Bank was the right bank to meet the needs of Taiwanese Americans. As part of my due diligence, I gave the board a list of reports and other data I wanted to review. When I evaluated the information, I immediately understood why the bank was in such a precarious financial situation.

One of the primary issues was the bloated organizational structure. There were simply too many employees doing unproductive tasks. The one bright spot, I thought, was that there wasn't any significant pending litigation, which would have created even more financial distress. After a few weekends of poring over reports, I believed the bank was salvageable, but it required an immediate infusion of capital. The bank needed a restart of sorts. It also needed to create a new image within the Taiwanese community. I went over every detail I could, but I knew there was no way I would know the full story until I saw things firsthand.

Challenge Accepted!

Before I formally accepted the offer, I had a meeting with the board to go over my findings and recommendations. I confirmed that General Bank would lose more than $4 million in the upcoming year, so the top priority should be strengthening the bank's capital. I promised the board that I would be directly involved in courting new investors. I also reiterated the need for unfettered decision-making, including employee hiring and firing. I knew all too well the Taiwanese custom of hiring people to curry favor instead of hiring based on talent and productivity.

My hope was to impress upon the board that they would have authority over high-level decisions and oversee the management, including me, while I would be in charge of bank operations. They agreed with my evaluation and recommendations. Which left only one major topic for discussion—my compensation. The annual salary the board offered was $65,000, a deep cut from what I currently earned at Western Airlines and even less than what I made at ANBN. The cold, hard fact was that General Bank couldn't afford to pay much given the financial constraints. I was passionate about this opportunity, so I wanted to find a way to make it work. I suggested that in addition to the salary, I would receive profit sharing based on the future financial performance of General Bank and a stock option package. The compensation package would only have value if I was able to turn things around and the bank did well. The board agreed.

I did make one other request that was personal in nature. I was about to be the face of a Taiwanese American bank where networking and socializing was part of the gig. I knew how much work turning General Bank around would take, so I respectfully asked the board not to be offended if I didn't attend such events. The board appreciated my candor and said they would leave me to the work.

Goodbye, Western Airlines—Hello, General Bank

It was time to let Western Airlines know I was leaving. I'd brought Western to a stronger financial footing over the past four months. This made it easier when I informed Neil Bergt, the chairman and CEO, that I was leaving for another opportunity. Neil had been extremely good to me when he hired me as his advisor. The last thing I wanted was to leave him in the lurch. But one of Neil's greatest strengths was adapting to new challenges. When I explained the new position at General Bank, he wished me luck.

Chapter Twenty-Six

FIRST HURDLE

The fifth of May has always been significant throughout my career. I joined NBoA on May 5, 1969, then ANBN on May 5, 1978. So when I joined General Bank on May 5, 1982, it felt like destiny. I'm not usually a superstitious person, but I had performed well in my previous positions, so I was optimistic that this opportunity would be the same. Little did I know that on my very first day, I would encounter a problem that almost ended my career at General Bank before it even started.

I arrived at the headquarters in downtown Los Angeles bright and early that morning. Gathered at the entrance of the bank was a throng of reporters and cameras from a number of TV stations. My first reaction was that the banking community had heard about my new position and wanted to welcome me. But when I walked into the bank, the looks on people's faces told me this was not a welcoming committee. Microphones surrounded me, and questions about a sexual harassment lawsuit were thrown my way.

What was happening? Was I being pranked? But it was obvious this was no joke. The reporters anxiously awaited my answer. After a few moments of silence, I muttered something about letting the legal system work through the process and quickly retreated inside my office. Just an hour earlier, I was thinking about the agenda for the day and key department heads I wanted to meet. But the only thing I accomplished that morning was giving the employees an impression of a man running around like a headless chicken, trying to get information on a lawsuit that he had just heard about.

I finally got the details. Ms. Peggy Joslyn, a Taiwanese American and former vice president and senior loan officer at General Bank, had filed a sexual harassment lawsuit against the bank. Ms. Joslyn was fired after complaining to bank executives about sexual harassment from her superior, then rehired in July 1981 to appease her when she made a discrimination and sexual harassment complaint with a state banking authority. But two months later, she was laid off again, this time allegedly because the bank was reducing staff for financial reasons. After this second go-round, Ms. Joslyn filed a public sexual harassment lawsuit against General Bank. How could I have not known about this? I'd looked over every report, document, and detail the board provided me. I'd specifically asked if there was any pending litigation of which I should be aware, and the answer had been no. Apparently this lawsuit had caught the board by surprise too.

Sexual harassment lawsuits had become more commonplace in the corporate world in the '80s. Ms. Joslyn's husband had very good connections with various media outlets. She'd also hired Gloria Allred, a famous discrimination attorney whose high-profile legal battles had led to many precedent-setting court decisions and hundreds of millions of dollars for her clients. This could potentially be devastating to General Bank.

The board called an emergency meeting to have our legal team provide an assessment. Our lead attorney summed up our situation with one simple phrase, "You have no chance of winning this case." One thing was clear to me. With this suit, my plan of raising capital would never get off the ground. No rational person would invest a penny with this kind of potential liability clouding the bank's future. I knew we needed to settle this as soon as possible.

I decided to reach out to Ms. Joslyn. Because of Ms. Allred's reputation, I knew a quick resolution would be unlikely if we communicated through the lawyers. My hope was that my limited history with General Bank would make our conversation more productive. The only problem was, I didn't know how to reach Ms. Joslyn or if she would even talk to me.

Fate intervened and threw me and General Bank a lifeline just when we needed it the most. I had become acquainted with C. C. Lee, the brother of an old friend, right around that time. During a casual conversation, C. C. mentioned that he was friends with Ms. Joslyn. I jumped at this opportunity and asked him to make an introduction on my behalf. C. C. was hesitant to get involved, but he somehow convinced Ms. Joslyn to meet with me one-on-one.

We met in a conference room at C. C.'s accounting firm. As soon as she stepped into the room, I stood and introduced myself, apologizing on the bank's behalf. "I'm terribly sorry. The bank was in the wrong. There's no excuse." I could see this was not the greeting she expected. The hard look in her eyes immediately softened. For the next thirty minutes, I listened with compassion as she told me about the grievances she endured during her time at the bank. When she was finished, it was as if a weight had been lifted from her. I didn't know what to say other than that it wouldn't have happened if I had been there.

I then told her why I'd joined General Bank and the vision I saw for its future. Ms. Joslyn agreed with me that the Taiwanese American community was in need of a bank since we often had difficulty banking with mainstream institutions. She too wanted to help people in our community improve their lives in our new home country. I was straightforward with her and explained that the sum she was seeking would effectively cripple General Bank. If that was what she wanted to do, she should continue with the lawsuit and destroy the bank. But because of the bank's precarious financial situation, it was going to be virtually impossible for her to receive a monetary award anywhere close to the $6 million she was asking for. I tried to convey that the bank's culture would change under my leadership and that General Bank would be a bank that she and other Taiwanese Americans would be proud to call their own. My hope was that she would consider a smaller amount so that both sides could move on.

I could tell she was trying to figure out if I was deceiving her. She said she needed to think it through, and we agreed to meet again in a few days. At our next meeting, she told me she didn't want to be the reason General Bank went under and wanted to know what number I had in mind. Ultimately, we settled on a figure of $400,000. I technically wasn't authorized to offer this amount, but I felt confident I would be able to convince the board to approve it.

Ms. Joslyn never involved her attorney during our settlement discussions. When we appeared in court to finalize the settlement and close the case, Ms. Allred approached me and said, "I don't know how you convinced my client to take that amount."

My response was, "That is the maximum amount my bank can afford to pay. I am humbled to see the case is settled and we can all move on."

Chapter Twenty-Seven

MAKEOVER

Just when I thought the sexual harassment lawsuit was behind us and I could finally focus on General Bank's operations, more lawsuits crawled out of the woodwork. It seemed because of General Bank's prior management, there was no end to the number of people or companies who were unhappy with the bank. I spent a good amount of time and energy dealing with angry customers and vendors.

My first year at General Bank was a blur of putting out fire after fire. Despite all the distractions, the one thing that had to be addressed in order for General Bank to stay afloat was raising fresh capital. I attended countless meetings to convince investors that General Bank was a worthy investment. By November 1982, we had raised approximately $9 million. We finally had the wherewithal to reverse the disparity between assets and liabilities and put the bank on a profitable track.

"I'll Lay Myself Off First"

The next step was taking a hard look at the organizational structure and identifying the areas where it could be more efficient. That meant laying people off. It was a devastatingly difficult process, and I wanted to approach the restructuring at General Bank in the most compassionate and transparent way possible.

The employees knew downsizing was inevitable. I needed time to evaluate every department and its function. To that end, I let everybody know that I had an open-door policy. I soon learned there was racial tension in the bank. Many of the Taiwanese American employees felt that the group of senior Caucasian bankers brought in by the previous president gave preferential treatment to their own. I wanted the culture to be based only on merit. I did not take any action at first but continued to observe. Six months into my evaluation, it was apparent that General Bank had ineffective communication between and within departments. No one knew what they were supposed to do. I was going to change that.

We ultimately reduced the personnel at the bank by 50 percent, a painful but necessary task. My next step was to address those still with the bank. I gathered the entire staff and said, "The downsizing we just went through was difficult, but it was necessary to make sure General Bank can survive. I have already mapped out the organizational structure and scope of your positions. We will work hard together to make this a bank you will be proud to be associated with." I concluded with a promise, which was later featured in a TV interview in 1993, "I'll lay myself off first before I lay off any of you!"

Not Your Typical Bank

Shortly after joining General Bank, I received a call from Liu Da-ren, director general of the Taipei Economic and Cultural Office in Los Angeles. He wanted to meet for lunch. As one of the senior US-based representatives of Taiwan's government, he and I had crossed paths a handful of times. At our lunch, Liu congratulated me on my new position. As our appetizers arrived, he said he was concerned that General Bank would be exploited by Taiwanese independence advocates and my reputation as a respected professional would be tarnished.

I put down my fork and said, "Director Liu, you are absolutely right. General Bank's mission is to serve Taiwanese independence supporters—as well as people like you." Liu was struck dumb with shock. I continued, "General Bank is a California state–licensed institution. This bank is bound by the law to not discriminate against any person based on religion, ethnicity, gender, or political affiliation." He had no response.

Although General Bank had a significant number of Taiwanese American investors and employees, we made sure that it was a bank for *all* customers. Early in my tenure, I addressed the staff on this subject. "We don't talk about politics here in the workplace." In the beginning, we did generate quite a bit of business from Taiwanese immigrants, among them many supporters of Taiwanese independence. But eventually we attracted other ethnicities, as well as high-ranking KMT officials and government officials from China. General Bank had earned a reputation for stellar service and maintaining privacy for all its customers.

A Niche Market

My vision was for General Bank to become the premier financial institution catering to the new immigrants from Taiwan who flowed into the US in the late '70s and early '80s. In order to implement my plan, I focused on a few key points. My first step was to make sure customer service was paramount, that everyone felt welcomed when they walked into any of our branches. We also offered an array of depository and loan products that were attractively priced. One of the keys to our success was that we were able to offer these new immigrants banking services when other mainstream banks found them risky. As long as they had a college degree, a good job, and resources brought over from Taiwan, we were happy to take on this "risk."

Word quickly spread within the immigrant Taiwanese American community. I used my old contacts at CCB, who provided me with valuable information on our new customers, and we were able to make lending decisions quickly. What could typically take days or weeks for other banks, we could do in a matter of minutes. Soon General Bank became known as the bank that could "approve a loan in a minute." We were able to access and use customer information better than other institutions. Furthermore, the strong growth in our loan portfolio rarely led to unmanageable loan delinquencies. In 1987 *Forbes* published an article titled "Mr. Wu Knows His Customers."

Chapter Twenty-Eight

BUILDING THE FOUNDATION

In my second year at General Bank, I established a management training program. It became an essential part of the bank's foundation and one of the main reasons for the longevity of our success. I knew from the beginning I wanted to recruit young people with little experience, generally newly minted MBAs. I wanted them raw so we could instill General Bank's culture in them. Many of the first trainees were from Taiwan, but eventually, as our program became better known, they came from all over the world.

The training program included a rotation in each department, and I oversaw it personally. I wanted to make sure the recruits knew every aspect of the bank before being assigned to a particular position. After the rotation period, the recruits were required to submit reports on areas in the bank they thought worked well and areas they thought could use improvement. I would review each report to get a better sense of their aptitude and overall business interest. At that point, I would assign them to their positions. I wanted these young professionals to feel that their observations and recommendations were taken seriously. I wanted them to feel empowered to make the bank the best it could be. We also sent each trainee to a multiple-week seminar at the Pacific Coast Banking

School in the Seattle area, one of the best executive banking programs in the country. I knew the investment would pay off in the long run.

At least twice a year, I would host the trainees at my home so I could get to know them better. During these gatherings, I purposefully didn't talk much. These were opportunities for me to hear from them. I usually warmed up the crowd with karaoke by singing an old Taiwanese folk song. After that, the trainees relaxed. Once the ice was broken, I'd tell them no subject was off limits. "Tonight, I'm not your boss. I want your honest opinion about anything at the bank." From these candid conversations, I was able to get an idea of what they were thinking and take their suggestions to improve upon future programs.

One of the most important aspects of the training was to have the recruits involved in the bank's annual planning process. We wanted our new employees to feel like they could make a significant impact on the bank's future. Getting these young people to buy into this process fostered loyalty and commitment. To this day, I still consider the training program the key driver for General Bank's success during my twenty years there. I'm proud to say that our high retention rate had much to do with the relationships our staff developed with one another. Many of the young people I mentored over the years continue to stay in touch. Being part of General Bank's financial success was gratifying, but I'm perhaps most proud of our young recruits who became successful business executives.

Integrity and Effort

In December 2000, *Investor's Business Daily* ran a feature on me, "General Bank's Li-pei Wu—Integrity and Effort Are Tops in His Books," aptly summing up the character traits I looked for in our employees. I valued integrity and effort more than professional competency.

This was put to the test not long into my tenure, when it was discovered that one of the bank's senior executives was receiving under-the-table payments from customers. I wanted to fire the executive, even though he was very productive and had landed numerous customers. The board was concerned about the potential loss of business if he was dismissed, but ultimately, we let him go. I knew General Bank's business would be hurt in the short term, but the damage in the long term if he were allowed to stay would be far worse. We would have been sending a message that our integrity could be compromised, and I couldn't let that kind of mindset grow at the bank.

Cultivate a Cost-Conscious Workplace with Incentives and Rewards

In order to reward the employees for their hard work, I suggested to the board that we implement an incentive program where 15 percent of the bank's earnings before taxes would be reserved for employee bonuses. General Bank's salary compensation was equal to or slightly lower than market rates, so this type of profit sharing would help differentiate it from other banks. Most importantly, the program was consistent with the company culture that we had worked so hard to develop: we are all in this together.

At the same time, I was notorious for being frugal. I made it crystal clear to all employees that waste would not be tolerated. We found numerous ways to reduce expenses. Right after I joined General Bank, I implemented a policy of economy travel only. As president and CEO of the bank, I needed to set the right example, so I insisted on traveling in economy class. This policy continued even when the bank was prospering. Being frugal was a philosophy that I held dear because I knew that every dollar we saved would be shared with shareholders and employees. This kind of frugality benefited our employees, and our year-end bonuses were among the most generous for commercial banks, sometimes equaling more than an employee's annual salary. As the bank's profitability improved, year-end bonus time became my favorite time of the year.

The corporate frugality measures were necessary early on for General Bank's survival, but they became an ongoing part of the company's culture. For years, General Bank was rated the most efficient commercial bank in the country by a number of industry periodicals. In April 1990, the *Economist* published an article titled "International Banking—Credit and Credibility," naming General Bank the most profitable American bank in terms of return on equity.

Everyone at General Bank Is a Sales Specialist

In order to involve the staff more, we created a referral incentive program whereby any employee who referred a new General Bank customer would receive a financial reward. We tried to keep the program straightforward and transparent so the interests of all parties were aligned properly. For example, in the case of employees referring prospective customers to the loan department, since the referring employee would not responsible for making the decision to grant the loan, a default down the road would not impact the reward received. In this way, the employees were empowered to help the company as well as themselves.

Open-Door Policy

I strove to make General Bank a collegial place to work, where fairness and transparency were the guiding principles among the employees. I wanted everyone to feel that they could bring any issue to my attention whenever they needed. During my twenty years at General Bank, my dream was for all employees to take pride in their work and in our company and ultimately feel like a part of the General Bank family. I can say without equivocation that this vision came true.

Chapter Twenty-Nine

CAPTURING OPPORTUNITIES IN A TIME OF ECONOMIC DOWNTURN

In 1990 General Bank celebrated its tenth anniversary and faced perhaps its greatest challenge. California was experiencing the most difficult economic conditions since the Great Depression. Many banks reacted by reducing personnel and shrinking their loan portfolios and product offerings. However, General Bank continued to stay profitable because we were in a great position to offer loans to business owners who were being turned away by the major banks. The theme that helped General Bank get off the ground years earlier—helping those underserved by traditional institutions—was once again providing opportunities.

While I understood why the major banks did this, I didn't agree with the way they left long-standing customers in the lurch right when these customers needed them the most. In September 1992, I published an essay in *California Business* titled "My Stand," in which I maintained that banks shouldn't bail on their customers when the going got tough. I urged my fellow bankers to figure out a way to ride out the storm with the customers, hopefully with government assistance.

Turn Crisis into Opportunity

Not long after my article in *California Business* was published, I received a call out of the blue from a real estate developer who had a thousand acres of land near Las Vegas just waiting to be developed. Despite his decades-long relationships with some of the largest banks in the country, he couldn't get financing. He was infuriated with his banks and unsure how to get his project off the groud, when he read "My Stand." It resonated with him, so he cold-called me.

I couldn't believe my ears. How could a developer with a track record and one thousand acres of prime real estate have a difficult time securing financing? The developer invited a couple of the board members and me to tour the property. He picked us up in his private jet, and after spending the day looking over the property and the development plans, we confirmed this was indeed a real prospect. The plan was to build more than a thousand new homes on the land.

I knew a project of that scale was way beyond General Bank's lending limits, but this was a great opportunity, and I didn't want to pass it up. Since he wouldn't require full funding for the entire project on day one, I proposed that he build the homes in phases. Once a phase was complete, he could begin selling those homes, repay General Bank, and then move on to the next phase. General Bank would then be willing and able to provide additional financing as he began building another phase. We would also insist the loan be secured by the full value of the property. Lastly, I asked that all lending and other administrative fees for the entire loan be paid up front. The developer agreed to every point, and both sides happily entered into the transaction.

This was one of the most successful real estate loans in General Bank's history, and it happened without a salesperson calling on the customer *and* during onc of the most difficult economic periods in US history.

Branching Out

A relative came to me in 1995 to seek my advice as he decided between two job offers. One was from a new technology company with promising prospects and the other from a well-established company. I told him that big companies offer job security, but small companies give you opportunities, especially if you negotiate for stock options. He ultimately decided to join the tech startup. Three years later, when the tech company was part of an IPO, those stock options made my young relative a multimillionaire.

I mention this story because at General Bank, we also saw opportunities in the high-tech world. Many of the young tech companies springing up in Silicon Valley were founded by Taiwanese Americans. My intuition led me to believe that there was a great opportunity for General Bank to offer them financial services. I decided the best approach was to establish a few branches in the Silicon Valley area and begin with basic banking services. Tech startups typically raise capital from venture firms because they are in the product development phase with no revenue to speak of. I established a lending program tailored to the financing of these startups. If these young companies were able to raise venture capital and deposited those funds at General Bank, we would extend them lines of credit. In addition to generating interest income on the loans, General Bank typically received stock warrants in the tech company, which could provide significant gain if the company did well in the future.

This program was unusual—many traditional banks didn't know how to assess the creditworthiness of these startups. We found that with the proper structure, these loans benefited both the bank and the clients. The bank increased its deposit base and loan portfolio with minimal credit risk. With a line of credit from the bank, the startup would be in a better position to solicit additional funds from venture capitalists. A few of our startup clients were extremely successful and through their IPOs, the bank profited handsomely from the stock warrants.

New Market Possibilities

In 1996 General Bank's net earnings were two and a half times higher than the previous year. It was named one of the top ten financial institutions by the California Export Finance Office. Considering the difficult economic environment, our success was a testament to the vision of the leaders of the bank and the hard work of the employees.

Inspired by General Bank's success within the Taiwanese American community, management and I decided to replicate this strategy with other new immigrant populations by creating a Multicultural Financial Services department. Japanese, South Korean, and Iranian immigrants, similar to their Taiwanese counterparts, had become mainstays of the diverse population in California. The immigrant story among all these different groups had many common themes. They all came to the States to find better lives for themselves and their families. They were ready and willing to work hard to pursue the American dream, and their determination knew no bounds.

General Bank's success was a reflection of the perseverance of all the immigrants we served. Because of our reputation that we would stand by our customers regardless of where they came from, our bank became known as a "commercial bank for new immigrants." I can't think of a moniker that more aptly reflects the culture of our employees and the type of institution we aspired to be.

Chapter Thirty

A TWO-DECADE LEGACY

A member of the General Bank board who is also a good friend once said about me, "For Li-pei Wu, anything worth doing is worth doing well." This pretty much sums up my aspirations in life. In 1994, after General Bank achieved the milestone of exceeding $1 billion in assets, a flurry of press activity followed. One banking periodical published a profile on me and General Bank titled, "A Taiwanese immigrant realizes the American Dream." The article touted me as being one of the most successful bankers in the US. It attributed General Bank's achievement of being one of the most profitable banking institutions to the observation that "Li-pei Wu knows his business and knows his customers." I always strive for excellence in all my endeavors, bar none. As a banker, I demanded the best from myself. While I worked hard, with diligence and persistence, I also kept my ear to the ground and had a keen eye for future trends and opportunities, always ready to make a strategic move.

From the Bottom to the Top

I took charge of General Bank in May 1982, when the bank was on the brink of collapse. By November of the same year, we were able to avert a shutdown. In only my second year, we went from bleeding cash to turning a profit. Our earnings growth and momentum continued on this trajectory for the next nineteen years. In 1988 General Bank went public on the NASDAQ to raise additional capital and expand its investor base. By the time I retired in 2002, General Bank's assets were $2.5 billion—twenty-five times the amount in 1982—and its equity had grown from near zero to $250 million. Our two original branch offices became a network of more than twenty branches. The initial investors enjoyed enormous returns and dividends on their stock holdings.

With General Bank's miraculous growth came various accolades and recognition. There were articles in the *Economist, Forbes, US Banker,* the *New York Times,* and the *Los Angeles Times.* In 1998 I was named Ernst & Young's Entrepreneur of the Year. Even though I was the one on the stage receiving the award, I truly believed it was a team effort. I was profiled on various local and national TV shows. In September 1998, I appeared in *World Business Review* with Caspar Weinberger. In May 1999, I was invited to Cambridge University to give a series of speeches on "Can Taiwan sustain its economic miracle?" and "The Taiwan and China Political Conflict vs. Economic Cooperation." In May 2000, the *Wall Street Journal* ran a profile of me. I was grateful and humbled to receive these accolades.

Soon after *Forbes* published the article on General Bank, I received a visit from the president of Fort Hays State University. He impressed upon me how helpful the media attention on me and General Bank was for raising the profile of our school and invited me to be the keynote speaker for its upcoming Presidential Speaker Series. When I looked out at the audience during my keynote address, I recalled my early days at Fort Hays State when I'd first arrived in the US. I was a foreign graduate student with broken English and poor health, trying to adjust to the bitter cold of Kansas winters. I thought of all the kind people who helped me during school, without whom I'm not sure I would have survived: Jennifer, the school counselor; Barbara, my English tutor, who also helped Jenny and my boys obtain a visa to come to the US; Ms. Kung, my friend and fellow student; and especially Professor Thomas, my mentor and teacher, who saw in me the potential that many others would have overlooked. I wished they all could have been with me at that moment so they could see how grateful I was that their efforts changed my life forever.

Years later, Fort Hays State University honored me with an Alumni Achievement Award for "outstanding achievement based upon meritorious service to society or the community." I was even asked to be the grand marshal of the homecoming parade. As my wife and I rode in the red convertible Cadillac slowly making its way through the narrow streets of Hays, Kansas, I wished Professor Thomas could have been sitting there next to me to share in the glory of the moment.

Chapter Thirty-One

CHAPTER CLOSED

When I negotiated my final employment contract with General Bank's board, we agreed that it would expire on my sixty-fifth birthday, which fell on September 9, 1999. I chose this date because of the numbers: 9/9/99. But my plan to ride into the sunset at sixty-five was put on hold when the board asked me to remain at the bank's helm for another few years. I agreed, and the board offered me another contract through January 1, 2002.

The main reason the board asked me to stay was to make a smooth transition to the next president. I had become the face of General Bank, and without a clear plan of succession, everybody associated with the bank—including employees, customers, and investors—would wonder about its future when I left. Why wasn't a plan in place prior to 1999? Discussions of finding a qualified successor to take over my post had surfaced long before my planned retirement, but we were never able to reach a consensus. Suffice it to say this problem created a rift between me and the board, which widened in the last two years of my twenty-year career at General Bank.

The Apprentice

Julian Wu—the man who first introduced me to General Bank in 1982—and his family were the largest shareholders of GBC Bancorp (GBCB), General Bank's holding company. They held numerous board seats and were extremely influential with the other board members. I knew when I first joined that they wanted me to groom Peter Wu, one of the sons of the patriarch, to eventually take over the bank as president. Peter was an executive vice president when I first joined the bank. I liked him. He was personable, and in all the years I worked with him, he always respected me and never tried to inappropriately influence banking operations. But being personable and respectful does not make one qualified to lead a billion-dollar organization.

There was no doubt that the disarray General Bank faced when I first joined was attributable to the previous management. Peter was part of that management team. When things were going bad, he had an opportunity to steer the bank in the right direction and watch over his family's investment, but he did not. In all the years I worked with Peter on a day-to-day basis, he did a good job of following orders, but he very rarely took initiative himself. If he had proven himself capable of independent and strategic thinking, then I would have been more than happy to groom him to one day take over, but I never saw that potential in him. I knew what the Wu family wanted, but I chose to defer the succession issue to a later time and focused on running the bank. I did come across candidates from time to time that would have made excellent presidents for General Bank, but whenever I broached the subject with the board members, they clearly indicated to me that they wanted to see Peter in that position. As time went by, whenever the board discussed Peter's future, I would try to explain that GBCB was a publicly traded company. The board and I, as chairman, had a fiduciary responsibility to make sure the next president was the most qualified candidate. We could not engage in nepotism. I emphasized that we had an obligation to all shareholders to conduct a proper, impartial executive search from candidates within as well as outside the bank.

Needless to say, my position did not sit well with the Wu family. General Bank was on strong footing from a financial standpoint, and they felt it was the right time for Peter to take over. They couldn't understand why I was making things difficult for them.

Loan Fraud

No matter how hard I tried to convince the board to conduct a proper executive search, the Wu family was adamant about grooming Peter. In 1998, during a board meeting, the Wu family added an item on the agenda to officially name Peter as the next president of General Bank, without first notifying me. I was livid. Even though I was chairman of the board, I had no choice but to put the resolution to a vote. The Wu family controlled six of the thirteen board seats, so it was no problem for them to convince one more member to side with them. Majority obtained, resolution approved. The approved plan was for Peter to officially become president in 2001, prior to which I would oversee the transition of responsibilities to him. Peter's ascension to the presidency seemed inevitable, but I still had a bit of time to play a few hands.

Not long after this meeting, an unfortunate incident arose that tainted General Bank's impeccable lending record. We had participated in a sizable syndicated loan led by United Commercial Bank, an Asian-owned bank based in San Francisco. As the lead lender, United Commercial introduced this opportunity to General Bank and conducted much of the initial due diligence on the borrower, an import–export company based in New York. We also conducted our own investigation by having our New York branch meet with the management team. We meticulously reviewed all the company financials and other investigative reports. Everything looked aboveboard.

Not long after we funded the loan, we discovered the borrower was a complete fraud. I was shocked and embarrassed that we could be conned in this way. I was a banker, an expert in underwriting loans with decades of experience, yet I was fooled along with everybody else. Anybody in the lending business knows bad loans come with the territory, but I can still feel the sting of this particular transaction. We immediately wrote down the loan, a $10-million loss—the worst of my career. Because this terrible event happened around the time of the board's vote to promote Peter, I couldn't help but think about the future of the bank in his hands. I was highly confident in my capabilities as a banker, but even I, with all my years of experience, was caught off guard on this particular loan. General Bank was able to overcome this setback, but I kept wondering how many more of these types of problems would occur with Peter in charge.

When GBCB went public in 1988, we expanded our shareholder base to include many high-quality institutional investors. All of these investors had confidence in the future of the bank, mainly because of my relationship with them. The bank's stellar financial performance led to great appreciation in GBCB's stock price, which meant happy shareholders. At least a couple of times a year, I would meet with the institutional investors to discuss the bank's operations and future plans. The subject of my successor was always brought up during these meetings. None of these investors knew much about Peter, other than his family owned a significant portion of the shares outstanding. If they suspected that I had no confidence in Peter as a leader, they would vote with their wallets and get out of the stock immediately, thereby driving the price down and hurting all remaining shareholders. So I did the only thing I could. I bit my tongue and tried to be as vague as possible, but I knew we had to face reality sooner or later.

My hope was to bide my time while I found an alternative. As the board directed, I oversaw the transition to giving Peter more responsibilities. Like the old saying goes—a leopard can't change its spots. The more I saw Peter in action, the more I was convinced he simply wasn't right for the job. I kept my concerns to myself. General Bank's financial performance remained stellar, and the stock price kept going up. The board, the employees, and the shareholders were all optimistic about the future. But it was increasingly clear to me that General Bank, an institution to which I had devoted a large chunk of my life, was in jeopardy.

The Sale

In 2000 I met with a handful of GBCB's largest institutional investors to provide a corporate update on the bank. Even though Peter would be taking over as president within a year, he still didn't have much of a relationship with shareholders outside of the board. They expressed concern when they learned of Peter's upcoming presidency. They told me point blank that if we couldn't be sure of General Bank's money-making future, then it might be time to consider selling to another bank. They emphasized that it was the board's responsibility to look after the interests of the shareholders. If there was a buyer out there willing to pay a good price, the board had an obligation to explore it. I promised to relay the message.

As much as I was devoted to General Bank, an acquisition by another institution would solve the primary problem I foresaw—lack of strong future leadership. When I spelled out to the board what the institutional investors had suggested, many of the members, including the Wu family, balked at the idea. It was clear their feelings were driven by pride, not based on rational business thinking.

The board couldn't reject this idea outright, but they were clearly resistant. They did what they could to prevent any kind of sale from happening. Although we didn't solicit offers from prospective buyers, it became known that we were willing to entertain the idea of selling, and offers were presented to us. But whenever a corporate suitor came along, the board of directors made sure to challenge the package being presented, picking it apart and not giving it a fair review.

Then Cathay Bancorp, an Asian-owned bank in the Los Angeles area that also focused on minority customers, contacted us. Cathay was slightly larger than our bank, so the transaction would technically be a sale of General Bank to Cathay, but the institutions were similar enough that it would look more like a merger of equals, which made the deal more palatable to the General Bank board. To appease the Wu family,

Peter would be named vice chairman of the newly formed Cathay General Bancorp but would not be the top executive managing the company. On March 7, 2003, the transaction was publicly announced, with the deal closing on October 20, 2003. I'm glad the board of General Bank came to its senses and did what was best for the shareholders. My role had come to its natural conclusion. It was time for me to move on and see what new opportunities awaited me.

A few months after the close of the transaction, I had lunch with a General Bank board member who had always been a good friend and ally. He told me that the board deliberately held off the acquisition until after I retired. When I signed on with General Bank, a contingency stock option was included in my employment contract. It provided substantial benefits to me if the bank was taken over by another firm during my term. Based on the acquisition price of the Cathay merger, my option was worth over $10 million. But since the merger didn't occur until I retired, the option expired. Of course, there was no way to prove their intent in a court of law, but it left a bad final impression. In spite of this, I reflect on my years at General Bank with immense fondness. Running this bank gave me a tremendous opportunity to shine a spotlight on what I could do as a banker as well as highlight the amazing success story of the Taiwanese American people.

Me (lower left) at about ten years old.

Me and my father during my college years.

*Graduating from National
Taiwan University, 1957*

Fresh college graduate, late 1950s

Early 1960s

Family portrait, early 1960s. Mother (lower left), Father (lower middle), Wen-pei (upper left), Jane (upper, third from left), Wuo-pei (upper, fourth from left), me (upper fifth from left), Shu-pei (upper, last from left)

*Leaving for the US -
Saying goodbye to my
father, 1968*

*Leaving for the US -
Saying goodbye to Jenny
and the boys, 1968*

Dr. Peng (right) visiting me in Alaska, early 1970s

Family portrait when visiting Taiwan, 1976.

Me and Senator Frank Murkowski, early 1980s

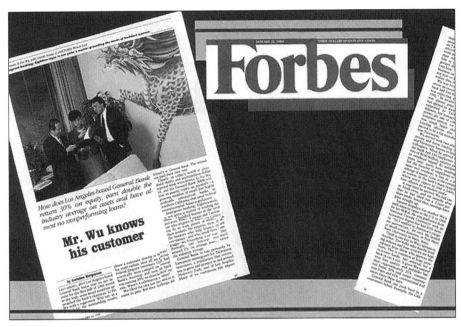

Forbes article - "Mr. Wu knows his customer," 1987

General Bank in the media.

LOS ANGELES BUSINESS JOURNAL™

WEEK OF JUNE 15, 1998

Li-Pei Wu

Li-Pei Wu's banking career began in 1960 at Chaghwa Commercial Bank in Taiwan. After immigrating to the United States in 1968, he led a successful turnaround of the Alaska National Bank of the North, which had been struggling in the post-pipeline recession.

He was recruited to lead another successful turnaround for General Bank (GBC), which had been founded to serve the growing Taiwanese-American community. Li-Pei Wu tripled the bank's assets within five years, then took the bank public. The bank is now the third-largest independent minority bank in California with $1.5 billion in assets. It currently has 16 branches in California, as well as loan production offices in Seattle and New York.

The bank's primary strength is linking California with Pacific Rim countries, with particular concentration on international trade financing for small- to medium-sized companies. On the domestic side, the bank concentrates on real estate, financing to high-tech companies and SBA loans.

Wu traces much of his success to his diverse background, which includes being an instructor of economics, accounting, finance and statistics, and being fluent in English, Mandarin Chinese, Japanese and Taiwanese. One of his strategies has been to appeal to people with diverse backgrounds. To serve the immigrant population, General Bank conducted background and credit checks through extensive networks within their home countries, which allowed it to make loans to deserving immigrants. The bank set up a multi-cultural group staffed with minority bankers to help fulfill the needs of Armenian, Iranian and Korean entrepreneurs as well as the Latino population.

GREATER LOS ANGELES AREA

1998

Entrepreneur

Of The

Year®

Awards

Ξ∥ ERNST & YOUNG LLP

GBC Bancorp

Role
Chairman and Chief Executive Officer

Company Description
The third largest independent minority bank in California

Location
Los Angeles

Major Innovation
Services and programs to serve Los Angeles' diverse cultural communities

Future Plans
Continued growth in Seattle and New York and expanding services for diverse immigrant cultures and businesses

To appeal to such diverse customers, services are based on flexibility and personal involvement. The bank has an expertise in its core products and each can be tailored to the customer's needs. Employees learn all facets of operations through a management training program, which rotates employees through key departments in a one-year span, providing opportunity while fostering loyalty. In addition, many of the officers have business experience in both the U.S. and Taiwan.

As the banking industry consolidates, GBC intends to capture customers who get lost in the mix of these mergers. Wu is leading a variety of efforts to double the size of the bank in the next five years. This growth will come from continued penetration of the technology market, expansion of target immigrant markets and growth in construction lending.

Now as Chairman and CEO of one of the most profitable commercial banks in the country, Wu has come a long way from the days he used to walk barefoot to grade school. Known as an expert on Asian business affairs, he works extensively with chambers of commerce, business associations and civic groups, encouraging ethnic harmony and partnership. Leadership, he says, is the willingness to make tough decisions and to work harder than everyone else in order to set a positive example.

Ernst & Young Entrepreneur of the Year, 1998

PART IV

OUTREACH FROM THE US TO TAIWAN

Chapter Thirty-Two

WUFI AND CHAI TRONG-RONG

I often tell people facetiously, "I'm a career activist for Taiwanese independence and a freelance banker." I say this because I'm better known as a successful banker rather than a political activist. That success afforded me more time and energy to advocate for Taiwan and support lobbying efforts with US policymakers. I put forth my best effort as a banker, but there was no question where my passion lay: fighting for freedom, democracy, and social justice for Taiwan.

WUFI Member in Alaska

When I first arrived in the United States, I joined the World United Formosans for Independence (WUFI). My old friend Chai Trong-rong was a founding member and elected as its inaugural chairman in 1970. At the time, I wasn't able to do much more than help distribute *Taiwan Youth*, a magazine advocating for independence. This volunteer work brought me great satisfaction because I felt like I was making a meaningful contribution to Taiwan.

I also published short essays whenever I could for *Taiwan Youth* under the pen name Si-min. Mr. Munakata Takayuki—a fellow writer using the pen name Song Chong-yang—and I had numerous debates about what was the greatest threat to Taiwan's democratic future. Although

Mr. Takayuki was Japanese, he had a long history of contributing to the Taiwanese movement. He was instrumental in Dr. Peng Ming-min's escape from Taiwan in 1970. Mr. Takayuki maintained that China was the biggest threat to Taiwan because its military capability would expand, and it was only a matter of time before it claimed Taiwan by force. Because of my personal experience, I was of the opinion that the KMT was the bigger threat.

Assassination Attempt of Chiang Ching-kuo

In April 1970, Peter Huang and his brother-in-law, Cheng Tzu-tsai, who were members of WUFI, made an assassination attempt on Vice Premier Chiang Ching-kuo, Chiang Kai-shek's son. A caravan carrying Chiang Ching-kuo arrived at the Plaza Hotel in New York City. Peter Huang managed to elbow his way through the crowd and draw his gun. But just as he was about to pull the trigger, a Diplomatic Security Service special agent slammed him to the floor. The bullet struck the hotel's revolving doors, and a team of special agents immediately rushed forward and restrained him. Huang shouted something that resonates with me to this day, "Let me stand up like a Taiwanese!"

Cheng Tzu-tsai tried to free his compatriot but was quickly overpowered. Before the pair was shoved into a police cruiser, they shouted, "Long live Formosa! Long live Taiwan! Down with Chiang Kai-shek!" Huang and Cheng were charged with attempted murder by American prosecutors. Even though violence should never be condoned, I do applaud their courage. Their attempt attracted worldwide attention and created great momentum for WUFI's mission.

Distancing Myself from WUFI

Not long after the assassination attempt, WUFI made an about-face because the members didn't want to be perceived as a violent organization. My friend, Dr. Chai Trong-rong, who was WUFI's president at the time, and an attorney hired by WUFI to defend Huang and Cheng, publicly asserted that WUFI was not involved in the attempt in any way.

This lack of support for Huang and Cheng angered many of the members, including Frank Lai, John Cheng, and me. It was unconscionable for WUFI to abandon members who had the bravery to take action. When Huang and Cheng were granted bail and fled US jurisdiction, we all cheered in support. Huang went into hiding for twenty-five years and reappeared in Taiwan in 1996. Cheng sought asylum in Sweden but was extradited to the US a year later. He was given a five-year prison term.

Even though WUFI was the most established Taiwanese independence organization in the world at that time, it lost a great deal of support after that. This really hurt the independence movement—without a strong organization to galvanize people, energy and enthusiasm were lost. WUFI continued on as an organization, but I was no longer as heavily involved.

Many years later, I paid $5,000 for a painting created by Cheng during his incarceration. The painting featured a red backdrop and a man silhouetted in white in the foreground. A circle was drawn over the man's heart, and his hands were raised as he was about to fall backward. To me, the painting signified Chiang Ching-kuo's demise. I later donated the painting to a fundraising auction to support Taiwanese independence. It was my own way of paying tribute to these courageous men.

Championing Taiwanese Independence

The battle cry of revolution and violent actions against the KMT resonated with many Taiwanese, including me. But the reality was, we were ill equipped to make a difference in any meaningful way. US authorities, however, were growing concerned that Taiwanese independence was becoming a radical terrorist movement. WUFI and other independence activists realized they had to change tactics. In 1982, recognizing that the US would be critical to the independence cause, Chai Trong-rong founded the Formosan Association for Public Affairs (FAPA), the largest lobbying organization in the US focused on Taiwanese affairs. It was created to promote international support for the people of Taiwan and to help Taiwan join the international community. It encouraged its members to be politically active and regularly attend local town hall meetings and events with members of Congress to educate them on relations between the US and Taiwan.

Trong-rong also founded Formosa Television in 1996 in order to counter the monopolistic hold that the KMT had over media coverage in Taiwan. I've rarely seen anybody as dedicated to Taiwan as Trong-rong, always operating at 110 percent. If he wasn't distributing literature or wooing new members, he was badgering his network of friends for donations. A wealthy friend once joked that when he passed, he wanted to be buried as far away from Trong-rong as possible, otherwise Trong-rong would forever harass him in the afterlife, hat in hand.

Democratic Progressive Party

In opposition to the KMT's one-party authoritarian rule under the party-state system, the Democratic Progressive Party (DPP) was founded in 1986 with a platform focused on human rights and Taiwanese identity. But since the DPP was formed during martial law, the political party was technically illegal. A year later, martial law was lifted, and measures regulating and limiting the establishment of newspapers and political parties were loosened. In 1988 Lee Teng-hui succeeded Chiang Ching-kuo as the first Taiwanese-born president. Although President Lee was the leader of the KMT in name, in reality, he met tremendous opposition from the old guard faction of the party. They felt his progressive tendencies were a threat to the stronghold the KMT had enjoyed for so many decades.

Back to Taiwan

In 1991 WUFI moved its headquarters back to Taiwan in order to influence the political process more effectively. Trong-rong visited me in Los Angeles to discuss this move. Many believed it meant WUFI would essentially be an extension of the DPP. I suggested it would be best if WUFI remained purely an advocacy group with no political affiliation. I even offered to help WUFI fundraise so that it would have the financial wherewithal to remain independent. I thought Trong-rong agreed with me, but the next thing I knew, he went to Taiwan and officially joined the DPP. He then announced his candidacy for a legislative seat in his hometown of Chiayi, stating that Li-pei Wu had promised to help him manage the finances and fundraise. That was Trong-rong—once he got an idea in his head, there was no stopping him!

Not long after his announcement, he faced his first test in the rough-and-tumble world of Taiwanese politics when an incident that took place seven years earlier came back to haunt him. In 1985 Dr. Peng had been the front-runner when FAPA was about to elect a new president, but WUFI had endorsed Trong-rong for the presidency. Trong-rong, as usual, threw everything he had into the election, and eventually Dr. Peng's lead began to lessen. Some of Dr. Peng's supporters, including Frank, were critical of Trong-rong. They felt that as a former student of Dr. Peng's, it was disrespectful of Trong-rong to compete against him in this way. They even called him a traitor. The tactic worked, and Dr. Peng won the election by one vote. Trong-rong's reputation took a hit, but that was not the end of it. When Dr. Peng was about to step into the role of FAPA's newly elected president, Trong-rong and a handful of other influential members changed the bylaws of the organization so that much of the president's power was diluted. Needless to say, Dr. Peng felt duped and was furious. He resigned immediately.

Trong-rong's foray into Taiwanese politics brought this bad blood back to the surface. As his campaign for the Taiwanese legislature gathered steam, he realized that he needed a high-profile endorsement in order to turn out the pro-DPP vote. The perfect person was Dr. Peng, who was about to embark on his much-anticipated return to Taiwan. Trong-rong thought it wouldn't be hard to convince Dr. Peng to help him, for surely his old friend and mentor had forgotten or forgiven him for the FAPA incident. But apparently Dr. Peng's memory was long, and the answer was a resounding no. In typical Trong-rong fashion, he was not deterred and asked me to make the request on his behalf. Dr. Peng's response painted a vivid picture: "The wound on my back where Chai stuck his knife is still bleeding." Even though I was more diplomatic when I informed Trong-rong of Dr. Peng's response, my friend was not discouraged.

I actually felt bad for Trong-rong. He had dedicated so much time and energy on behalf of Taiwan, and having like-minded people in Taiwan's legislature should have been the priority for everybody. I suggested a compromise to Dr. Peng. We would go to Trong-rong's headquarters early in the morning when very few people were there. Dr. Peng would sign one of the banners so that all could see that he supported Trong-rong. We would then leave to avoid any active campaigning. The professor reluctantly agreed.

My idea should have worked, but when it came to Trong-rong, very few things were ever straightforward. On the morning of Dr. Peng's quick visit, Trong-rong was waiting with a mob of his supporters. As soon as Dr. Peng exited our car, he was swept up into an enthusiastic crowd, side by side with Trong-rong, and led into an open-topped campaign van. The vehicle was fully equipped with a public-address system, and the teacher and his former student stood hand in hand as the car slowly progressed down the streets of Chiayi, surrounded by a mass of people chanting "Dr. Peng endorses Chai Trong-rong!" As Dr. Peng was about to disappear from my view, he looked back at me helplessly. I shrugged my shoulders and waved goodbye.

Trong-rong won that election against the KMT candidate by less than two hundred votes. He knew he needed something dramatic to put him over the top, and to his credit, he found a way.

A Law without Teeth

During President Chen Shui-bian's (affectionately nicknamed A-bian) first term, an idea regarding a referendum on Taiwan's future began to take hold. The purpose of the referendum was to give the people the right to choose the national flag, the official name of the country, the national anthem, and essentially suppress anything that referenced unification with China. If Taiwan's legislative body passed the referendum, by law the people of Taiwan would finally be able to consider a path toward true independence. This was exactly the kind of issue that Chai Trong-rong could sink his teeth into. He was directly involved in drafting the referendum, which would be presented to the Legislative Yuan (the congressional body of Taiwan). The KMT held a majority in the legislature at the time, so it took tremendous pressure and effort from people like Trong-rong to advance the referendum for consideration.

On November 30, 2003, the Referendum Act advocated by Trong-rong was up for deliberation. But the KMT, masters at playing political games for their own benefit, also introduced a version of the act for deliberation. Their version was essentially worthless and gave no power to the people of Taiwan to vote on any matter of importance. But with the KMT's majority, the emasculated version of the Referendum Act easily passed. On December 31, 2003, A-bian signed the act into law. I know many were disappointed with his decision, but he was under tremendous pressure, not only from the KMT legislature but also from the international community, including the US. I know A-bian had wanted to push through Trong-rong's version of the Referendum Act. As consolation, he presented Trong-rong with the pen he used at the signing ceremony and called him "Mr. Referendum." Trong-rong put his heart and soul into this effort, and all he had to show for it was a pen.

Media Liberalization

Of all of Chai Trong-rong's achievements, I believe his greatest was founding Formosa Television in March 1996. Establishing this television network was challenging and full of internal power plays, but Trong-rong overcame them with a will of steel. The network thrived, and the Taiwanese people were finally able to access a media resource that wasn't just KMT propaganda.

Unfortunately, the KMT used its legislative majority to force A-bian into yet another impossible battle. In 2003 it sought to "liberalize the media" and painted Formosa Television as nothing more than an ideological apparatus controlled by the DPP. The DPP couldn't withstand the KMT's overwhelming pressure and eventually caved. A DPP committee that regulated its own membership proposed that no standing politician should have an interest in any media company. This would obviously affect Trong-rong, since he was still a legislator at the time and chairman of Formosa Television.

As soon as I heard about this, I gathered Dr. Peng and Li Hong-hi, an NTU professor emeritus and renowned constitutional expert, and asked to meet with A-bian privately. We had carefully scripted the message we wanted to relay. The KMT had dominated the country's media outlets for decades, and now that Formosa Television was succeeding, they were suddenly concerned with political influence? The hypocrisy was unbearable. Formosa Television was the only outlet providing information and perspectives based on Taiwanese nationalism. We needed to preserve that, and we needed Chai Trong-rong to continue as chairman to ensure that the integrity of the network remained intact. Why should the DPP be forced to make accommodations, when the KMT never had?

Unfortunately, our argument was ignored. A-bian asked Trong-rong to set the right example and abide by the new rules. Trong-rong reluctantly gave up the chairmanship of Formosa Television, and the KMT's furor over government-controlled media conveniently subsided. A-bian's willingness to capitulate did come back to haunt him. In 2008, when he and his family were embroiled in numerous financial scandals and other improprieties, the newspapers, airwaves, and internet were inundated with stories skewed against him. Formosa Television wasn't able to provide the sorely needed counterbalance against these attacks. Ultimately, A-bian lost the public relations battle, and the DPP candidate for president that year, Frank Hsieh, was easily defeated.

It Is What It Is

These defeats were difficult for Trong-rong considering how much blood, sweat, and tears he gave for Taiwan. Despite the disappointment, he continued to aim high. He ran for the chairmanship of the DPP on three separate occasions but lost each time. After his last defeat, to a rising star named Tsai Ing-wen, he invited me to dinner to commiserate. Throughout the evening, he kept wondering why he'd lost to Ms. Tsai. "What does she have that I don't? She has a doctorate, I have a doctorate. She used to be a professor, I used to be professor—in the US, no less. She served as a legislator, I served as a legislator. In fact, I served more terms than she did. When it comes to Taiwanese independence, she's not even in my league. So what is it about her?"

I didn't know how to console him. "It is what it is," I said to my old friend. "You're right about your qualifications, but she seems to know how to pull the right strings. That's what elections are about, having connections and pulling the right strings." Trong-rong fell silent. It was perhaps the first time I had seen him without his usual boundless, optimistic energy. In the next legislative election, Trong-rong lost his seat as well as his position with the DPP Central Standing Committee, one of the most powerful groups within the party. He tried to make a comeback, but the political pendulum didn't swing his way again.

Chai Trong-rong died of multiple organ failure on January 11, 2014, at the age of seventy-eight. It's been many years since his passing, but I can feel his indomitable spirit each time I turn on Formosa Television or see political activists exercising their rights on the streets of Taiwan. Trong-rong may not have been able to see his full vision of Taiwan come to fruition, but because of his effort, passion, and will, he cemented his legacy as a great advocate for Taiwan.

Chapter Thirty-Three

LIN YI-HSIUNG

In 1979 I met and hosted Lin Yi-hsiung when he passed through Alaska on his way back to Taiwan after visiting Washington, D.C., on the invitation of the US State Department. He was a member of the Taiwan Provincial Consultive Council (TPCC) and had made a name for himself within Taiwan's democratic movement. A lawyer by trade, he was soft-spoken and introspective, with the soul of a poet and the mind of a philosopher. During our week together in Alaska, we got to know each other very well. We went sightseeing during the day and spent the evenings by the fireplace talking about how to accelerate democracy in our home country. We were completely in tune when it came to Taiwanese politics. Our discussions often went long into the night, always with great enthusiasm and plenty of scotch. I did my best to keep up with Yi-hsiung glass for glass, but I was no match for him. He would be halfway through a bottle and completely lucid, going on about the evils of the KMT and the danger of China, while I was trying to stay upright in my chair. The next day, he was ready to do it again!

A Letter and Two Photos

A few days after Yi-hsiung returned to Taiwan from Alaska, I received a letter from him thanking me for my hospitality. He promised that he would use his position on the TPCC to ensure the voice of the Taiwanese people was represented. He also enclosed two pictures. The first was a photo of the entire Lin family spanning multiple generations. The second was of his three beautiful daughters. On the back of it he wrote, *I'll save two of my girls to be your future daughters-in-law.*

Imprisoned

Two months later, on December 10, 1979, a crackdown on pro-democracy demonstrations known as the Formosa Incident—because it involved members of *Formosa* magazine—occurred in Kaohsiung. The day began with Yi-hsiung and a throng of supporters demonstrating to commemorate Human Rights Day, an annual worldwide celebration. This would be the first time that Taiwan recognized it. Although the demonstrations were peaceful, the KMT viewed this as expressing discontent, which was against the law. They indiscriminately arrested many leaders, including Lin Yi-hsiung. My friend was imprisoned and tortured for doing nothing more than voicing his support of human rights. Through the KMT propaganda machine, reports implied that Yi-hsiung had succumbed and become a most "cooperative political prisoner." We learned later that Yi-hsiung was perhaps the strongest of those arrested. He refused to cooperate and, as a result, was subjected to the harshest torture. His unbreakable spirit frustrated the KMT to such an extent that they retaliated.

On February 28, 1980, a few months after Yi-hsiung's arrest, a nameless assailant broke into the Lin household off Xinyi Road in Taipei and stabbed his sixty-year-old mother and six-year-old twin daughters to death. The eldest daughter, nine-year-old Huan-chun, was critically injured but miraculously survived. When I first heard the news, shock, despair, and anger hit me like a tidal wave. I couldn't get the photo of his three smiling daughters out of my mind. For a father to lose a child in any manner is tragic, but to lose innocent children at the hands of a murderous government is beyond comprehension.

There is no doubt in my mind that the KMT ordered the murder of Yi-hsiung's family. The KMT had the Lin home under surveillance twenty-four hours a day, yet somehow the murderer was able to slip into the house undetected. The KMT also wiretapped the Lin home telephone, yet all the recordings at the time of the murder were inexplicably destroyed. The KMT even went so far as to implicate Jeffrey Bruce Jacobs, a friend of the Lins and a known democracy supporter. Jacobs, an American-born Australian scholar trained in Taiwanese studies, was arrested not long after the killings. Witnesses claimed he visited the Lin home the day of the crime. After Jacobs had been detained for three months, Amnesty International intervened, and the authorities released him for lack of evidence. The Lin Family Massacre remains officially unsolved to this day.

Help from Senator Murkowski

The KMT's plan to tarnish Yi-hsiung's reputation and quell the pro-democracy movement did the exact opposite. Yi-hsiung became a hero among the Taiwanese. At the grassroots level, more and more Taiwanese became active in the political process as advocates or politicians. The barrage of media articles and reports on the Lin Family Massacre exposed the KMT's immoral and corrupt history to the international community. Yet Yi-hsiung remained imprisoned. My fellow Taiwanese Americans and I realized we needed to do something. The KMT valued their relationship with the US, so we contacted every member of the House and Senate who was sympathetic to our cause and asked them to pressure the KMT to release Yi-hsiung. I asked Frank Murkowski for help. We also contacted US mainstream journalists, hoping to counteract the false narrative put out by the KMT-controlled media. Our goal was to humanize the story. We didn't want Lin Yi-hsiung to simply be another faceless political prisoner. We wanted people to know that he was a husband, a son, a father. I personally contacted numerous journalists to provide additional background on Yi-hsiung and gave them copies of the two photos of his family. Our plan worked—every news article on the massacre was accompanied by the picture of Yi-hsiung's three daughters. With help from Senator Murkowski and others, we were able to push for Yi-hsiung's release.

In 1984, four long years after his arrest, Lin Yi-hsiung was granted parole. We rejoiced that he was finally free. Yi-hsiung returned a hero, but while the public celebrated, he did not join in. The first thing he did after leaving prison was to attend the funeral services for his murdered mother and daughters. Because of his incarceration, he had to wait four years before he could properly say goodbye to his loved ones.

My Friend in Exile

Lin Yi-hsiung tried his best to put his life back together, but it was difficult. He and his daughter, Huan-chun, moved to the US for a change, settling in Laguna Niguel in Orange County, California. Yi-hsiung's wife, Fang Su-min, remained in Taiwan and became a well-respected politician. I was in Los Angeles at General Bank when Yi-hsiung moved to Southern California and looked forward to spending more time with him. Whenever I visited, I would bring a bottle of scotch in hopes that we could rekindle our fiery discussions. But Yi-hsiung was no longer the same man. He rarely spoke, and much of the passion he'd had for Taiwanese politics had waned. Oftentimes, we would just sit in silence. I didn't know how to help him. He needed to grieve in his own way.

Yi-hsiung essentially shut himself off from the rest of the world for two years. He stopped communicating with friends and refused all interview requests from the media. There was so little information about him that wild rumors swirled, including unfounded stories of his mental instability. It got to the point that Dr. Peng contacted me because he and so many others were worried. I reached out to Yi-hsiung, telling him people just wanted to know he was all right. His response was simple. "Judge me by how I live my entire life, not how I am at this moment."

Time can help heal deep wounds, and in 1986, Yi-hsiung emerged from his self-imposed exile and entered the Harvard Kennedy School as a graduate student. A year later, he received his master's degree in public policy. While at school, he rediscovered his passion for Taiwanese politics and joined the DPP. His wife completed her term as a Taiwanese legislator and reunited with her family in the US. The couple went on various study tours, including to Cambridge University in the UK and the University of Tsukuba in Japan. During that time, Yi-hsiung wrote "The Outline for the Basic Law of the Republic of Taiwan," which to this day remains widely recognized as the de facto constitution of the republic.

Yi-hsiung and Su-min returned to Taiwan in 1989, and in 1991 the couple established the Chilin Foundation and the Chilin Cultural Center in Yilan. They created these organizations to raise awareness of social issues in Taiwan. The impact Yi-hsiung had as a social advocate was inspirational. He and fellow DPP stalwarts Hsu Hsin-liang and Shih Ming-teh joined forces in the early 1990s to pressure the KMT to hold direct elections for president and vice president. They organized numerous demonstrations, rallies, and sit-ins, to the point where the KMT caved and included this landmark democratic reform in its legislative agenda. But of all the social issues for which Yi-hsiung advocated, he is best known for his staunch opposition to nuclear power.

Antinuclear Movement

In 1999 construction began on a nuclear power plant—Taiwan's fourth—which was to be based in New Taipei City. After inspections found defective construction and unsafe waste disposal, there was a public outcry to halt the project. In addition to the poor construction, design issues, vendor disputes, and budgetary overruns mired the project in constant delays. A-bian's platform during the 2000 presidential election included an antinuclear stance. Public opposition to the power plant grew, yet the project continued, mainly because the KMT, with its majority in the legislature, wanted to see the plant completed. Yi-hsiung became a vocal critic of the project and partnered with religious entities, environmental groups, and social advocacy communities to establish the Referendum Process for the Fourth Nuclear Power Plant. Their mission was to force the Taiwanese government to allow a full vote by the people to determine whether the controversial power plant should be completed.

Yi-hsiung's strategy was to begin with a small group of volunteers who would hand out leaflets and hold rallies and sit-in demonstrations. He had studied and greatly admired Gandhi and his nonviolent approach to protesting. In all our years of friendship, we generally always agreed about Taiwanese politics, but not in this case. I didn't think this form of quiet protest would apply the kind of pressure necessary to make the KMT capitulate. But one should never underestimate the will of a man like Lin Yi-hsiung. He and a handful of his supporters began a hunger strike on April 22, 2014, and called upon President Ma Ying-jeou and his administration to halt construction of the fourth nuclear power plant. The strike was held at Gikong Presbyterian Church, a house of worship converted from Yi-hsiung's former residence, where the Lin Family Massacre took place.

On the seventh day of the strike, I visited the church with a note I had handwritten for Yi-hsiung. I was worried about my friend's health, and I couldn't stand by and let him deteriorate without letting him know how important he was to me and Taiwan.

Yi-hsiung, my brother. When you said you would fight this battle to your last breath, I believed you. I'm writing this today because I want you to know how much you have inspired me. The whole country has awakened to your call against the development of the nuclear power plant. Your character and dedication to the cause have earned you nationwide respect. But our beloved country is beset with a myriad of problems. We need you and your leadership to continue to inspire change. Let's give Taiwan all we have in our final years until we see the last of the KMT. Stay alive, stay healthy!

I knew the strength of Yi-hsiung's mind and will, and I hoped my note would persuade him to end the strike before it was too late.

Fortunately, the public pressure from Taiwanese citizens was more than the KMT could bear. The hunger strike began just as the Sunflower Student Movement ended, the largest civic protest in Taiwan's history. The timing was perfect. People were already immensely dissatisfied with President Ma and his administration, and the hunger strike was exactly what was needed to push the government over the edge. Eight days into the strike, President Ma and Premier Jiang Yi-huah visited Yi-hsiung. Soon after, the KMT announced they would halt further construction on the fourth power plant. What a great victory for the people of Taiwan and a clear demonstration of how the will of one man *can* make a difference.

Side by Side

Though reticent by nature, Yi-hsiung has always been remarkably observant and thoughtful. He is a man grounded in substance over superficiality, and his friendship for me shone through even when I didn't expect it. When my mother passed away in 1997, I didn't make a formal announcement because I wanted to keep the service small and private. When I returned to Taiwan for the funeral, to my great surprise, Yi-hsiung had found out about it and come to pay his respects. When I donated a significant portion of my yearly bonus to his Chilin Foundation, he invited me to join the board of the foundation as a sign of his appreciation. And when I renounced my US citizenship in 2004 and moved back to Taiwan, he would check on me from time to time to make sure I was settling in.

He was equally selfless in the political arena, a rarity among politicians. In 1998 he was elected the chairman of the DPP. Under party rules, as chairman, he would automatically be designated as the candidate to represent the party in the upcoming 2000 presidential election. He was very popular, and all the leaders within the DPP—except for Hsu Hsin-liang—encouraged Yi-hsiung to run. But there was evidence in the polling data that another young, popular DPP member, Chen Shui-bian, had a better chance of victory in the upcoming election. In typical Yi-hsiung fashion, he declined the nomination and personally asked A-bian to run. He cared more about the greater good. A-bian was hesitant to take the place of a man he considered to be an elder and revered by so many, but Yi-hsiung was able to convince him that it was the right thing for the country.

Yi-hsiung stepped down from his post as DPP chair one month after A-bian's first presidential inauguration. He said he had successfully completed his mission and it was time for the next generation to take the lead at the DPP.

Supporting Shih Ming-teh in Running for President

I've known Yi-hsiung long enough to understand how principled he is in his convictions. It is because of his integrity and strength of character that I have usually supported whatever cause he has taken on. That is why I was so shocked to open the newspaper on May 21, 2015, and see the headline, "Lin Yi-hsiung throws his weight behind Shih Ming-teh's presidential bid in 2016." I reread the headline multiple times, hoping that my eyes were deceiving me.

The Sunflower Student Movement, the nuclear plant debacle, and the historically low approval ratings for President Ma meant the DPP had a golden opportunity not only to win back the presidency but also gain majority in the legislature in 2016. Tsai Ing-wen was the chairperson of the DPP and its presidential nominee. The last thing anybody in the pan-Green camp (those parties who support an independent Taiwan) wanted to see was division within the party. Shih Ming-teh throwing his hat in the ring would do exactly that. At one time, Shih was considered a prominent voice in the democracy movement and a leader within the DPP. But as I came to know him better, I viewed him as a self-serving opportunist. To me, his presidential bid was another example of him trying to attract attention for the sake of glory. Shih was arrested along with Yi-hsiung in the Formosa Incident, so they had a long history together, but it was difficult to fathom how Yi-hsiung, a man known to put country above all personal gain, would support a man like Shih.

I wrote a note to Yi-hsiung the following day to express my concern and ask that he clarify his stance to the DPP supporters. A few days later, he wrote the following in response:

I'm well-aware of Shih's reputation, which is why I have had no dealings with him the past ten-plus years. But we will forever be brothers-in-arms because of the Formosa Incident. During that difficult time, we faced danger together and encouraged and supported each other. It's a camaraderie that few can understand. Although I hadn't communicated with Shih for many years, when he asked for my help, I was compelled to do so. I will cast my vote for Shih, even though I know there are better candidates out there.

I read the note and sensed Yi-hsiung's internal conflict but felt that it was a mistake for him to show that kind of loyalty to Shih. For something as important as the presidency of Taiwan, the greater good must outweigh personal loyalties. This endorsement tarnished Yi-hsiung's impeccable reputation to some degree, but as he said many, many years earlier, judge him for his entire life, not just one moment. The respect I've always had for my dear friend would not be swayed by this one decision. To be able to face the adversities he has and come out of that dark tunnel with a sense of purpose and achievement is something we as Taiwanese should honor and cherish. I'm so fortunate to have a friendship with Yi-hsiung that started more than four decades ago when we sat by a fireplace, talking about the future of Taiwan with a glass of smoky scotch in hand.

Chapter Thirty-Four

TEMPEST IN A TEACUP

In the forty years I've known Frank Murkowski, we've been through thick and thin, both personally and professionally. Our friendship is one of the most important of my life, and our cultural differences created an opportunity for each of us to learn from the other. This friendship extended to his family and friends as well. Frank's daughter, Lisa, used to wash my car to earn money for school. Lisa followed her father's path in politics. She served in the Alaska House of Representatives and was appointed to the US Senate after Frank resigned his seat in December 2002 to become the governor of Alaska. Like her father, Senator Lisa Murkowski has always been a strong advocate for Taiwan.

During our numerous discussions about foreign affairs, Frank developed an interest in world politics. With Asia's proximity to Alaska, Frank became very knowledgeable and influential regarding Asia–US relations. He was a member of the Senate's Committee on Foreign Relations from 1983 to 1995 and chaired the Subcommittee on East Asian and Pacific Affairs from 1983 through 1987.

Quiet Diplomacy

In the early '80s, Senator Edward Kennedy, Senator Claiborne Pell (chair of the Senate Foreign Relations Committee), Congressman Stephen Solarz (chair of the Asian and Pacific Affairs Subcommittee of the House Foreign Affairs Committee), and Congressman Jim Leach of Iowa were four of the most outspoken supporters of Taiwan in the US Congress. They were concerned by the deprivation of rights of Taiwan's political prisoners and Taiwanese exiles who were opposed to the KMT. They also strongly believed the people of Taiwan should have the right to determine their fate and were considered by the KMT as a "pro-Taiwan" force in Congress.

Frank, a member of the Republican Party, chose to stay on friendly terms with the KMT. He believed this would give him leverage should he ever need anything from them. He was invited to Taiwan every year to meet with high-ranking government officials. The KMT always did their utmost to make him happy during his visits. One time, after returning to the US following a particularly pleasant visit to Taiwan with his wife, Nancy, Frank enthused about Taiwan's wonderfully cheap commodity prices. I didn't have the heart to tell him the KMT probably quoted well below market rates just to please him, so I laughed and let it slide.

As sympathetic as Frank was to the plight of the Taiwanese people, he believed that what Kennedy, Pell, Solarz, and Leach were doing wasn't effective. Frank always said: "Saving face is important to the KMT. It's an organization with tens of thousands of members, and leadership would lose credibility if it compromised too easily." I learned over time that Frank's quiet diplomacy was quite effective. Frank knew how to tread the fine line between denouncement and tactful negotiation.

"What can I do for Taiwan?"

When Lee Teng-hui rose to the presidency in 1988 after Chiang Ching-kuo's fatal heart attack, Frank led a delegation of representatives to Taiwan to express his condolences as well as to make sure there was a smooth transition of power. As a Taiwanese, President Lee faced the possibility of the predominantly Chinese KMT threatening his power.

En route to Taiwan, Frank called me unexpectedly. He didn't mince words. "I'm on Air Force Two. What can I do for you and Taiwan?" I asked for two favors. First, I urged Frank to speak with Hau Pei-tsun—a lifelong KMT member and career soldier who fought in the Chinese Civil War during his youth and was then the chief of the General Staff in the Ministry of National Defense—about the US stance against Taiwan regressing to military rule. It would be invaluable for Frank to tell him that the US was watching him. Second, I asked Frank to publicly commend Lee Teng-hui for his commitment to full democracy. Frank was quick to say he would get it done.

True to his word, he did exactly that. During a news conference, Frank acknowledged Taiwan's sustained democratization progress and praised Lee Teng-hui for being the right leader for Taiwan. I believe Frank's public remarks helped keep the KMT in check, preventing them from plotting to sabotage Lee's presidency.

Lee Teng-hui was likely unaware of these backroom conversations that took place during the beginning of his presidency. I'm grateful for what my friend did, providing a much-needed watchful eye during a delicate time in Taiwan's history.

Setting up a Meeting between Murkowski and the DPP

In November 1990, Frank went to Taiwan at the invitation of the Ministry of Foreign Affairs as the keynote speaker for the Fourteenth US–ROC Economic Council Convention. Ironically, this was the same convention for which I was denied a visa exactly ten years earlier. The political environment had changed quite a bit, and this time, I planned to accompany my good friend.

Because the KMT had always arranged Frank's itinerary on previous visits, he never got a full picture of Taiwan. He had yet to meet the self-made entrepreneurs born and bred in Taiwan or members of the opposition party, the DPP. I suggested he let me plan the latter half of his trip. Frank agreed, but neither of us foresaw the trouble to come with that plan. To facilitate communications, Frank named me one of his advisors and included me in his delegation. But when he presented his roster to MOFA, they promptly crossed out my name. When Frank inquired why I had been excluded, they replied, "This is an official visit by an official delegation, and Mr. Wu is merely a civilian."

The KMT clearly had a hand in excluding me. I told Frank, "There are two civilians in the delegation—me and your friend John Daly. Why did MOFA ax only me?" When Frank brought this up with MOFA, they acknowledged their mistake and crossed out Mr. Daly's name also. Since Frank was a guest, his hands were tied. Although I couldn't be an official part of Frank's team, I would still make the trip to Taiwan and looked forward to hosting the second part of his visit.

Frank's delegation received noticeably less fanfare this time compared to his previous visits. He usually met with the president of Taiwan, yet this time, MOFA claimed that President Lee's schedule was full. Vice President Lee Yuan-tsu would do the honors instead. Later that day, President Lee called my friend to apologize for not meeting him. He wanted to arrange another time to meet, but because of Frank's commitment to me, this was not possible.

On the evening of November 17, 1990, I hosted a dinner party including several celebrated Taiwan-born business people at a banquet hall managed by one of them. Frank and I stayed at a villa in Yangmingshan, a national park and resort area in northern Taiwan, owned by my good friend Eric Wu. The next day, Eric held a lunch reception for Frank attended by more Taiwanese business people. The following day, Hsu Hsin-liang and Roger Hsieh picked us up for a cocktail party hosted by the DPP at the Ambassador Hotel in Taipei. Just about every DPP bigwig showed up for the party. Frank's attendance garnered quite a bit of attention, and several reporters turned up to interview him.

Mr. Kao Tian-sheng from the *Liberty Times* was one of the reporters in attendance. He interviewed Frank, and a couple of the questions touched upon democracy and self-determination.

Q: The *New York Times* urged the US to reconsider its One China policy the other day. What do you think about this?

A: The US is concentrating on the Persian Gulf crisis now. It's not the right time to reconsider the One China policy. The "two Chinas" issue is a Chinese problem, and China insists on "one nation, two systems." However, the US emphasizes self-determination by the people. This is a democratic approach. But Taiwan must work on its democratization first.

Q: Cries for Taiwanese independence are getting stronger. What is your view on this?

A: This must be decided by the people themselves.

Q: Will the US support it?

A: The US advocates for democracy and self-determination.

Frank's replies were consistent with established US foreign policy to Taiwan, exactly what you would expect from a seasoned politician. This interview made the front page of the *Liberty Times* the next day with the headline: "The US Supports Democracy and the Right of the Taiwanese People to Self-Determination, Said Frank Murkowski, Member of Subcommittee on East Asian and Pacific Affairs."

The piece also mentioned that Frank was displeased because President Lee had not met with him on this visit. The interview portion was straightforward and truthful, but the journalist used the headline to take Frank's comments out of context. Mr. Kao credited me for being a tactful liaison for the meeting between the DPP and Frank, which "established breakthrough diplomacy for the opposition DPP of Taiwan and the Republican Party of the United States."

Frank's entourage and I returned to the US on November 20, 1990. MOFA translated the newspaper articles into English and sent them to Frank's office in a show of protest. The KMT was clearly annoyed by Frank's visit with the DPP and my relationship with him and expressed their displeasure through MOFA. MOFA highlighted portions of the articles in which they believed Frank showed support for Taiwanese independence. They also highlighted Frank's supposed "unhappiness" that President Lee didn't meet with him, putting Frank in an even more awkward position. Frank forwarded the MOFA letter to me, and I knew it was the work of the KMT. They used this opportunity to twist Frank's statement into support for Taiwanese independence, thereby justifying their protest against him. What's worse, the translated document implied I was the culprit and somehow manipulated Frank into this situation.

On December 10, 1990, Frank sent a letter to Ding Mou-shih, director of the Taiwan Council for US Affairs and top diplomat in the US representing Taiwan. Frank told Ding that his opinions were grossly misrepresented by the Taiwanese press and that he had never hosted a news conference in Taiwan. Most importantly, he stated that he had enjoyed himself and the treatment he received was very welcoming, contrary to what the article claimed.

"Are you falling into their trap?"

Frank sent me a letter the day after he lodged his complaint with Ding Mou-shih. The fact that he didn't simply pick up the phone to call me was an indication that the KMT's ploy to drive a wedge between us was working. My friend wrote that he was very disturbed by MOFA's missive to him, but I could tell by his tone that he was annoyed with me. He did not know there would be reporters present at the dinner engagement held by the DPP.

It weighed heavily on me that Frank was put in this position and, more importantly, that the situation had caused a strain on our friendship. In my reply to Frank, I told him I would never sabotage the positive relationship he had with the Taiwanese government. He had, however, earned quite a bit of respect from the people of Taiwan for supporting their right to self-determination. I clarified with Frank that I did not know the reporters had been invited, but it was understandable that they would be there because his visit was highly publicized and his meeting with the DPP members was the biggest news event of the year.

The meet-and-greet that I set up for him with prominent Taiwanese business leaders was arranged so that he could be exposed to more diverse perspectives and backstories. As for what happened with President Lee, I told Frank that it was very likely the KMT prevented them from meeting for two reasons: to taint Frank's visit and drive a wedge between us. I asked him, respectfully, not to fall into their trap.

Frank felt he was unjustly cast in a poor light. He wrote a letter to the *Liberty Times* and demanded clarifications for the distortion of facts. The *Liberty Times* published Frank's letter verbatim, which satisfied him for the time being. We thought that this tempest in a teacup was behind us, but we were wrong.

More Chicanery

Back in Taiwan, a journalist named Hsu Po-hsiung wrote a special feature, "Truth Unveiled on the Report of the US Senator Murkowski's Visit to Taiwan," and published it in *Taiwan Daily*, the overseas edition of the *Central Daily News*, the *Washington China Post*, and the *News Mirror Weekly*. The article was based completely on lies and had the KMT's fingerprints all over it.

Hsu's special feature, written in the style of tabloid journalism, alleged that Senator Murkowski was uncomfortable with the meetings with the DPP and the Taiwanese business people arranged by Li-pei Wu, but he reluctantly agreed because he could not refuse an old friend. Without prior notice from Li-pei Wu, Senator Murkowski was surrounded by press from the *Liberty Times* and *Ming Chung Daily*. He felt deeply betrayed by his friend and was furious over the deliberate misquotation of his opinions by the reporters. The piece also quoted Frank's aides, who accused me of having ulterior motives by bending Frank's ear with incendiary talk about the KMT and the ROC government, thus putting the senator in a difficult position. The article painted Frank as somebody who was willing to be manipulated by an old friend and me as somebody willing to use a friendship to get what he wanted.

On February 7, 1991, Frank wrote an official letter to the aforementioned papers and Ding Mou-shih demanding a clarification. In his letter, Frank pointed out they had quoted words he never said, which misled the readers. He stressed again that neither he nor anybody from his staff were interviewed by Hsu Po-hsiung, nor had Frank provided any information to him. Frank included this statement in his letter:

> Your article repeatedly indicated that my good friend Li-pei Wu had on several occasions influenced me to make certain political decisions. I consider the implications false and misleading. I, being a United States Senator, have always made independent decisions in the best interest of the United States. I solicit advice from many people, including Li-pei Wu, whose opinions I respect.

> I resent the statement in your article saying that I "felt betrayed by Wu," that I was enraged with "extreme dissatisfaction in Wu," and all the innuendos that suggest distrust in my friendship with Mr. Wu. He and I have been good friends for a very long time, and I do not like the suggestion that he has tried to use this friendship for personal gain.

Frank asked that his official letter be published in the papers that reprinted the original tabloid piece. Given his position as a prominent American politician, the four papers did as they were told and published it between February and April 1991.

No Pushover

Upon seeing his letter in print, Frank was at last pacified, but I had been injured as well, and my battle was far from over. I asked the reporter, Hsu Po-hsiung, and the newspapers that published his article to issue an apology to me. They refused. But I was not deterred. Instead of wasting time arguing with them, I hired a renowned human rights attorney in

New York, Leonard Weinglass. He was sympathetic to my plight and took my case, charging me a symbolic retainer of $1,000, and filed a libel suit on my behalf.

To clear my name, Weinglass reached out to the newspapers and Hsu Po-hsiung, who was living in the US. He also contacted the Taiwan Council for US Affairs and went as far as writing to James Soong, who was serving as the KMT secretary-general, asking them to correct the erroneous reporting, but we were ignored. I even reached out to Mr. Cheng Chung-mo, President Lee's trusted aide. I told Cheng that if no apology from those responsible was forthcoming, I would hold them legally accountable. Frank suggested to me that diplomatic leverage would be more effective than filing a suit. He contacted the Taiwan Council for US Affairs, asking the KMT officials there to intervene. Mr. Weinglass continued to exert pressure where he could. My strategy was to be as loud and annoying as possible, because otherwise I would be ignored.

Victory Earned

As I had hoped, the pressure from me, my attorney, and Frank was effective. The first paper to cave was *Taiwan Daily*. The editor-in-chief, Chao Li-nian, agreed to issue an apology on behalf of the paper and the author. There was no way I would trust a KMT-controlled newspaper that easily, so I insisted on seeing the draft before the apology was published. As expected, I was extremely dissatisfied with the mock-up Chao sent. Hsu Po-hsiung's tabloid piece and Frank's official rebuttal letter had been given front-page prominence, but the draft apology for me was the size of a postage stamp.

Chao finally capitulated after I protested. I wrote a letter to *Taiwan Daily* and insisted the letter be published in its entirety. It was published on September 28, 1991, with the appropriately prominent headline, "An Official Apology to Mr. Li-pei Wu." Other papers quickly followed suit. Even though this struggle felt at times like that of David versus Goliath, it was a fight worth fighting. For my victory to come at the expense of the KMT was extraordinarily sweet!

My Chosen Family

In May 1995, Frank and Hank Brown, a Republican senator from Colorado, introduced House Concurrent Resolution 53, which would allow the president of Taiwan at the time, Lee Teng-hui, to visit the United States. Five months later, H. Con. Res. 53 was passed in the House and the Senate. This resolution demonstrated that congressional and public support for visits by Taiwan's most senior officials was continuing to build. That was just one example of how my friend has championed Taiwan. His advocacy for my beloved country is well known in both American and Taiwanese politics and media. His loyalty has always been with the people of Taiwan, regardless of the political environment. What astounds me is that even though Frank has been retired since 2006, he is still ready and willing to go to bat for Taiwan.

Prior to Taiwan's 2012 presidential election, he came to its aid once again. At my request, he canceled his annual vacation to Mexico and traveled to Taiwan with his wife, Nancy, to join the International Committee for Fair Elections in Taiwan, where he was made the honorary chairman. The purpose of the committee, which consisted of twenty-one observers from eight countries, was to objectively monitor the election process in Taiwan's developing democracy. The committee needed somebody with a strong political background to ensure the elections went smoothly and fairly.

My friend's presence on the committee proved necessary. On January 12, 2012, two days before the election, Douglas Paal, former director of the American Institute in Taiwan—the de facto US embassy in Taiwan— told CTiTV Cable News, a Taiwanese network, that Washington, D.C. would be uncomfortable with an election victory by DPP candidate Tsai Ing-wen. The comments appeared in print the following day and put a dent in Tsai Ing-wen's campaign. Frank was on his way to Taichung to monitor campaign activities when I called him to explain what had happened. When he arrived in Taichung, he immediately took the next northbound train back to Taipei, where he called a press conference.

Frank criticized Paal for trying to swing the campaign favorably toward Ma Ying-jeou, the incumbent KMT candidate. At the time of Paal's comments, Ma and Tsai were polling neck and neck. Frank was forceful in his criticism. "I challenge the credibility of Mr. Paal to speak for me or my government, or for the vast majority of Americans, who have great admiration for the advancement of democracy in Taiwan." Citing his twenty-six years in public service, he further drove home the point that Paal no longer had any official position with the US government. He also assured the reporters that what the US wished to see was an election that fairly represented the voice of the people. Frank's comments made the papers the next day. Although Tsai wound up losing this election to Ma, I was extremely grateful to my friend for setting the record straight.

Chapter Thirty-Five

PRESIDENT LEE TENG-HUI

I first met Lee Teng-hui one evening in the mid-1960s. I had just won my third hand of mahjong in a row when the doorbell rang. Our host, Chen Chen-ji, answered the door. In walked a tall, lanky young man beaming with pride. He was holding a bamboo birdcage with a live chicken inside. I watched as they spoke in hushed Taiwanese in the doorway. The young man thrust the cage at Chen-ji, but my friend pushed it back to him, only to have the man try to give it back. This dance went on for some time until I ran out of patience. I was on a hot winning streak, and I shouted, "Chen-ji! Quit messing around. Let's get the game going again!"

The stranger finally bowed politely to Chen-ji and left with the chicken. My friend came back to the table and explained that the man had wanted him to recommend a friend for a government job at the Joint Commission on Rural Reconstruction, where Chen-ji worked. The stranger assured him that the candidate was highly qualified and, more importantly, Taiwan-born. The chicken was his way of showing appreciation for the favor. While it may be an odd choice for a gift today, in the midsixties in Taiwan, a gift like that was extravagant. Chen-ji wouldn't accept it, though. He, like the rest of our circle of friends, was more than happy to help a fellow Taiwanese.

I look back on that night and can't help but shake my head in amusement. Here I was, worried about nothing more than my hand of mahjong. I had no idea this tall, lanky Taiwanese was none other than Lee Teng-hui, who in a little over twenty years would become Taiwan's first Taiwanese president, successor to the Chiang regime, and known to the rest of the world as Taiwan's "Father of Democracy."

Rising Star

When Lee Teng-Hui was appointed president in 1988, I met with Dr. Peng to discuss where President Lee's loyalties lay, with the KMT or the people of Taiwan. We weighed the pros and cons and ultimately felt it made sense to support him. He had an obvious pro-Taiwan policy agenda, despite his career affiliation with the KMT. I believed President Lee would remain faithful to Taiwan, but providing any kind of support for a KMT official was going to be a delicate balancing act. The last thing we could afford was to create dissent among our own people, but we felt the potential gain was worth the risk. After my meeting with Dr. Peng, we phoned President Lee to let him know he would have the support of the Taiwanese American community.

President Lee's star was rising within the KMT party in the late seventies when he was appointed mayor of Taipei and, later on, governor of Taiwan province. I knew of him mainly because it was so rare to see a Taiwanese rise so quickly in the KMT ranks, which was predominantly waishengren, Chinese immigrants who came to Taiwan in 1949.

We weren't formally introduced until 1984, not long after he was appointed vice president of Taiwan by President Chiang Ching-kuo. He was planning a stopover in Los Angeles during a diplomatic trip, and the director of the Taipei Economic and Cultural Office in Los Angeles, Ouyang Rui-hsiung, called and invited me to a reception for the vice president. I had no interest in meeting a KMT official and politely declined. To my great surprise, I received another phone call the very next day from Mr. Ouyang telling me that Vice President Lee was hoping to have a one-on-one private meeting with me during his visit. I was intrigued, so I accepted, but I was on guard.

Our meeting was nothing like what I expected. I assumed he wanted to use my relationships within the Taiwanese community to further the KMT's agenda and was prepared to dismiss the overture. But he surprised me. The vice president spoke of democratic reform and how he and President Chiang wanted to insert more Taiwanese into the higher levels of government. President Chiang's appointment of him as vice president was an example of his sincerity, and Lee wanted to build upon that foundation. They realized the KMT's old way of governing was not sustainable or good for Taiwan. I could barely believe my ears! I never would have imagined these words coming out of the mouth of a KMT official who was next in line to be president. Lee emphasized that he and I wanted the same things for Taiwan; only our approach and timelines were different.

Initially, I was reticent to share my thoughts with Lee because I wasn't sure if I could trust him. But the passion and sincerity in his voice won me over. He asked if there was anything that he could do to help in my work with Taiwan. I seized the opportunity and told him about the numerous political prisoners suffering behind bars for doing nothing more than opposing the KMT. Not long after our meeting, Lin Yi-hsiung was released from prison, after having spent the prior years incarcerated for the Formosa Incident. I believe Vice President Lee was instrumental in Lin Yi-hsiung's release. From that point forward, despite our political differences, I knew Lee Teng-hui was a man of great integrity who cared deeply for Taiwan and its people.

Taiwan's Father of Democracy

Early in his presidency, President Lee pledged his commitment to full democracy in Taiwan. He supported direct elections of the president and vice president, which became a reality in 1996. These changes were exciting and something I had envisioned only in my dreams. Taiwanese

Americans like myself used our relationships with US policymakers to influence change and assist Taiwan's burgeoning democracy.

Taiwan experienced impressive economic growth under Lee Teng-hui's leadership. True to his word, Lee oversaw liberalization of the electoral process, granted pardons to political criminals, and lifted the blacklist on Taiwanese activists. This progress was significant, and even though he failed to carry out full institutional reforms within the KMT, I applaud his efforts.

President Lee often said one of his great honors was giving the commencement address in 1995 at Cornell, his alma mater. During the speech, he spoke to an enthralled audience of a few thousand about his ascension to the presidency of Taiwan. He spoke of his duty where he "sought to ascertain what the people of Taiwan wanted and to always be guided by their wishes."

Because of pressure from China, President Lee didn't make many trips to the US during his presidency, but I was honored to help him plan a two-week visit after he left office. He was finally able to see the one place he had always wanted to visit—Washington, D.C. The trip was a resounding success, during which President Lee received the recognition from the international community that he so richly deserved. What I remember most from that trip were the times when the two of us found time to simply sit and talk. We spent hours conversing on politics, family, and business. I will always cherish those times I had with him.

With the success of his visit to the US, President Lee asked me to lead a delegation for the 2006 Japan–Taiwan All-Party Parliamentary Group (*Nikka giin kondankai*) meeting in Japan. The purpose of the event was to strengthen the unofficial ties between Taiwan and Japan, and I was honored by this request. My Japanese counterpart was Motoo Shiina, a famous conservative politician. His fellow members of the delegation had equally impressive backgrounds, coming from both the House of Representatives and the House of Councillors. The meeting was extremely productive, but it would be the last time I would see President Lee in person.

Lee Teng-hui passed away on July 30, 2020. When I think of him, I'm filled with many emotions. I naturally grieve for a man who I considered a friend, but I'm also heartened that I was fortunate enough to spend time with such a remarkable person. Given our political differences, I could easily have dismissed him when we first met. If I had done that, I would never have had the privilege of knowing a man who was so instrumental in furthering Taiwan's democracy. He was profoundly dedicated to the Taiwanese people and for that, he will always be a true inspiration to us all.

Chapter Thirty-Six

DR. PENG MING-MIN'S HOMECOMING

In 1970, Dr. Peng escaped confinement in Taiwan and was granted asylum in Sweden. The ROC considered him a fugitive and exiled him indefinitely. Various governments throughout the world sympathized with his plight and gave him traveling visas. Dr. Peng spent his first year in exile traveling and attending conferences. After the US granted him a traveling visa, he visited me in Alaska. Although my banking career was going well, I told him I would drop everything to support his efforts without hesitation. He turned down my offer, telling me the time was not right and I should focus on my work.

Dr. Peng was so well respected within the Taiwanese expat community that he was constantly recruited for different causes. His former student Chai Trong-rong persuaded Dr. Peng to become the chairman of WUFI in 1972. He was the chairman for only one year because, while he excelled as a scholar, he didn't as the head of a political activism organization. He was able to articulate his bold and inspirational vision for Taiwan, but he wasn't good at the administrative side of operating an organization. He did impart, however, a leadership style characterized by integrity and virtue.

He served as the president of the Formosan Association for Public Affairs between 1986 and 1988 and was crucial in strengthening the organization's presence. Membership more than doubled, and the number of chapters swelled twofold under his leadership. FAPA's growth unexpectedly and unfortunately created friction with WUFI, which viewed FAPA as a rival organization. Instead of tainting himself with petty infighting, Dr. Peng decided to move on and launched the Asia–Pacific Democracy Association in 1989 with Hsu Hsin-liang.

Revolution Redux

Dr. Peng's personal experience with various Taiwanese associations left him wanting more direct action against the oppressive government of Taiwan. He visited me in Alaska along with another friend, John Cheng, not long after stepping down from his post as chairman of WUFI. None of us were happy with WUFI's change to a less aggressive approach. We wanted something more radical—we believed a revolution was needed.

The three of us huddled in my living room throwing out any and all suggestions. John said he knew of a Mr. Liu who actually had his own guerrilla force in a mountainous region near Seattle. Dr. Peng said he had some connection with a Palestinian militant group who could train our own revolutionary force. Then came the question—who would fund our project?

We thought maybe Mr. Liu could help. After all, how many people have their own guerrilla force? John returned to Seattle to ask him, and he seemed interested in helping us. But one day when I tried calling Dr. Peng, all I got was a recording that his number had been disconnected. This made no sense. My mind raced with questions. Could the KMT have found out about our mission? Were we being monitored by other intelligence agencies, like the CIA? I considered contacting Dr. Peng through other means, but I didn't want to potentially involve other people. Time slipped by, and without Dr. Peng's involvement, our momentum effectively ended. To this day, Dr. Peng has not spoken about what happened during that time. I respect his reticence, but those questions still linger.

When I think back, I can't help but chuckle at our naïveté and half-baked plans. Although we had no clue how to execute a revolution, I can say with pride that we were earnest in our convictions and ready to lay down our lives for Taiwan.

Taking on Dr. Peng's Commission

When Lee Teng-hui took over Taiwan's presidency, he convened the Conference of National Affairs in 1990, a groundbreaking event to discuss further steps for Taiwan to make democratic reforms. Invitations were sent to many political and business leaders, including myself and Dr. Peng. Dr. Peng had publicly voiced his support for President Lee, which was widely criticized by WUFI. But Dr. Peng believed President Lee would be able to further freedom for the Taiwanese.

Dr. Peng did not feel comfortable attending the conference because he was technically still wanted by the KMT, but the invitation was a sign that he would hopefully see his home country again soon. In July 1991, he hosted a conference on Taiwan's political future with the Asia–Pacific Democracy Association at the University of Hawaii's East–West Center. It was a gathering of more than one hundred, a who's who of politics from Taiwan and the US. He asked me to attend because he had an important matter to discuss.

We met over coffee with the beautiful Hawaiian coastline in the background. As he looked upon the gentle waves crashing on the beach, he said, "I'm ready to go back to Taiwan." I was elated. To have one of the great pioneers of democracy for Taiwan finally returning to the homeland he'd been banned from for more than twenty years would be a monumental event. Dr. Peng continued, "I'd like you to organize this for me."

I was honored to be asked, but the enormity of this task was difficult to grasp, and I was hesitant. Failure was not an option—it simply had to go well. I wasn't sure if I had the wherewithal to pull this off, so I was noncommittal. But when Dr. Peng asked again later, how could I turn down my old mentor and friend? I said I would take on the project.

A Mentor and a Friend

I accepted the job on one condition: everything had to be done my way. Dr. Peng agreed. Years later, in 2013, at a dinner we had with Reverend Milo Thornberry and his wife, Judith Thomas—the American missionary couple who played a key role in his escape from Taiwan to Sweden in 1970—Dr. Peng told me I'd been extremely bossy during that time. He said I had made him sign over power of attorney on the project. I do remember making the professor promise not to intervene, but I have no recollection of asking him to sign such a thing.

Peng Ming-min was in his thirties when he became the youngest tenured professor and chairman of the Department of Political Science at National Taiwan University. He had been appointed by Chiang Kai-shek as the advisor to the ROC's delegation to the United Nations. In 1963 he was one of the recipients of the Ten Outstanding Young Persons award in Taiwan. Before his arrest in 1964, he was on top of the world. Yet he gave all that up to pursue his dream of a democratic and independent Taiwan. He has dedicated his life to seeing those dreams come to fruition.

Rolling with the Punches

Once I committed to spearheading the project, I was determined to make it a success. Our target return date was late 1992, so we only had about a year to make all the arrangements. It became clear in the early stages of planning that we would need the support of Taiwanese people both overseas and in Taiwan to make this a success. It was also complicated because of the fraught relationship between Dr. Peng and key Taiwanese organizations.

My work at General Bank kept me busy, but I managed to find time to take leave and fly back to Taiwan to make preparations. I visited WUFI's leadership—Chang Tsan-hung, Kuo Pei-hung, and Lee Ying-yuan—at a detention center in Tucheng. At that time, WUFI had recently moved its headquarters back to Taiwan, and the KMT promptly incarcerated these key members for sedition and other trumped-up charges.

My goal was to convince them that Dr. Peng and WUFI were on the same page in terms of seeing the downfall of the KMT and that it was in their best interest to support him. His homecoming would inspire and energize the people of Taiwan to rise up against the Chinese Nationalist Party in ways that had never been achieved before. I hoped WUFI would rally its membership and release a welcome announcement for Dr. Peng.

I also wanted Chairman Chang Tsan-hung to greet Dr. Peng at the airport when he arrived, should Chairman Chang be released by then. If he was still incarcerated, I would arrange for Dr. Peng to visit him at the detention center upon arriving in Taiwan. As convincing as I thought I was, Chairman Chang never confirmed his commitment, but I refused to give up. I was able to get Roger Hsieh to convince Lee Ying-yuan, who was serving as acting chairman of WUFI, to release a welcome announcement. This was a critical step in building a coalition among all the people and organizations we would need for this endeavor. There was still a long way to go, but the progress was exhilarating.

The other issue was acquiring travel documents for Dr. Peng, since his Taiwanese passport was no longer valid. The symbolism of Dr. Peng returning to Taiwan as a recognized Taiwanese citizen was critical. The only person who could make this happen was none other than President Lee. This required me to meet with him in Taiwan.

I hadn't realized how challenging President Lee's first years in office were until I met with him to discuss Dr. Peng's return to Taiwan. Because of the controversial nature of Dr. Peng's return, we met in secret. George Huang, secretary-general of the General Association of Chinese Culture (GACC) and sympathizer to the cause, suggested we meet at the GACC office. The president routinely made spontaneous stops there, so Mr. Huang could arrange a meeting for us in private.

I arrived at the GACC office at seven in the morning to avoid undue attention and settled in for the long wait. President Lee finally entered the office that afternoon. After our greetings, I handed him a letter written by Dr. Peng. I told him that it was Dr. Peng's dream to live his remaining years in Taiwan and give what he had left to his beloved home. President Lee immediately picked up the phone and called Ding Mou-shih, head of the Taiwan Council for US. Affairs. He ordered him to fast-track a Taiwanese passport for Dr. Peng. President Lee then suggested that upon Dr. Peng's return, he would be appointed president of the prestigious Academia Sinica. I told President Lee that I would relay his suggestion to Dr. Peng.

The whole matter took only five minutes, and I assumed that was the end of our meeting, but I was wrong. For the next three hours, President Lee confided in me on myriad topics, mostly about the pressure he was under from members of his own administration and other high-ranking party members. Once he began talking, it was as if the floodgates had opened. I recall the one phrase he repeated over and over again, "I need to persevere just a little longer." There was a look in his eyes when he spoke, the same look he'd had when we met eight years earlier, that spoke of his vision for Taiwan. His great love for Taiwan was clear, and he was doing his best to lead the country into a brighter, more democratic future. I boarded my flight back to the US relieved that we were one step closer to our goal of a successful homecoming for Dr. Peng.

Numerous Loose Ends

Another key component to Dr. Peng's return was drumming up excitement among the Taiwanese people. I reunited with my old friend Roger Hsieh on this endeavor, along with John Cheng and my musician friend, Leonard Hsu, to reach out to various organizations. Roger coordinated from Taiwan, and we worked enthusiastically and tirelessly toward the common goal of creating an event worthy of Dr. Peng. Mobile phones were not common at that time, so my niece, Sharon Huang, flew back to Taiwan from San Francisco to manage the phones.

As the momentum began to build, more and more people wanted to be part of the entourage accompanying Dr. Peng. All the details needed to coordinate such a large group had to be done behind the scenes so that Dr. Peng could focus on rallying and inspiring the Taiwanese people. Fortunately, my executive assistant at General Bank, Ms. Lin, was able to take care of many of the details for me. The travel arrangements alone were fraught with challenges, especially when our original carrier, Singapore Airlines, canceled our booking without providing a reason. I suspect the political nature of the trip scared them. We did find an alternative in Cathay Pacific, but with a layover in Hong Kong.

The number of people escorting Dr. Peng to Taiwan reached one hundred. These Taiwanese Americans not only contributed time and resources to the overall project but also paid for their own airfare and lodging just so they could be there when Dr. Peng set foot on Taiwanese soil. In spite of the risks, they were willing to stand by him as witnesses to a glorious homecoming that was twenty-two years overdue.

The Incident with Li Ao

Given that Dr. Peng had been gone for so many years, we were concerned the young people in Taiwan might not know of his sacrifice and contribution to their country. We wanted to reprint *A Taste of Freedom*, a memoir authored by Dr. Peng, and distribute one hundred thousand copies for free. But *A Taste of Freedom* was originally written in English during Dr. Peng's exile in the US, and there was no official Chinese translation.

However, many publishers had translated the English version into Chinese without authorization by Dr. Peng. We were in a position to choose a version that would suit us best. We narrowed our choices to two: one by Li Ao, a controversial Chinese Taiwanese writer, social commentator, historian, and independent politician; and one by Vanguard Publishing, whose version was considered one of the better translations.

Li Ao and Dr. Peng had been friends for decades. He was part of the group that helped Dr. Peng escape from Taiwan in 1970. His version was the logical option because of his familiarity with the work and personal relationship with Dr. Peng. With Dr. Peng's blessing, we approached Li first through Roger Hsieh, who was an old classmate of his. But to our disappointment, Mr. Li's quote was exorbitant. He wanted $400,000 for one hundred thousand copies. I felt we needed a second opinion and approached Vanguard Publishing, which gave a quote that was approximately $133,000 less. We had no choice but to go with Vanguard.

Li Ao was offended and angry when he learned of our decision. Roger in turn was upset—at Li for the unreasonable pricing and me for choosing Vanguard over his old friend. From my perspective, it was a simple matter of budget, yet somehow, this incident widened a chasm that was starting to grow between my old friend Roger and me.

I gave Li the opportunity to lower his quote, but he refused, and things got ugly. He sent Dr. Peng a message, "If you decide to go along with that Wu character, so be it. This shall be the end of our friendship." In the end, we tabled the reprint of the memoir. The Manifesto of Formosan Self-Salvation was reprinted instead.

Dr. Peng did not want this to ruin a friendship that had spanned so many years. In spite of Li's spiteful message, Dr. Peng tried to visit him during the homecoming, only to be turned down. But Dr. Peng's kind heart would not be deterred. He extended an olive branch and commissioned Li to reprint a limited edition of *A Taste of Freedom*. Unfortunately, things did not end well. In 1996, when Dr. Peng represented the DPP to be its presidential candidate in Taiwan's first direct presidential election, Li Ao stabbed Dr. Peng in the back by publishing *An Exposé on Peng Ming-min*. The book was full of malevolence and slander, intended only to malign Dr. Peng's reputation for monetary gain. Dr. Peng was furious, and the friendship he had tried so hard to preserve was over.

Home at Last!

The day of Dr. Peng's homecoming to Taiwan finally arrived. It was October 30, 1992. After more than a year of planning, our efforts were about to become reality. Our entourage arrived first in Hong Kong, as planned, to rendezvous with friends and supporters from all over the world. Our arrival time was late in the day, and we considered spending the night, since by the time we made it to Taiwan, Dr. Peng wouldn't get a proper reception. The other issue was if we continued immediately to Taiwan, we would have arrived on October 31, the birthday of Chiang Kai-shek. Dr. Peng was adamant that he not set foot on his homeland on the birthday of his persecutor.

We stayed the extra night in Hong Kong despite the risk to Dr. Peng's safety. We took extra precautions and asked my good friend Liao Wu-sing to switch rooms with Dr. Peng in the middle of the night. Fortunately, the night was uneventful.

I had done my best to plan for all contingencies, but my biggest worry was that with all the excitement and passion the event would stir up, there was a chance of violence. Six members of the DPP met us in Hong Kong dressed in army fatigues and offering to protect Dr. Peng. Our worry was not unfounded. In August 1983, Benigno Aquino Jr., a former Philippine senator, returned to the Philippines after three years in exile and was assassinated on the tarmac of Manila International Airport. We pleaded with Dr. Peng to wear a bulletproof vest on arrival, but he refused, saying he wanted to step back into Taiwan unencumbered.

Despite our worries, we were met at Taoyuan International Airport on November 1, 1992, by a roaring crowd of supporters numbering in the tens of thousands. Banners and streamers waved. Taiwanese people chanted Dr. Peng's name. I tried to stay close to him but was soon elbowed away by the crowd. In a news conference hosted a couple of hours later, Dr. Peng announced publicly that I would be his only spokesperson in Taiwan.

On November 6, 1992, a handful of us accompanied Dr. Peng to pay respects at the burial site of Lin Yi-hsiung's mother and two daughters. The cemetery where the three were laid to rest was littered with rocks and pebbles. Dr. Peng and Yi-hsiung walked at a steady pace, while I lagged behind, laboring to catch my breath. Lin said to me, "Taiwan's journey to democracy is treacherous and bumpy." His statement resonated with me in that moment as I struggled to keep pace and has stayed with me throughout the years.

Dr. Peng's return coincided with Taiwan's legislative election, and many candidates representing the DPP wanted to take advantage of his celebrity status. We traveled throughout Taiwan to visit supporters and give speeches and were met with the warmest reception at every location. In Kaohsiung, countless supporters cheered for Dr. Peng as his caravan wove through the city streets. In Taipei he gave a speech at Chungshan Stadium to a standing-room-only audience. It seemed the entire country came out to welcome Dr. Peng home. My heart swelled with pride and joy as I witnessed these indelible moments. It was a homecoming long overdue and everything Dr. Peng had hoped for.

Running for President

The first direct presidential election was to be held in Taiwan in 1996, and the DPP was looking forward to putting forth a candidate who had the first legitimate opportunity to unseat the KMT. There were many who believed the only person who could fill that role was Dr. Peng Ming-min. He had never aspired to be in politics, but the pressure on him to run was intense, and he finally agreed to put his name in for consideration as the DPP's presidential candidate in 1996. I believe he understood the historical significance of having his name on the ballot and what it would mean for Taiwan. Not long after, he called and urged me to head back to Taiwan and join him and his campaign team when he officially announced his candidacy. As usual, I found it very difficult to say no to my old mentor and did as he asked.

Because Dr. Peng was so new to Taiwanese politics, he had yet to build his coalitions and relationships within the DPP. Although he had name recognition and a strong following among the populace, there was no guarantee the DPP membership would elect Dr. Peng as their nominee, despite the countless members who had persuaded him to run.

Hsu Hsin-liang, Lin Yi-hsiung, and You Ching, all stalwarts within the DPP, were also interested in running for president, so a primary was held. Hsu Hsin-liang emerged as the top candidate, with Dr. Peng coming in second. A political platform presentation by Hsu and Dr.

Peng was conducted to determine a final candidate, and another round of voting was held. This time, Dr. Peng won by a large margin.

Dr. Peng was the consensus candidate for the DPP, but Hsu did not concede right away. I wrote an op-ed titled "Hsin-liang, It's Time to Let Go" and submitted it to a Taiwanese paper for publication. I urged Hsu and the DPP to throw their full weight behind Dr. Peng for the uphill battle against the KMT. In the US, after a primary contest, the party unifies in order to gain momentum for the general election. I expected the DPP to do the same for Dr. Peng, but Hsu never responded to my urging. Instead, his friend—a Mr. Hung—published an article to rebuke me, claiming that I had no right to meddle in DPP's affairs since I was not a member. Hsu eventually conceded, but I felt he should have lent his support to Dr. Peng once the primary was over. Regardless of my party affiliations, I had every right to publish my opinion piece.

A Glorious Defeat

Upon officially accepting the DPP nomination, Dr. Peng received a hero's welcome throughout Taiwan. Polling showed him trailing President Lee, but as the campaign gained momentum, there was hope he might actually pull off the upset. He called me from Taiwan two weeks before the election. "Get ready, we're taking over the government. I'm going to win this!"

It was rare to hear Dr. Peng so excited. Conviction was strong, and the positivity was overwhelming. He wanted me to return to Taiwan to help him with the transition after his win. I had my reservations but kept my feelings closely guarded because it was so wonderful to see my old friend in such an upbeat mood. Instead, I provided realistic encouragement. "That's great, but let's not get ahead of ourselves. Just focus on shoring up support."

I'd set up an organization in the US called the Overseas Committee for Dr. Peng's Campaign to fundraise and mobilize our friends in Taiwan to get out the vote. As the election drew near, I led an envoy back to Taiwan to give the campaign a final push. When I ran into President

Lee from time to time on the campaign trail, he was always courteous to me, despite our being on opposing sides. He treated me as an old friend rather than a political rival. Frank Murkowski acknowledged often that President Lee always spoke affectionately of me.

Those were memorable days. We launched guerrilla campaigns to reach out to voters. Each day, our legion of volunteers would melt into the populace to ask for support. On one particular evening, as we wrapped up a visit in Chiayi and got ready to head out for our dinner break, I ran into an old friend—Li Hong-hi, the revered constitutional theorist. Wanting his opinion on Dr. Peng's prospects, I took Professor Li aside and asked, "Is all this optimism for real?"

Li affirmed, "I think it is. You would not believe the turnout."

"But have you seen the latest polling on Dr. Peng?" I countered.

"No need." He fluttered his hand dismissively. As much as I wanted to believe Professor Li and the rest of Dr. Peng's supporters, were things too good to be true?

It soon became apparent why Professor Li and others felt so confident. A persistent group of supporters had doggedly followed Dr. Peng wherever his campaign trail took him. They cheered and whooped their encouragement, fortifying Dr. Peng's faith that an upset was in the making. The feeling of enthusiasm was real, but it could not overshadow the challenge of the polling data facing Dr. Peng. For the fledgling DPP to defeat a KMT incumbent president in Taiwan's first multiparty presidential election would take a miracle. The resources President Lee had at his disposal were virtually limitless. The practical side of me couldn't help being skeptical, but I realized that while the election results were important, having someone of Dr. Peng's clout and stature on the ballot representing Taiwan's democratic movement was even more so. This race, regardless of outcome, would give Taiwan's democracy a boost.

Ultimately, Dr. Peng came in second to President Lee, but what a great election it was! With all the odds stacked against us, those millions of votes for Dr. Peng reminded us of what was possible for Taiwan.

Lifelong Sidekick

Since then, Dr. Peng and I have remained the closest of friends. We worked together as national policy advisors under President Chen Shui-bian's administration. Dr. Peng is now well into his nineties, and we speak often. Over the years I've heard many people call me the best sidekick Dr. Peng has ever had. I'm honored to have that moniker.

These days, instead of going out, I prefer to watch TV or read the newspaper at home. But when Dr. Peng calls to get together, I feel a renewed sense of energy, and I can't help but heed his call. If Jenny answers the phone when he calls, she will say to me, "Your big brother wants to pick your brain again!" She'll then hand me the phone knowing I'm not to be disturbed for the foreseeable future. I always flash her a smile and pick up the phone to talk to my friend.

Chapter Thirty-Seven

THE TAIWANESE AMERICAN STORY

Among Taiwanese Americans, the two favorite topics of discussion are democratic progress in Taiwan and the social and economic standing of Taiwanese Americans in the United States. Many of my friends have children or grandchildren who were raised and educated in the US. They are Americans in every sense of the word, more focused on their future in the States and less on the current events of Taiwan. As the older generation, we have asked ourselves how we can help these young Taiwanese Americans be the best they can be as citizens of the US. How will they fight for their rights and equality? What can we do for them as their parents?

Over time, we began to pool our ideas and resources and agreed that we needed to create organizations to make our voices heard and our impact felt in the US. Not only did we want our progeny to stand on their own, we also wanted them to remember where they came from.

Inaugurating the Taiwanese American Citizens League

With that in mind, I partnered with a few like-minded Taiwanese Americans and created the Taiwanese American Citizens League (TACL) in Los Angeles on January 14, 1985. By focusing on American political and societal discourse, TACL set itself apart from WUFI, FAPA, and other Taiwanese associations that focused primarily on Taiwan-centric issues.

Self-identity is one of the biggest challenges for the next generation of Taiwanese Americans. My own children are an illustrative example. My eldest son, George, was always outgoing and made friends easily. But when he attended UCLA for college, I was surprised to learn that he had trouble connecting with his peers. The international students from Taiwan didn't think he was truly Taiwanese, and the American students thought of him as a foreigner. This made George reflect on his own identity. He published an essay in the *Daily Bruin*, the student newspaper at UCLA, titled "I Am a Banana," describing himself as having the skin color of a Taiwanese but the cultural upbringing of a Caucasian. I imagined George's experience was not uncommon among young people with parents from Taiwan. This need for a deep sense of self-identity was what inspired us to set up TACL. Our hope as parents was that our children would have the strength of character to earn and demand respect for themselves.

Following the establishment of TACL in Los Angeles, I reached out to Taiwanese Americans with the same vision to expand the organization's presence to other parts of the US. In 1989 we consolidated different community groups and established a national TACL, and I served as its first chairman. Local chapters were born successively in Atlanta, San Diego, San Francisco, Seattle, Houston, Kansas, and St. Louis. TACL had thirteen chapters across ten states by the time it celebrated its twentieth anniversary in 2005. Its mushrooming presence in the US helped our collective voices be heard. Through TACL we were able to mobilize at a moment's notice and engage with politicians and other community organizations to make sure they knew of our presence.

Fighting Racial Injustice

Shortly after TACL was established, our mettle was tested in an incident in Monterey Park, California. In 1996, the Monterey Park City Council vetoed a proposal to erect a housing complex for senior citizens. Monterey Park, nicknamed Little Taipei, had one of the largest Taiwanese communities in California at that time. In addition to rejecting the senior center, the city council also approved a new statute that permitted city police to intercept people they suspected to be illegals. This obviously targeted all minorities, violating the rights of anybody that didn't look "mainstream."

TACL took action immediately. The Monterey Park City Council did not anticipate how effectively and aggressively we'd fight for our rights. TACL mobilized a coalition called the Committee against Age and Racial Discrimination made up of other ethnic Asians, Latinos, and African Americans, numbering approximately a thousand, to rally against the Monterey Park City Council. We demanded the city police honor the rights of minorities and stop racial profiling. TACL also pressured the council to resume construction of a complex for senior citizens and add bilingual capabilities for various government services. Our actions were successful. The impressive turnout forced the city council to review and eventually approve the proposal for the construction of the residential complex. TACL was off to a great start.

Other than fighting racism, TACL also worked to protect Taiwan's business reputation. In 1987, a movie called *Fatal Attraction* was released. It was one of the top-grossing films of the year. In one of the scenes, Michael Douglas's character is trying to open an umbrella that has flipped inside out. Glenn Close's character comments with disdain, "Is it made in Taiwan?" This kind of comment hurts the business reputation of Taiwanese manufacturers and gives consumers the perception that Taiwanese-made products are inferior. TACL wrote a protest letter to Michael Douglas and demanded an apology, and he wrote back with a heartfelt acknowledgment, promising he would rewrite that line if he could.

A similar incident occurred in 2006. The city of Irvine, California, was scheduled to sign a sister-city agreement with Xuhui District in Shanghai, China. These sister-city agreements were purely cultural, nonpolitical relationships to create goodwill between cities of different countries. However, one of the conditions Xuhui insisted upon was that Irvine uphold the One China policy, thus eradicating the fact that Irvine has been a sister city of Taoyuan, Taiwan, since 1990. Once word got out, numerous Taiwanese American organizations, TACL included, lodged a protest. My son, George, a resident of Irvine, spoke on behalf of ten thousand protesters at a public hearing. Irvine eventually agreed to stick to its original sister-city agreement with Taoyuan.

I'm proud that TACL has safeguarded the rights and interests of Taiwanese Americans on many fronts. We were always there to meet new challenges, but perhaps the greatest test for TACL occurred at the national level in 1990.

Legitimizing Our Identity: The TACL Census Campaign

The US census is administered by the federal government every ten years to collect data on its citizens. The survey asks participants to identify their ethnic origins. The larger the ethnic community, the more government funds and services are apportioned. Also, the president of the United States, in order to promote diversity when staffing the cabinet and other positions in the administration, uses the results as a guideline. That is why being counted in the census is important for America's ethnic minorities. TACL made a commitment for the 1990 census to make sure that every Taiwanese American designated themselves as such.

For decades Taiwanese Americans identified simply as Asian American or even Chinese because there was no option on the census form to specify Taiwanese American. Besides the lack of specificity, another major issue was that many Taiwanese Americans didn't identify themselves as such. The decades-long indoctrination by the KMT to use "ethnic Chinese" in Taiwan's official education curriculum effectively suppressed any sense of Taiwanese identity among the people. Even though there were some Taiwanese Americans who chose the Other Asian option and wrote in "Taiwanese," most did not. As a result, Taiwanese Americans were undercounted in the US census, which translated to reduced federal funding and an overall underrepresentation in politics and American culture.

The Formosan Association for Public Affairs, TACL, and other partner organizations sought out Senator Edward Kennedy and Representative Stephen Solarz to lobby the US Census Bureau to add Taiwanese to the form. Dr. Chai Trong-rong was invited to a hearing at the House Committee on the Census on May 19, 1987, where he listed ethnic and historic distinctions between Taiwanese and Chinese. Our lobbying efforts were successful. We were thrilled to see Taiwanese listed as an option in question 13 of the 1990 US census: "What is this person's ancestry or ethnic origin?"

Once we had successfully added Taiwanese to the form, our next step was to make sure that Taiwanese Americans made the proper selection. TACL launched a campaign to raise awareness on how to identify ourselves and why it mattered. I took a leave from General Bank to spearhead the campaign and hit the road. For more than a month, I traveled all over the United States to coordinate with other Taiwanese American organizations. We produced four versions of campaign announcements, in Taiwanese, Mandarin, Hakka, and English. I even used my own voice in the Taiwanese version. Everyone on the campaign worked tirelessly to have our identity correctly represented.

When the census results were tallied, approximately 211,000 US citizens identified themselves as Taiwanese Americans. Even though I was proud of our campaign and viewed our efforts as a success, I knew that figure was far below the real number. As much as we tried to educate and influence, many immigrants from Taiwan still identified themselves as Chinese.

When the 2000 census was administered, Taiwanese no longer appeared as a choice. Taiwanese Americans had to once again resort to checking the Other Asian box and writing in "Taiwanese." That year's census resulted in a count close to 145,000 Taiwanese Americans.

The same thing happened in 2010. TACL intensified its campaign by setting up booths at Taiwanese American gatherings and producing online public service announcements. That year's result indicated that self-identified Taiwanese numbered 234,000. The population of self-identified Chinese, on the other hand, was approximately 3.8 million.

Although the numbers in the census are still far below our actual population, we have come far. Taiwanese Americans are arguably the best-educated ethnic group in the US. We engage in high-end occupations and do well from a socioeconomic standpoint. According to the US Census Bureau data released in 2010, 73.6 percent of all Taiwanese Americans have attained a bachelor's degree or higher, compared to 51.8 percent for Chinese Americans and 28.2 percent nationally.

Despite this, Taiwanese Americans still face many hurdles. Very few have reached the status of upper management in corporate America. My firsthand experience in a Caucasian-dominated industry taught me that regardless of the challenge, one must stand up and be counted. We have an obligation to ourselves to be proud of our identity and to pass that pride on to the next generation.

Excellence Is a Taiwanese American Tradition

My greatest hope for first-generation Taiwanese Americans is that they support their progeny to be not only culturally, economically, and politically involved in America life but also advocates for all Taiwanese Americans. While at TACL, I established a program where outstanding college students would intern for various organizations, including political offices, media outlets, and film production houses. This program helps young Taiwanese Americans strengthen their sense of identity, impact their communities, and gain leadership and networking experience. What's more, TACL offers scholarships to graduating high school seniors and hosts summer camps for a unique, confidence-boosting experience of identity building.

In 1991 TACL's Los Angeles chapter created a sister organization, the Taiwanese American Professionals (TAP), out of a need for a Taiwanese professional networking organization. TAP has prospered. With chapters across the nation, it is currently the largest network of young Taiwanese

American professionals in the US and has thousands of members. Its online communities, career search, and counseling services are just a few examples of the power of this network.

Taiwanese United Fund

The Taiwanese United Fund (TUF), first established in Chicago, is an arts-and-culture foundation devoted to promoting Taiwan's cultural heritage. Dr. Lin Jer-shung, TUF's president from 1988 to 1990, was a music aficionado and incredibly passionate about promoting arts and culture. In 1986, Dr. Lin partnered with Mr. Symeon Woo to set up a TUF office in Los Angeles.

As a newly founded nonprofit organization, TUF relied exclusively on donations. It hosted an annual cultural night and fundraiser, where famous people would give speeches and well-respected musicians and other artists would perform. Early in TUF's history, Dr. Lin preferred showcasing Western classical music. This approach puzzled me. Why would TUF promote music that had nothing to do with Taiwan? I discussed this with the board and encouraged them to promote Taiwan's arts and cultural heritage instead.

TUF switched gears and began providing scholarships to Taiwanese American students studying music and created programs featuring prominent Taiwanese American musicians like violinists Cho-liang Lin and Nai-yuan Hu and noted pianist Gwhyneth Chen. When a choir from Taiwan performed at one of TUF's concerts, they sang one Taiwanese folk song after another, filling the auditorium with beautiful music that many of us had listened to in our youth. There wasn't a dry eye in the audience when the show ended.

TUF's refocus on Taiwanese culture did wonders to garner support and enthusiasm for the foundation and the film festivals, operas, and countless other Taiwan-related cultural events it held. It was a reminder to me and many other Taiwanese Americans that our struggle to enhance and preserve Taiwanese democracy was not only for political purposes but to also preserve and recognize Taiwan's distinct history and culture.

I served as president of TUF for two years, from 1991 to 1992, and recognized how challenging it was for organizations like this to fund their operations. I decided to help. In October 1997, TUF organized a farewell banquet to honor Dr. Lin Jer-shung, who was moving back to Taiwan. I had earned a substantial year-end bonus from General Bank that year and, after speaking with my family, decided to make a donation on the day of the banquet. Half a million dollars to TUF and half a million to Chilin Foundation, the charity founded by Lin Yi-hsiung that promoted Taiwanese democracy and cultural education. This donation gave the two organizations a financial footing that they'd never had before. My hope is for TUF to continue to play a role as a cultural intermediary and inspire Taiwanese all over the world to preserve and honor our heritage.

Chapter Thirty-Eight

TAIWAN CENTER: OUR HOME AWAY FROM HOME

Although our work on the US census didn't provide an accurate count of Taiwanese Americans, we knew Los Angeles had more Taiwanese Americans than any other city in the US. The Taiwanese government had set up two Culture Centers in Los Angeles, yet those centers, with their strong KMT leanings, held little appeal for expatriates. We wanted to establish a center where a sense of community could be forged by Taiwan-centric programs.

This would require funds and personnel. An opportunity arose when Ken John Wang, who was a board member of General Bank and interested in promoting public affairs for Taiwanese expats, planned to donate one of his buildings in Rosemead for the purpose of a community center. This was exactly the initiative we needed to establish the Taiwan Center of Greater Los Angeles. A preparatory committee was quickly formed to solicit donations.

However, there was a mortgage of $528,000 on the building, which was valued at $1.65 million at the time. Wang would not be able to donate the building unless the committee raised enough money to pay off the mortgage. The goal was to raise $1 million to pay off the mortgage, with the remainder to fund the center's operating costs.

To encourage people to donate, the committee announced that those who personally contributed or were able to raise $20,000 could become founding directors of the board. But the funds raised were nowhere close to the target. Wang suggested to the members of the committee that they approach me to lead the fundraising. On May 6, 1998, they asked for my help, but I was hesitant to shoulder the responsibility at that time.

Sticking My Neck Out

A few days later, one of the committee members and a very good friend of mine, Dr. Simon Lin, tried to convince me that I was the only person who could raise enough money to see this project come to fruition. Against my better judgment, I agreed to lead the fundraising, but I wanted Wang to sign an agreement containing three items.

First, Wang had to pay off the mortgage before the donation was made. Second, as a nonprofit organization, the Taiwan Center's board had to make all decisions on management and operations without any outside intervention. And third, the property would be owned by the Taiwan Center Foundation, and any alteration, renovation, expansion, relocation, or sale of the property would be decided by the board only. I would walk away from the whole project if any of these conditions were violated. I don't think Wang was happy with these conditions, but he agreed that the donation of the building would be unconditional.

On May 11, 1998, three committee members, including Simon Lin and me, met with Ken John Wang at the Radisson Hotel in downtown Los Angeles. Freeman Huang, a reporter for *Asia News* in Los Angeles, was also present to witness the signing of the agreement. The following day, we hosted a press conference to announce my role in the project. Wang made a statement saying, "United we will win," and invited me to be the chairman of the Taiwan Center's preparatory committee.

In response to Wang's generosity, I accepted the position, knowing I would be shouldering a great responsibility. In order to kick off the fundraising, I announced in a press conference that General Bank would be donating $100,000 to the project and made the statement that we were all making "selfless contributions for the benefit of Taiwanese Americans." The preparatory committee also named Wang as the center's honorary chair. Excitement gathered, and the establishment of the Taiwan Center was well on its way.

To keep the momentum going, the preparatory committee decided to solicit founding members for a fee of only $1,000. Within a very short period of time, we had more than six hundred founding members, the eldest being Madam Lai Gao An-si, at ninety-two years of age. The youngest was Simon Lin's twelve-year-old boy. Everyone was excited to have a true Taiwanese community center to call our own. An inaugural banquet for the Taiwan Center was held on June 12, 1998, with an expected turnout of one thousand. That night, almost two thousand attended the event. It was certainly a night to remember.

Previous Dealings with Ken John Wang

In 1982, when General Bank was raising additional capital, Wang's family invested $1 million and became board members. The position of chairman of the board was not filled after the former president left. Wang told me on numerous occasions that he felt a calling to serve as chairman. I replied that as president, I was handling the chairman's responsibilities. I also pointed out that it wouldn't serve the bank to have a chairman with no experience in banking. Wang was not happy with my response.

He went to the board of directors and lobbied for them to appoint him as the chairman. But the board voted to make me the chairman. Needless to say, this did not please Wang, and our relationship became tense after that.

Ups and Downs

At the Taiwan Center's first board meeting, I was asked to serve as the chairman. I had agreed to chair the preparatory committee, but I felt it was time to hand the reins to somebody else. But the members of the board were concerned that if I left at this early stage, faith in the organization would wane, and it would affect the center's operations. Wang also urged me not to leave. In spite of my hesitation, I agreed to stay.

Wang had promised to transfer the title of the property to the Taiwan Center before the inaugural banquet, but it didn't happen because he had to wait for the nonprofit tax-exempt status to be approved by the IRS. Our accountant, Chen Tian-shou, worked tirelessly, and the 501(c)(3) tax-exempt status was finally approved by the IRS on October 13, 1998. We expected the transfer to take place soon after the approval, but there were more delays, causing discontent within the Taiwanese American community. Accusations and complaints about the delayed transfer appeared in newspapers, and rumors swirled that the board planned to sell the property as soon as it was transferred. Without the transfer of ownership, the relationship between the board and the Wang family grew tense.

Since I was the face of the organization, I felt a duty to rectify this situation. I was the reason so many people had made their donations to this project. I reminded Wang of the agreement we had signed on May 11. But he insisted he had never seen or signed the agreement. When we produced the statement with his signature, he claimed that he'd signed it before he had a chance to review it. But we had witnesses to the signature. We had a press conference confirming his commitment to the project.

I was frustrated and wanted to resolve this by taking legal action against Wang, but the others didn't want to escalate the situation. The board asked me to meet with Wang to see if we could come up with a solution. I preferred not to, but because of what was at stake, I reluctantly made the visit to Wang's home three days before Christmas.

His son greeted me at the door. He was one of the board of directors of General Bank, and we made small talk until his father appeared. Before I had a chance to say a word, Wang said, "I agreed to make you the chairman of the preparatory committee because the others claimed you'd donate significant dollars to the project. You donated pocket change, but you took all the credit!" With that, he turned and went back upstairs. We hadn't even discussed the transfer of property title, the purpose of my visit. Wang's son went to speak with his father while I stood there waiting. When the son finally returned, he said, "I'm sorry, but my dad won't be coming downstairs." I left, humiliated and sad, exasperated beyond words.

Time to Go

I realized that Wang's true grievance against me was that I got more attention than he did. As the conflict over ownership transfer escalated to an irrational level, Wang's attorney sent a notice to the Taiwan Center proclaiming he would only agree to transfer the property title if the center immediately purchased the property next door for parking, and that the center could not sell or mortgage the property without his permission for ten years. The Wangs also wanted the right to conduct a review of Taiwan Center's operations and reclaim the property for $1 if they didn't find the operations to their satisfaction.

The board agreed to purchase the adjacent property in order to allay Wang's concern that the center would sell the property immediately after the ownership transfer. It wouldn't have been right to use the donations we'd already raised to purchase the property because they were solicited for the center's general operations. This meant we had to raise additional funds. Asking for more money so soon after the first pledge drive would have been challenging, so I contributed $50,000 to set things in motion. Jackson Yang and Keng Lu, both honorary presidents of the Taiwanese American Chamber of Commerce of Greater Los Angeles, managed to raise $220,000 to purchase the adjacent property. The board also passed a resolution not to sell or mortgage the property for at least five years. The property title was finally transferred to the Taiwan Center on March 11, 1999.

Ken John Wang passed away in 2012. Simon Lin suggested that the board name the library in the Taiwan Center the Ken John Wang Memorial Library. If not for his generosity, the Taiwan Center would not have happened. As the founding chairman of the board, I'm proud of what the center was able to accomplish. I resigned from the board a year after my second two-year term in 2001.

United for Taiwan

The Taiwan Center Foundation of Greater Los Angeles has lived up to expectations in many ways and provides a much-needed bridge between our adopted country and Taiwan. Whenever an opportunity arose for Taiwanese expats to show their spirit and generosity toward Taiwan, the community and the center rose to the challenge.

On September 21, 1999, a 7.7 magnitude earthquake occurred in Nantou County in central Taiwan, resulting in a death toll of 2,400. Many organizations, including the Buddhist Compassion Relief Tzu Chi Foundation and the American Red Cross, launched fundraisers for disaster relief in the Los Angeles area. The Taiwan Center raised more than $400,000 within a short time, showing the generous spirit of the Taiwanese American community. But unfortunately, what should have been a time to focus on humanitarian purposes ended up highlighting China's bullying hold over Taiwan.

As rescue groups with supplies from around the world arrived in Taiwan, racing against time to rescue victims buried under the rubble of collapsed buildings, China tried to politicize the tragedy. China's Red Cross chapter asked other international chapters to "consult" with it before providing aid to Taiwan so as to dispel "possible international confusion that there are two Chinas."

Unfortunately, the president of the American Red Cross, Dr. Bernadine Healy, confirmed during an interview on ABC's *Good Morning America* that there would be no aid to Taiwan without approval from China. To hear that level of callousness come from the head of the American Red Cross, on network television no less, was not only cruel but defied a fundamental principle and the mission of the International Red Cross movement: to alleviate human suffering wherever it may be found, without discrimination as to nationality, race, religious beliefs, class, or political opinions.

The Taiwanese American community was outraged. The Taiwan Center, along with other Taiwanese American organizations, released press statements and convened news conferences demanding that Dr. Healy apologize to the people of Taiwan and Taiwanese Americans. We also insisted that she confirm that the Red Cross would provide aid to Taiwan regardless of pressure from China. If she did not comply, we would call for her immediate resignation and boycott the American Red Cross.

I followed with letters on behalf of the Taiwan Center to the International Federation of Red Cross and Red Crescent Societies in Geneva to protest the statements and actions by Dr. Healy. We continued to put pressure on all these organizations, but we were disappointed in how slow they were to respond during this crisis. In the end, $100,000 was donated by the American Red Cross for Taiwanese aid, but those funds were first remitted to Geneva instead of sending the donation directly to Taiwan, apparently for fear of offending China. In spite of all our protests, this so-called humanitarian organization cared more about political sensitivities than expediency and saving lives. As for Dr. Healy, she did eventually reply to us. She listed a summary of relief supplies procured and emphasized that political concerns would not hinder or delay the Red Cross's emergency assistance to Taiwan.

A Taiwanese expat friend of ours in Los Angeles contributed $10,000 when the Taiwan Center first launched its fundraiser for earthquake relief. Incensed by what Dr. Healy did to Taiwan, he donated an additional $100,000, matching the American Red Cross. When he dropped off his check, he said, "Who needs the Red Cross when Taiwan's got us?" The character of the Taiwanese community was tested, and I'm proud to say we stood strong.

The center has also stepped in when other disasters struck Taiwan. It raised funds and provided much-needed face masks and personal protective equipment for Taiwan's first responders when an outbreak of severe acute respiratory syndrome (SARS) was reported in 2003. It also raised relief funds when disasters struck around the world, including the September 11, 2001 attacks on the World Trade Center, Hurricane Katrina in 2005, and the Tōhoku earthquake and tsunami in Japan in 2011.

On the political front, the center has also mobilized people to voice their concern and anger whenever China flexed its muscles against Taiwan. On March 14, 2005, China ratified its Anti-Secession Law, whereby China could legally use force to quash any move toward independence by Taiwan. As expected, the Taiwan Center was at the forefront of this blatant act of intimidation. The center organized a demonstration and mobilized local Taiwanese American associations to demonstrate in downtown Los Angeles around the Chinese consulate office.

I am proud of all that the Taiwan Center has accomplished, and I can say with fondness that it will always hold a special place in my heart. I was happy to return in 2011 as a keynote speaker for its annual fundraising banquet.

Chapter Thirty-Nine

BUILDING NEW ALLIANCES

I had the privilege of networking with many political pundits, opinion leaders, think tanks, and scholars when I was in the United States. After my move back to Taiwan in 2004, I found these connections extraordinarily valuable in my continued fight for freedom, democracy, and human rights in my birth country. The friendships I cultivated over the years reinforced for me that we, the people of Taiwan, must band together before we can enlist international support. I also learned that true friendships with American politicians must be founded on mutual benefit.

While I dreamed of a brighter democratic future for Taiwan, I understood that this future could not happen overnight. In the meantime, I focused on projects that were realistic in the short term to further my goals for the long term. Two projects that I was heavily involved with were the Tibet Fund and the Formosa Foundation.

Friends of Tibet

I have always admired the Dalai Lama, the spiritual leader of Tibet. In 1959 the fourteenth Dalai Lama fled to India with other Tibetans and continued the resistance movement against China. I was always amazed at how he was able to achieve such a high level of respect and popularity among such a wide range of followers. Friends of Tibet, an organization promoting human rights and Tibetan independence, has approximately sixty thousand members in the US, many of whom are members of Congress, prominent academics, media moguls, or Hollywood celebrities. The parallels between Taiwan and Tibet are eerily similar, yet Taiwan hasn't been able to acquire that level of visibility in the United States, even though we share the Tibetans' dream of full sovereignty.

When the Dalai Lama visited Los Angeles in November 1999, I was able to meet him in person and asked if he would speak to the Taiwanese American community. We coordinated with Lodi Gyari, his special envoy to the United States, and the Tibet Fund for a speech and fundraising luncheon to take place on June 25, 2000, at the Hilton Universal Towers. The speech was titled, "Love, Compassion, and Universal Responsibility." The morning prior to the luncheon, the Dalai Lama and I spent nearly forty minutes in a private talk. I found him to be an affable, kindly gentleman with a great sense of humor. He also expressed interest in forming an alliance between the Taiwanese and the Southland Tibetans. I was thrilled.

More than $30,000 was raised during the event, which was attended by over eight hundred Taiwanese Americans, including many who rarely attend these kinds of events. I was amazed at His Holiness's ability to attract an audience. His remarks during the luncheon centered primarily on human rights issues, as well as the volatile and complex political dynamic between China, Taiwan, and Tibet. His Holiness also remarked that he hoped Taiwan, Japan, and Southeast Asian nations—with their newfound wealth—would invest more resources in spiritual pursuits. Lastly, he urged the Taiwanese American community to support the Tibetans in preserving their distinctive history, culture, and religious legacy.

The attention this event garnered was beyond my expectations. About a dozen or so media outlets, including the *Los Angeles Times* and various Chinese-language papers, covered it. We had many noteworthy guests, including well-known politicians and business people, but by far the most famous was Richard Gere, celebrated American actor and producer. His advocacy for human rights in Tibet has been an inspiration to many. He told the audience that Tibet and Taiwan shared many similarities. I was extremely impressed with Mr. Gere's passion. I had always dreamed of making a movie with a historic backdrop set in Taiwan, so I stayed in touch with him in the hopes that he could be involved in such a project.

In spring 2004, on the eve of the reelection of President Chen Shui-bian, China—as usual—tried to use its political and military clout to influence the election against the DPP incumbent. The polls at that time were very close, and I felt that an appearance by Mr. Gere on President Chen's behalf could generate much-needed voter enthusiasm and a will to stand up to Beijing's intimidation tactics. I contacted the actor and asked if he'd be interested in traveling to Taiwan for a speech. He agreed without hesitation.

President Chen initially loved the idea of a celebrity as well known as Mr. Gere standing with him. But then he worried he'd be labeled as an independence activist, not only for Taiwan but for Tibet as well. President Chen didn't want to give his political rivals in the pan-Blue camp (the KMT and other parties who support reunification with China) any ammunition. Mr. Gere waited for more than a week, thinking that the arrangements for his trip to Taiwan were being completed. He even contacted me directly to reiterate that he was happy to go. In the end, President Chen's campaign office notified me that it'd be best if Mr. Gere did not visit Taiwan. I was extremely disappointed and embarrassed when I had to inform Mr. Gere of these developments. Needless to say, I never brought up the subject of my movie idea with him.

The Formosa Foundation

When President Chen Shui-bian was elected in 2000, it was the first time in Taiwan's history that a member of the opposition party was president. While the US government was courteous to the new administration, it was unfamiliar with the new president. My relationships with President Chen and government officials in the US put me in a position to bridge that gap. It seemed the best way to facilitate this opportunity was to create a US-based organization to foster stronger ties between Taiwan and the US. With that in mind, I established the Formosa Foundation.

Originally, I wanted to name the organization the Taiwan Foundation, but that name was already taken, so the Formosa Foundation it was. I didn't foresee what a headache a simple thing as a name would become. Unknown to me, the Formosa Foundation happened to have a name very similar to an organization established in Taipei City by President Chen, the Formosa Cultural Foundation. The rumormongers in the pan-Blue camp began inventing stories that President Chen had stashed tens of billions of NT dollars from illegal gains in the Formosa Cultural Foundation, confusing his organization with mine. The Formosa Cultural Foundation consisted of Taiwanese entrepreneurs and independence advocates. That foundation organized and facilitated President Chen's campaigns and causes, a completely different purpose from the Formosa Foundation I had established.

The Formosa Foundation was a US-based nonprofit with federal 501(c)(3) status created to strengthen ties between Taiwan and the US. In order for our organization to be granted this status, it had to go through rigorous scrutiny, including ensuring its activities were within government guidelines and filing annual donation and tax reports. The Formosa Foundation was an advocacy organization that had a singular focus, debunking the US's One China policy and phasing in a new policy, "One China, One Taiwan."

Rethinking the One China Policy

In order to challenge the One China policy, we needed to reexamine the core of the concept by inviting noted scholars, think tank representatives, and other high-profile influencers to public policy forums and roundtables hosted by the Formosa Foundation. I hoped to steer the American policymakers toward supporting One China, One Taiwan, which would bolster security in the Taiwan Strait, a benefit to both the US and Taiwan.

Many detractors thought my concept was Mission Impossible, but I felt this was our only way out of the political confusion that had been happening between Taiwan and the US for years. When the US established official relations with the PRC in 1979, it adopted the One China policy, expecting the issues between China and Taiwan would be resolved internally. As a result, Taiwan, which had been recognized by the US since 1949, was no longer officially recognized. However, the US did pledge military aid if Taiwan needed to defend itself against China.

But by creating a policy that was both ambiguous and self-serving, the US essentially punted its responsibilities down the road in hopes that this issue would resolve itself. As time passed, this poorly constructed policy became dangerous. Once the Cold War ended, the world's balance of power shifted. China's military buildup and economic growth in recent years completely rewrote the power narrative in the Asia Pacific, and China became the greatest existential threat to the US in the twenty-first century.

As threats from China loomed large, some of America's political elites began to take note of my appeal to reexamine the One China policy. Republican Tom Delay, House majority leader from 2003 to 2005, for instance, publicly supported my One China, One Taiwan policy. John J. Tkacik Jr., with the Heritage Foundation, authored *Rethinking One China*, which inspired widespread discussions among American academics and think tanks. Mr. Tkacik wrote in the copy he gave me, "This book would not have been possible without your inspiration!" After leaving public service, former Deputy Secretary of State Richard Armitage founded Armitage International LLC, a global business advisory firm, with former Assistant Secretary of Defense for East Asian and Pacific Affairs Randall Schriver as one of the founding partners. They often reference my One China, One Taiwan discourse in their keynote speeches and publications.

In Congress

The Formosa Foundation's programs advocating for One China, One Taiwan made an impression on Capitol Hill. In January 2011, Ileana

Ros-Lehtinen, chair of the House Foreign Affairs Committee, spearheaded two congressional hearings that emphasized the strategic importance of the United States' relationship with Taiwan. The Formosa Foundation, through its executive director, Terri Giles, played a key role in urging Congress to hold these hearings.

On August 1, 2013, the Taiwan Policy Act, introduced by Representative Ros-Lehtinen was passed unanimously in the House. The Taiwan Policy Act strengthened and clarified the commercial, cultural, and other mutually beneficial relations between the people of the United States and the people of Taiwan.

Goodwill Ambassadors

I believe the Formosa Foundation's greatest legacy was its Ambassador Program. Every summer, the Formosa Foundation welcomed approximately thirty undergraduate and graduate students of all backgrounds from the United States, Taiwan, and around the world to an intensive advocacy training program. Many of these ambassadors were Taiwanese or Taiwanese Americans, but there were also non-Taiwanese students. It was extremely gratifying to see young people work as a team to learn the important art of public advocacy.

The Ambassador Program was recognized by many on Capitol Hill as a top advocacy program. It combined advocacy and education and enabled our young ambassadors to work directly with experts on democracy and human rights, including elected leaders in Congress who created the policies that charted US–Taiwan relations. The ambassadors spent two weeks on Capitol Hill, the first week consisting of hands-on training regarding current US–Taiwan issues and how to communicate effectively with Congress, the media, and the public. The ambassadors spent their second week using that training in face-to-face meetings with members of Congress, their office directors, and staff to explore policy insights concerning US–Taiwan relations. I'm proud to say each class developed the tools and confidence to really make a difference in the world.

The Formosa Foundation closed its doors in 2016 after the victory of Tsai Ing-wen, the second DPP member to be elected president in Taiwan. By that time, the Ambassador Program had produced more than three hundred alumni. These advocates for Taiwan continue to engage through social media and other networking apparatus. It is my hope that these young ambassadors who have walked the halls of Congress will continue to be the blueprint of Taiwan's transformation and a formidable force of champions for the rights and interests of Taiwanese everywhere.

Taiwanese American Political Action Committee

Given the Formosa Foundation's nonprofit status, the organization could only engage in educational and advocacy programs. Using the foundation for campaign activities would be inappropriate. The reality of US politics is that politicians require significant campaign funding in order to win elections, and those who provide that funding can influence policy. If Taiwanese Americans wanted to have the ear of US policymakers, we needed an entity that actively funded campaigns that would help the Taiwanese cause. This entity would be able to aggregate donations from many Taiwanese Americans and establish itself as a fundraising resource for different candidates and political parties. With that in mind, I set up the Taiwanese American Political Action Committee (TAPAC).

While the Formosa Foundation was set up to foster understanding and exchange of ideas between the US and Taiwan, TAPAC was founded to legally and financially support parties or candidates with whom it was in political agreement. There was a clear operational distinction between the two entities, yet they complemented each other beautifully. In the United States, a political action committee (PAC) is a tax-exempt organization that pools campaign contributions from members and donates those funds to campaigns for specific candidates, ballot initiatives, or legislation. Simply put, the donations are ways to influence public policy and legislation at the congressional and executive levels. There is strength in numbers—connected PACs can accomplish what individual contributors cannot achieve, and that was what TAPAC hoped to attain for Taiwanese Americans and Taiwan.

The Trump Era

Things took a surprising turn after Donald J. Trump was elected US president in November 2016. On December 2, 2016, the telephone conversation between President-elect Trump and Tsai Ing-wen, president of Taiwan, marked the first time since 1979 that a US president or president-elect had directly spoken with a Taiwanese president. Although I dare not say for sure whether the US One China policy is to undergo a shift, I believe it's possible that the historical moment could enhance Taiwan's position within the international community.

On March 16, 2018, President Trump signed into law the Taiwan Travel Act (H.R. 535), which allows high-level officials of the United States to visit Taiwan and vice versa. The bill was passed by the House and Senate with no opposition, signifying a milestone in Taiwanese and US diplomacy. By signing the bill into law, Mr. Trump was sending a clear message, in my opinion, that the US would no longer stand idly by as China threatened stability in the Taiwan Strait region.

Immediate US Action

As I reflect on my work to debunk the One China policy, it has become abundantly clear to me that the US must take action *now*. This outdated and ambiguous policy has led the US down a road on which there can be no good outcome. The hope that the One China policy would create stability and status quo in the Taiwan Strait region is a fallacy. Where is the status quo? China continues to be an even greater threat to Taiwan by flexing its economic and military might. Relations between the US and China are at an all-time low. Today even the general public recognizes the existential threat that China poses to the world. US policymakers must take action now by replacing the One China policy with an unambiguous, proactive policy of One China, One Taiwan. My hope is that Taiwan, as a beacon of democracy, can play an integral role in the region to balance the destructive force that China represents.

PART V

BEGIN ANEW

Chapter Forty

A-BIAN AND ME

Shortly after Lee Teng-hui became Taiwan's first popularly elected president in 1996, I was asked if I was interested in joining President Lee's cabinet. I respected President Lee and was flattered by the offer, but I couldn't bring myself to work for a KMT administration. Little did I know that only a few years later, I would be appointed as a senior advisor to the first DPP president of Taiwan, Chen Shui-bian.

A-bian (the name Taiwanese people affectionately call Chen) won the presidential election in 2000 and made history—this was the first time the DPP took political power from the KMT. On the evening of the election, with victory firmly in place, the air was electric with excitement. The overseas group of Friends of A-bian that I had brought to Taiwan to help persuade relatives and friends to vote for him was overwhelmed with joy. I congratulated President-elect Chen and returned to the US.

North America Friends of A-bian

My association with A-bian started years earlier—before he became mayor of Taipei, when he was a member of the Legislative Yuan and an up-and-coming star for the DPP. I met him for the first time when he was invited by TACL to be the keynote speaker at its annual convention in 1992 in Los Angeles. Since I was heavily involved with TACL, I invited him to stay at my home. Because of his rushed schedule, it was a very short stay, with little time to get to know each other.

Later that year, I was back in Taiwan just prior to Dr. Peng's homecoming. I called A-bian to see if he had time to meet and discuss Dr. Peng's schedule. A-bian impressed me with his distinctively polite manner. Even though he garnered a lot of attention, he never let it go to his head. In fact, when I invited him to be a member of Dr. Peng's homecoming reception committee, he said he didn't feel qualified. He insisted that I not include him. I was impressed with his humility.

As democracy began to take hold in the 1990s, DPP politicians such as A-bian made a strong impression with Taiwanese voters. He became a political phenom and was elected mayor of Taipei in 1994, a position viewed as a stepping-stone for higher office. During his reelection bid for mayor in 1998, I was asked to organize the fundraising and voter drive among overseas Taiwanese, who pinned so much hope on A-bian. To help coordinate our efforts, we established North America Friends of A-bian. The organization mushroomed quickly to more than sixty chapters around the world. This level of endorsement for a mere mayoral candidate spoke volumes about A-bian and his political charisma.

As momentum grew, the numbers in the support group swelled. Fellow Taiwanese expats ran fundraisers and flew back to Taiwan to canvass for votes. We roamed through streets and alleys, waving our pennants, shaking hands, and chanting our campaign slogan. The atmosphere was charged with a combination of excitement, anticipation, and exhaustion.

A-bian was widely thought to be the best mayor Taipei had ever had. His poll numbers were through the roof, and it seemed his reelection was a foregone conclusion. But politics can be extremely unpredictable. The day of the elections, my overseas campaign group planned a huge celebratory feast at Hai Pa Wang restaurant for that evening. But as the vote tallies came in, our optimism faded. Despite his high poll numbers and stellar administrative performance, A-bian lost out to the KMT candidate, Ma Ying-jeou.

Ascension to Presidency

Despite the setback, A-bian was ready to move on to the next challenge, running for president. His performance as the mayor of Taipei did wonders for his visibility and put him in the forefront of Taiwan's national political scene. The DPP and the pan-Green camp were hopeful this next presidential election would end more than six decades of KMT rule. President Lee had hit his term limit, so the KMT had no distinct advantage in the 2000 election. The executive office was up for grabs, and our hopes rested on A-bian as our candidate.

After his loss to Ma in the 1998 mayoral election, A-bian wrote me a lengthy letter to thank me for supporting him. As I had observed many times before, he showed remarkable humility in this loss. He embarked on a postelection overseas tour. Every venue he visited was filled with Taiwanese people listening to him with rapt attention. During a visit to Los Angeles, more than three thousand people packed an auditorium with a maximum seating of twenty-five hundred. Attendees spilled out into the hallways and the reception area, where they watched A-bian speak on mounted televisions. His popularity had surged after the defeat.

A-bian seized the moment and announced his intention to run for president. He won the DPP nomination in April 1999. His poll numbers and public support continued to grow. Several friends and I set up a campaign organization in the US called the Overseas Support Group for A-Bian's Presidential Bid. We used this entity to raise funds and mobilize every Taiwanese person we could to return to Taiwan to vote for A-bian.

As the general election drew closer, the excitement grew. It was predicted to be a very close race, and it was imperative that we continue to encourage all our friends to vote. I flew back to Taiwan a few days before the election, accompanied by countless other Taiwanese Americans. This was truly a call to arms—to make sure our voices were heard. When we arrived in Taiwan, we boarded a caravan of campaign Jeeps that had been fitted with banners and loudspeakers. We put on canvasser uniforms as "expat representatives." We began our days visiting traditional farmers markets frequented by local grocers and housewives, handing out fliers and courting voters. At day's end, we beelined for the pep rallies, where I was honored to address thundering crowds of tens of thousands. Between dawn and dusk, I would join my friends at the Taipei Main Station, handing out flyers to drum up support.

And then the evening of the election was finally upon us. Several Taiwanese expat friends of mine and I decided to watch the results at an event hosted by Dr. Peng. As we had anticipated, it was an extremely close race. We were glued to the TV all night. The food that Dr. Peng provided went untouched—who could eat in all the excitement? At the end of the night, A-bian became President-elect Chen Shui-bian, the first non-KMT member to be elected president of Taiwan. Our dream of unseating the KMT had finally come true! Heaving a collective sigh of relief, we packed our bags and returned to the US. But unlike A-bian's last election, this time we returned victorious and hopeful.

Senior Advisor to the Office of the President

In May 2000, I led an entourage of members of North America Friends of A-bian to Taiwan to attend President-elect Chen's inauguration ceremony. The number of expat groups planning to attend the ceremony was surprisingly large, so I asked to meet with A-bian's staff several days ahead of time to discuss ways to accommodate the group. One of A-bian's aides met with me and handed me two invitations with the presidential seal. He also assured me our group would have a great view of the inauguration. I was puzzled by the invitations. One was for the inauguration ceremony, the other for a banquet after the inauguration I didn't know about. On the banquet invitation were my name and Jenny's in elegant calligraphy. Upon further inspection, the invitation detailed a special ceremony where I was to be named a senior advisor to the president.

I was conflicted. It was nice to be recognized, but I was confused as to why A-bian hadn't told me of this appointment personally. In the days immediately following his victory, he'd taken the time to meet senior and national policy advisors of the KMT to ostensibly "ask for advice." I knew A-bian was grappling with the challenge of a KMT majority in the Legislative Yuan. Despite his true feelings, he had to put on an act of conciliation because he needed a certain degree of support from the KMT to fulfill his administrative vision. I tried to keep things in perspective. The title of senior advisor was honorary in nature—unpaid, with virtually no responsibility.

A-bian's roster of senior advisors and national policy advisors included great political minds and extraordinary entrepreneurs such as Dr. Peng, Tsai Wan-tsai (founder of Fubon Group), Shi Wen-long (founder of Chi Mei Corporation), Lin Rong-San (founder of Union Bank of Taiwan and the publisher of *Liberty Times* and *Taipei Times*), Morris Chang (founder of Taiwan Semiconductor Manufacturing Company), Stan Shih (cofounder of Acer Inc.), and Nita Ing (president of Continental Engineering Corporation). This was a noble group that I was proud to be a part of, especially given my humble roots as a Taiwanese independence advocate.

Chapter Forty-One

TOUGH BEGINNINGS

In August 2000, three months into his first term, President Chen Shui-bian went on a diplomatic trip to visit Taiwan's allies in Latin America. The number of countries around the world that had official diplomatic relations with Taiwan had dwindled dramatically due to China's political and economic pressure. Given the complex nature of US–Taiwan relations, a Taiwanese president had to be given permission by the US State Department in order to step foot on US soil. A-bian was granted permission to land in the US en route to Latin America, but under strict conditions. There would be no private meetings with US politicians or any press coverage. And there would be no official welcome or pageantry that would have normally been typical of such a visit. The State Department was extremely sensitive to how China would view President Chen's visit and wanted to keep complaints from Beijing at a minimum.

Despite these conditions from the State Department, the Taiwanese American community was not deterred from welcoming the newly elected president to the US. We made sure to fill A-bian's schedule so that all his supporters would have a chance to see him. I hadn't seen him since the inauguration ceremony and was looking forward to catching up. On the afternoon of August 13, 2000, A-bian's delegation traveled to

Long Beach, California, and I met with him privately that evening. I was eager to speak to him about his reform agenda.

But when we met, I hardly recognized him. Normally upbeat and optimistic about the future, A-bian looked deflated, as if he did not have the drive to push for the reforms that were part of his campaign platform. I tried to give him a pep talk. "You won a very close election with 39 percent of the vote. Despite that, your approval rating has jumped to over 60 percent since you took office. The public is clearly behind you. What's stopping you from moving forward?"

He didn't have a good explanation. After such a hard-fought campaign, it didn't make sense for him to be so hesitant to put forth his agenda. Lien Chan and James Soong, the candidates he defeated in the general election and his chief rivals, had gone to the US with their tails between their legs. Morale had hit rock bottom in the pan-Blue coalition. The timing couldn't have been better for A-bian to fulfill his campaign promise and root out "black gold," a euphemism for political corruption associated with the KMT. If his administration took a hard stance on exposing the KMT's collective profiteering and apprehended those responsible for betraying the public's trust, a new wave of moral responsibility would ripple through Taiwan's civil servants. I wondered what was holding A-bian back. Unknown to me, something was brewing within the administration that would be disastrous for Taiwan and the democratic reforms that had been achieved.

A-bian As the New Chief of the National Unification Council?

Just as President Chen and his delegation left the US to continue their diplomatic mission, back in Taiwan, Chen Che-nan, acting secretary-general to the president, told the press that A-bian would make a key announcement while traveling. Rumors began to spread quickly that A-bian was to serve as head of the National Unification Council (NUC). The NUC was established by Lee Teng-hui in 1990 to pacify pan-Blue hardliners who still believed in unification with China. The NUC was the antithesis of everything the pan-Green camp and President Chen stood for, or so we thought.

Meanwhile, Beijing interpreted this gesture as A-bian's willingness to reunify with China. My phone was ringing off the hook with inquiries from Taiwanese expats who, just a day earlier, had rolled out the red carpet for A-bian in the United States. None of us could believe it. How could A-bian make a 180-degree turn like this? This was not the same man we had helped get elected just months earlier.

I was beside myself with fury. I called Dr. Peng, who was in Taiwan at the time. I had rarely witnessed my old mentor as angry as he was that day. He wanted to submit his resignation as a senior advisor right away, but I was able to calm him down. We had spent all that time and hard work to get our candidate elected—we were not going to let things fall apart without a fight. We would first try to privately convince A-bian to change his mind. If we couldn't, then we would fight him publicly.

We wrote him a letter, stating in no uncertain terms that serving on the NUC was not the way to go. By taking such a position, he was giving the impression that unification was an inevitable outcome for Taiwan. We argued that unification was one possible outcome, not a foregone conclusion. A true democracy would take the path of unification if, and only if, Taiwan's citizens chose that path by a majority vote. We implored him to think about what kind of message he would be sending to all the people of Taiwan if he took this post. We hoped he would make the right decision.

Dr. Peng delivered our letter to President Chen via the help of Chang Rong-feng, one of the members on the advisory board of the National Security Council. In twenty-four hours, the note made its way through the various security protocols and into the hands of President Chen, who was in the Dominican Republic at the time. On August 17, 2000, A-bian hosted a news conference, announcing that he had yet to decide whether to head the NUC since the people of Taiwan were not resolved to reintegrate with the People's Republic of China. He stressed that unification with China was not the only choice for the Taiwanese people. I was pleased that he'd taken our advice and used a lot of the points in our letter. However, it was disconcerting how close we had come to disaster. Although I had known A-bian for years, I was still figuring out my relationship with him. This was an early indication that my tenure as senior advisor would be extremely challenging.

From Senior Advisor to Senior Consultant

Not long into President Chen's first term, the secretary-general of the office of the president informed me that, according to guidelines governing the employment of senior advisors, I would have to renounce my American citizenship within a year and move back to Taiwan. I had been a naturalized American citizen for more than twenty-five years. While Taiwan was my birth country, the United States was my adopted country and home for more than three decades. Also, I was still CEO of General Bank and could not simply pack up and leave. I had hoped to act as a bridge between President Chen and my network of American politicians and opinion leaders. Giving up my citizenship would hinder that work. I decided it was best to give up my senior advisor position instead.

After my resignation, someone in President Chen's administration came up with the idea to appoint me as a "consultant to the Office of the President." I soon learned that no such position existed, but I did receive an official letter of appointment. Since this position was created outside of the official protocol, I would not have to renounce my American citizenship or answer to any regulatory bodies other than the president. I appreciated A-bian's effort to keep me as a part of the team. I would continue to advise him as best as I could while still focusing on my job at General Bank. When people asked me what "consultant" meant, I joked that I had been demoted. I had no idea what the title meant either!

Shortly after my "demotion," I mobilized a group of Taiwanese Americans, all members of the North America Friends of A-bian, to accompany the president during his visit to the Republic of El Salvador. There were so few Taiwanese living in El Salvador that we felt it would be a nice show of support for the president. We all paid our own way, but A-bian did treat us to dinner the evening we arrived. During the chat after dinner, Simon Lin blurted out, "Mr. President, our chief, Li-pei Wu, has always been your most faithful defender. Why did you demote him from senior advisor?" The politician in A-bian rose to the occasion. Brows furrowed, he shook his head and declared, "There must have been some mistake! I have the utmost respect for Mr. Wu. I will get to the bottom of this."

He was true to his word. Upon his return to Taiwan, he sent me a new letter of appointment. I had been "promoted" from consultant to the Office of the President to *senior* consultant to the Office of the President.

A Tinge of Disappointment

I remained President Chen's senior consultant through his first term. During that time, I never shied away from offering my opinion on a wide array of issues. But A-bian very rarely asked me for advice; I was always the one to approach him when issues arose. Given my background, I would have expected A-bian to seek my advice in business and economic matters, but that never happened. This advisory relationship which had started with so much promise was overall a disappointment because I wasn't as productive for Taiwan as I had hoped.

Chapter Forty-Two

OLD SOLDIER ON A NEW BATTLEFIELD

Because of interference by China, it was hard for Taiwan's president to get permission to enter the US. And when the US State Department did grant permission, the president was only allowed an unofficial transit stop.

A notable incident happened in May 1994, when President Lee Teng-hui stopped in Hawaii en route to Nicaragua. Per the US State Department's order, President Lee was blocked from staying overnight in Hawaii to avoid angering Beijing. The president's aircraft was allowed to land in Hawaii and refuel only. To make matters worse, he was given a perfunctory reception in the air force base lounge. President Lee, in order to preserve Taiwan's dignity, insisted on staying in the cabin and met with visiting American officials in his pajamas as a show of protest. It was demoralizing for Taiwanese people to see their president demeaned in this way. It was also an embarrassment for the US, and many members of Congress from both parties condemned the State Department. The Clinton administration faced considerable pressure from Congress to not kowtow to Beijing because of this incident. In late May 1995, they reluctantly decided to issue a visa to President Lee so that he could deliver his speech at the Cornell University alumni reunion on June 9.

Hardships

When A-bian was elected president, China was very aggressive in marginalizing Taiwan within the international community. Each planned transit stopover in the US was met by the typical State Department response—no overnight stay and no meetings with US officials. But the worst situation A-bian had to endure was in 2006, when he was only allowed to transit in Alaska, a very obvious downgrade from locations like Los Angeles. A-bian, in a show of protest, made a last-minute decision to bypass the transit in the US. Since this was unplanned and he had so few countries he could visit, the aircraft had trouble finding a place to refuel. It was in the air until it finally landed in South America. The media dubbed this trip "Star Trek," since the president's plane seemed to be on an endless voyage.

The KMT, other pan-Blue officials, opinion leaders, and media outlets jumped at the chance to criticize and ridicule A-bian's Star Trek adventure. I thought this criticism was unwarranted and damaging to Taiwan. Regardless of political leanings, this was an insult to the entire country. All of Taiwan, including President Chen's detractors, should have been outraged at the way their president was treated. But instead of coming together on an issue that should have been nonpartisan, the pan-Blue coalition poked fun at their president doing his best to make Taiwan relevant on the world stage. A-bian refused to be disrespected by the US and China, but the media called him a fool nonetheless. Taiwanese Americans understood all too well the challenges A-bian faced in the US and were proud of the way he stood up for Taiwan.

A Great Honor

Not all of President Chen's visits to the US were disasters. One visit in late October 2003, three years before his Star Trek trip, was particularly memorable. President Chen was given an award from the International

League for Human Rights (ILHR) in front of one thousand guests, and I was honored to be a part of it.

Each year, the ILHR honors a person who demonstrates notable human rights advocacy. Previous recipients include the Dalai Lama, Nelson Mandela (former president of South Africa), and Kim Dae-jung (former president of South Korea). Dr. Lung-chu Chen, a renowned professor of law in New York and coauthor of *Formosa, China, and the United Nations: Formosa in the World Community*, served on the Executive Committee and Governing Council of the ILHR. Through his recommendation, the ILHR selected Chen Shui-bian to be the 2003 award recipient. The ceremony was to be held in New York City, and A-bian asked that I oversee his reception. He also asked me to coordinate meetings with American politicians during his stay.

The ILHR ceremony was a notable event for all Taiwanese. It not only honored their president, but it also recognized the strides the Taiwanese people had made in the areas of democracy and human rights. This US trip would finally ensure that A-bian and Taiwan received the international exposure that had been so elusive in the past. To rally support, members of the North America Friends of A-bian joined me in New York for the awards banquet. I also invited a group of young Taiwanese Americans to attend the banquet. It was important for these young people to see Taiwan's president honored in this way.

The evening of the banquet, the Waldorf Astoria Hotel in New York City was bustling with Taiwanese Americans eagerly anticipating A-bian's arrival. In the background, there was a smattering of overseas PRC students and elderly, pro-reunification Chinese expats, shouting and chanting for A-bian to "get out." How ironic that this display from protestors from a country notorious for abusing human rights came on the eve of a ceremony recognizing a champion of those rights. Fortunately, their antics couldn't dampen what was an exciting evening for A-bian and Taiwan.

As one of the three cohosts of the event, I was asked to give a speech, in which I praised A-bian as deserving of this most prestigious award.

My cohosts were William S. Cohen, former US senator, secretary of defense, and chairman of the US–Taiwan Business Council; and Thomas Rabaut, president and CEO of United Defense Industries (UDI), a well-known defense contractor. During dinner, Mr. Rabaut asked if I could get A-bian's autograph for him. A-bian glanced at Mr. Rabaut as he scribbled his name across the program. That was our first, last, and only exchange with Mr. Rabaut. Yet the next day, splashed across the front page of Taiwan's pro-unification newspapers was a sensational and laughable story proclaiming A-bian's visit as shady, implying that he was involved with an arms dealer. The papers even speculated that I was somehow bankrolling UDI. We joked that the reporters were wasting their talent in journalism. With such vivid imaginations, they could have found work in Hollywood as screenwriters.

This smear campaign showed how desperate the pan-Blue camp was to taint President Chen. The awards ceremony was only months from the 2004 presidential election, and the KMT was using every tactic possible to undermine him. My work at the Formosa Foundation was also affected. The pan-Blue camp created a rumor that A-bian was getting hundreds of millions as commission for signing an arms deal, claiming the illicit proceeds were stashed somewhere at the Formosa Foundation. It was difficult to imagine these sensationalized, fictitious stories would have any effect on voters; however, the barrage from the press was constant. I made a trip back to Taiwan to be interviewed by Cheng Hung-yi, host of a popular political commentary show, to refute these rumors. I produced mounds of evidence, including the Formosa Foundation's bank statements and tax filings with the IRS, showing that these rumors were completely unfounded.

A Trip Worthy of a Head of State

After the ILHR awards ceremony, A-bian enjoyed a few additional days in New York City. He had numerous meetings with members of Congress, rang the opening bell at the New York Stock Exchange, and interacted with members of the media. It was so refreshing for all Taiwanese Americans to finally see the US welcome a president from Taiwan. During a cruise on the Hudson River, Therese Shaheen, chairman and director of the American Institute in Taiwan, hinted to A-bian that a "secret guardian angel" had played an important role in making the trip go smoothly. That angel was President George W. Bush.

A-bian left New York to continue his visits with Latin American allies. He was exceedingly appreciative of the hospitality he received in New York. On his way back to Taiwan, he transited in Anchorage, Alaska. Governor Frank Murkowski, along with a team of his top aides, rolled out the red carpet for A-bian. This treatment touched A-bian deeply. In his impromptu speech, he said, "Alaska has truly shown me what a great state and friend it is to Taiwan." We later boarded a glass-ceilinged train for a tour and took in the breathtakingly beautiful Alaskan landscape in the company of Governor Murkowski and Director Shaheen. What a perfect note to conclude A-bian's transit.

As I look back on that trip, I can't help but think about Director Shaheen's words regarding A-bian's guardian angel. Where was this angel when President Chen was on his Star Trek flight just three years later? How could A-bian have had such a successful US visit in 2003, but in 2006, under the same US administration, be treated so poorly? This was further proof that diplomacy can be a fickle thing, especially when it comes to the ambiguous status of Taiwan, the inconsistency of US policy, and the aggressiveness of China.

Return Home

A-bian was reelected in 2004. However, just like in 2000, it was an extremely tight race, with a margin of less than half a percent. After the election, A-bian again offered me a senior advisor position. Once again, I had to decide if I would renounce my US citizenship in order to take on this position. My circumstances, however, were different this time around. I'd officially retired from General Bank at the end of 2001. My plan was to stay in the US and enjoy a simple life. I was about to complete a renovation of my home, and I had nothing on the schedule but relaxation and spending time with my grandchildren. President Chen's offer forced me to reevaluate my future. I had spent the last thirty-six years in the US, but a longing to return to my roots in Taiwan was always stirring within my heart. On top of that, I was in relatively good health, and my mind was still active. Retiring wasn't appealing since I felt I still had a lot to contribute.

I kept going back to the same questions: What would I actually do for Taiwan once I moved back? In what way could I contribute? A-bian's reelection success suggested a heightened awareness of Taiwanese nationalism among the people. The political climate in Taiwan was changing. I felt my background lent itself to facilitating opportunities between US businesses and Taiwanese companies, which would lead to additional investments in Taiwan's economy. Given my relationships within the Taiwanese American community, I felt there was a strong possibility of bringing significant investment dollars from expats back to Taiwan.

Besides economic relationships, I believed I would be able to use the political connections I had built in the US to help Taiwan. I could still act as a liaison between Taiwan and the US and establish deeper US relationships for A-bian and other Taiwanese politicians. By inviting America's political elites to Taiwan for international conventions or seminars, we would open their eyes to the democratic reforms that had been enacted. These gatherings could also serve to raise Taiwan's visibility within the international community and provide much-needed global perspectives for the Taiwanese.

The more I thought about my potential role as senior advisor, the more I felt hope. I thought back on countless meetings I'd had with US policymakers trying to convince them to support Taiwan's sovereignty. I'd often been confronted with the same questions: Do the majority of Taiwanese people share your view? Don't the Taiwanese want to reunify with China? Don't people in Taiwan view themselves as Chinese? These questions deflated me because it was clear that the Taiwanese people had not done a good enough job expressing their hopes for the future.

There is only so much that Taiwanese expats can do for the cause if the Taiwanese people don't speak up for themselves. In spite of this, a silver lining appeared after Taiwan's 2000 and 2004 presidential elections. A-bian's victories were a clear signal that the Taiwanese people's longing for democracy and freedom had taken root. I felt it was my duty to help cultivate this spirit of nationalism in Taiwan so that it would last well beyond A-bian's presidency.

As I thought of these possibilities, a relaxing retirement no longer seemed appealing, and I discussed A-bian's offer with my family. My wife, like me, had spent the better part of her adult life in the US, so she was naturally apprehensive about moving back to Taiwan. After a lengthy discussion, though, she agreed with me. Our two boys were grown and had families of their own. They worried about us living so far away, but they understood my desire to help my country. With my family's blessing, I decided to renounce my US citizenship and move back to Taiwan to accept A-bian's commission as one of his senior advisors.

New Challenges Await

I officially accepted President Chen's offer in the summer of 2004 and prepared for my move back to Taiwan. My wife returned to Taiwan ahead of me to find us a new home. The remodeling on our house in Los Angeles had just been completed before we put the house on the market. The decision to move back to Taiwan happened quickly, but I did have a chance to reflect on my time in Southern California. I will always remember Los Angeles as the place I had called home for so many years, where I'd passed so many milestones and so many kindred spirits had crossed my path.

On July 24, 2004, my friends in Los Angeles threw me a farewell party with about a thousand in attendance. The event was quite a production, with singing, dancing, and speeches. Friends and compatriots overwhelmed me with their graciousness and blessings. These were the people I had been in the trenches with, working side by side to try to make Taiwan a better place.

Frank Murkowski and his wife made a special video for me, to be played during the party. He called my departure "America's loss and Taiwan's gain." I usually don't show much emotion, but it was overwhelming. So many conflicting feelings battled for center stage in my heart. I was so excited to return to Taiwan, yet I was saddened to leave my friends in the US. I only hoped that everything I planned to do for Taiwan would be worth it.

As for renouncing my US citizenship, my trusted friend and accountant C. C. Lee had handled the paperwork for me. He'd filed my final tax return, reported my annual net income, and compiled multiple years of tax transcripts in preparation for the process. The final step was to visit a US diplomatic office in a foreign country, per the US State Department regulations. On August 4, 2004, I arrived in Vancouver, Canada, with two pieces of luggage. I went directly to the US consulate to sign an oath of renunciation. It was then official; I was no longer a US citizen.

When I boarded the plane in Vancouver for Taiwan, I couldn't help but recall the flight I took more than thirty-six years earlier, traveling in the opposite direction. I was once again leaving my home, this time going back to Taiwan with a mission to do everything I could to help it become an independent nation. In a way, it was comforting to have the same feelings of excitement, sadness, and anxiety coursing through my seventy-year-old Taiwanese body as I entered a new battlefield.

Chapter Forty-Three

HANDS TIED

With these aspirations in mind, I settled in Taiwan and began working in the Presidential Office, committed to making a positive change for my reclaimed country. I could barely contain my excitement when I walked into my office, an official employee of the Taiwanese government and part of the Chen administration. I was ready to offer my expertise in finance and the economy to the president. However, the position did not pan out as I envisioned. Instead of feeling honored and fulfilled, I was disappointed and frustrated.

Powerless

Even though I had direct access to the president and he was very accommodating when I wanted to discuss something, I didn't feel that I was accomplishing anything. A-bian was always exceedingly polite, listening with patience to my suggestions. But in all the time that I worked as a senior advisor, the president never once approached me for advice or help on anything. It was just like his first term when I served as his senior consultant.

I had naïvely assumed that with our offices so close, A-bian would call upon his few senior advisors and national policy advisors to consult on key matters. But no such meetings ever took place. I had given up my

US citizenship and moved to Taiwan for nothing. I reached out to Dr. Peng, who had been senior advisor since A-bian's first term, and asked him why the president kept us around if he had no need for our opinions. Dr. Peng's resigned response was telling and disappointing. "I don't know who he confides in, but it's not me." Dr. Peng was clearly as disturbed as I was at being ignored. What were we doing here, if they didn't think we had anything to contribute?

I wasn't sure how to handle the situation, but I knew one thing—I needed to stay productive. I researched and wrote memos for the administration. I gave frequent speeches on various current issues and policies. On occasion Dr. Peng and I took it upon ourselves to visit A-bian. During these meetings, Dr. Peng would break the ice, and then I would follow with my long-winded suggestions. A-bian listened but never took our advice. I didn't give up. I met with him often, bringing various reports or essays I'd written. I reminded him how quickly the world was changing and how little time his administration had left. I also emphasized my concerns regarding Taiwan's growing economic reliance on China. But he only replied with "I know" or "I see," and then he'd put my reports away.

I was usually respectful toward him, but after I presented my thoughts in one such meeting, I lost my patience. I asked him bluntly, "Mr. President, is this all a waste of time for you?" A-bian sensed the frustration in my voice, and he sighed. He said, "You don't understand how difficult my position is. There are so many issues and problems that I'm not at liberty to disclose to you." This was his polite way of telling me the meeting was over. I quietly took my leave.

Meeting between A-bian and James Soong

What was most disappointing about A-bian's administration was China's unconstrained and unabashed influence over Taiwan's economy. Even though A-bian had unsurmountable pressures from all sides, he did have the power in this situation to protect Taiwan's interests. Unfortunately, he wasn't aggressive enough, and China took full advantage. Another great disappointment was his meeting on February 24, 2005, with James Soong, one of his chief political rivals. His actions infuriated not only me but also most of his supporters.

On March 14, 2005, China ratified its Anti-Secession Law, a set of laws meant to counteract the "One Country on Each Side" concept proposed by A-bian in August 2002. President Chen's concept stated that the entities on each side of the Taiwan Strait were separate countries, while the Anti-Secession Law essentially reasserted the One China principle. China's new law included a host of ominous verbiage, the most noteworthy of which was in Article 8, which read:

> In the event that the Taiwanese independence secessionist forces should act under any name or by any means to cause the fact of Taiwan's secession from China, or that major incidents entailing Taiwan's secession from China should occur, or that possibilities for a peaceful reunification should be completely exhausted, the state shall employ non-peaceful means and other necessary measures to protect China's sovereignty and territorial integrity.

Taiwan's Mainland Affairs Council and the Ministry of Foreign Affairs condemned the promulgation of the law as "disregarding the sovereign rights of the Republic of China, unilaterally changing the status quo, escalating tension between Taiwan and China, and triggering a Taiwan Strait crisis." The US State Department also expressed concern to Chinese officials that the Anti-Secession Law would be counterproductive and hinder a peaceful resolution to Taiwan's status.

The passage of the Anti-Secession Law compounded a string of problems that President Chen faced in the first year of his second term. In December 2004, during Taiwan's legislative elections, the pan-Green coalition failed to win the majority. The pan-Blue coalition in the Legislative Yuan, consisting of the KMT, the People First Party (founded by James Soong), and the New Party, retained its majority by winning 114 seats, compared to 101 seats won by the pan-Green camp, comprising the DPP and the Taiwan Solidarity Union (founded by Lee Teng-hui). The remaining ten seats went to independents and other smaller factions. The threat from Beijing and the election results inevitably put A-bian under a lot of stress. He had to figure out a way to find compromise with the pan-Blue majority. This led to the meeting with Soong.

Former President Lee Teng-hui was of the belief that A-bian needed to find a way to work with the opposition party and James Soong in order to get the Legislative Yuan to function and enact policies. Lee advised A-bian to smooth things over with Soong. "Let Soong have minister of finance or any other ministerial position. Just find a way to work with him." When A-bian told me this, he declared emphatically that he would not give Soong anything.

That was why I, and so many others, were shocked by what he did next. A rendezvous between A-bian and James Soong took place the morning of February 24, 2005, at the Taipei Guest House, a historic government building. After more than two hours of discussion, the two men signed a ten-point agreement and joint statement. A-bian and James Soong reached a consensus to acknowledge and respect the current definition of Taiwan's status and ensure a cross-strait peace mechanism with the Constitution as the highest legal principle. A-bian also agreed to honor the "Four Noes and One Without" pledge, a principle effectively assuring China that there would be no steps toward Taiwanese independence.

This was a slap in the face to the voters who'd elected A-bian in the 2004 presidential election. How could this have come from our president, who was supposedly part of the pan-Green camp? For A-bian to concede in such a fashion was indefensible and crushing.

As expected, there was an immediate outcry from most of the pan-Green camp after A-bian released the documents. The opening words from the joint statement were especially disheartening:

In a move to ensure the overall national interests of the Republic of China and safeguard the rights of the Taiwanese people to pursue freedom, democracy, peace and prosperity . . . the highest guiding principle of cross-strait relations at this stage . . . under the premise of cross-strait peace . . . President Chen will not declare independence, change the national title, nor promote a referendum on unification or independence.

I immediately confronted A-bian. "Who drafted this declaration? Where did it come from? Who have you talked to about this?" I needed answers because he'd taken this action without consulting anyone in his inner circle. A-bian told me that the documents were drafted by a staff member and reviewed twice by Chiou I-jen, secretary-general of the Executive Yuan. But what really disturbed me was that he said we should be thankful that Soong was willing to accept this joint statement. I tried to remain calm, imploring him to think this over carefully because his actions went against everything every one of his supporters believed in.

I read the declaration over and over again. It was disturbing that A-bian had chosen to cooperate with Soong in this manner, but the specific wording within the declaration was even more troublesome. Why had he used the words "the national interests of the Republic of China" when something like "the wellness of twenty-three million Taiwanese" would have shown the people that they were the priority? Also, in the press conference following the summit, A-bian's silence when Soong stated, "Taiwanese independence will not be an option," indicated that he agreed with Soong's view. Soong also said, "I was born and bred in Hunan province. Hunan is my ancestral home." Soong made a point to emphasize that he is "Chinese, through and through." A-bian could have responded in kind that he was 100 percent Taiwanese and 100 percent for the Taiwanese people, but he didn't. He allowed Soong to get the upper hand, and I felt betrayed. Had I made a big mistake backing this president?

Protest over China's Anti-Secession Law

To my surprise, A-bian was unapologetic when I confronted him. This was one of the few times he wasn't his usual polite self. He felt he was being unfairly judged since he had essentially followed President Lee's suggestions to meet with Soong. He thought he'd done a good job negotiating since he hadn't offered Soong a cabinet position. I was speechless, realizing that he was thinking more like a politician than the leader of a country.

President Lee was also critical of the summit. He was fine with them meeting, as long as it was constructive for the country's political stability. His opinion was that the ten-point agreement would create more instability. Lee suggested that A-bian had been outmaneuvered by Soong, the leader of a "small political party," which wouldn't inspire confidence in his supporters. Lee also pointed out that it was unclear who A-bian represented when he signed the agreement. Did he represent himself, the DPP, or someone else? The agreement appeared to be a "memorandum of understanding" between two countries, yet it bore no such legitimacy. Lee's daughter jumped into the fray and was much more pointed with her criticism. "We encouraged Chen to talk to Soong—we didn't ask him to sleep with him!"

Perhaps another motivation for A-bian to sign this agreement with Soong was the pending adoption of China's Anti-Secession Law. I believe the president was hoping to appease the public and counter China with this passive tactic, when a more direct, forceful approach like the Anti-Aggression Parade would have been more effective.

After China ratified its Anti-Secession Law, the citizens of Taiwan took it upon themselves to express their outrage. The Taiwanese people were tired of China's threats. In a sign of solidarity, the DPP, the Taiwan Solidarity Union, and several hundred civic groups formed the Alliance of Democracy and Peace to Protect Taiwan and announced the Anti-Aggression Parade to be held on March 26, 2005. This was an inspirational idea, the perfect antidote for the Taiwanese at a time when most felt like their destinies were not in their own hands. I gladly paid for a large advertisement in the newspaper to support the parade with the words "Say NO to China! Join the March 26 Anti-Aggression Parade!"

The parade was a tremendous success. The sight of hundreds of thousands of protesters taking over the streets around the presidential building was breathtaking. The participants divided themselves into ten processions, signifying the ten articles of the Anti-Secession Law. It was a family affair, with children of all ages and even pets participating in the parade. Chants of "Protect democracy, peace, and Taiwan!" filled the air. In a surprising move, President Chen ignored critics from the pan-Green and pan-Blue camps to join the crowd and became the first head of state in Taiwan to take to the streets and protest against Beijing's military threat. The Taipei Police Department estimated the crowd at over 270,000, and I was proud to be one of them.

Resignation Request Denied

Despite our differences, I have always held A-bian in high regard. The difficulty of his job and the enormous pressures he was under were not lost on me. As time passed, however, the chasm between our beliefs and convictions grew too wide. I continuously provided what I believed to be sound advice to help the administration and Taiwan, but it went unheeded. All my reports, memos, and letters were ignored. All the meetings I had with A-bian and his other policy advisors went nowhere. I felt like I was wasting time. There were moments when I wondered whether I should continue as senior advisor, but I vowed to press forward because I had made a commitment to President Chen and Taiwan. I did my best to refrain from publicly disagreeing with him. But all that changed when he had the meeting with James Soong. That fateful meeting and the public statements that followed were a fundamental betrayal of everything I believed in. I could not keep quiet any longer.

I accepted interview invitations from quite a few radio and TV stations, where I explained in detail why the Chen–Soong meeting was extremely inappropriate and condemned the ten-point statement. It was very unlike me to think about giving up and walking away from my advisory position, but every time I recalled his actions, my throat tightened, and frustration and anguish washed over me. What A-bian did was wrong, but I also wondered if I had fallen short in my responsibility as senior advisor. On March 1, 2005, five days after the Chen–Soong meeting and two weeks before China adopted the Anti-Secession Law, I handed in my resignation, on which I wrote, "As senior advisor, I should be up front with the president about his agenda and the progress his administration has made for Taiwan. Regrettably, there has been very little opportunity for me to offer input to your policies since my return to Taiwan. The weight of my frustration is staggering; thus, I formally submit this resignation, effective immediately."

I also used this letter to provide one last piece of advice to the president. I urged him to pay special attention to three particular matters. One, never underestimate the power of public opinion. I encouraged him to always put the love of Taiwan and Taiwanese people as his upmost priority. Two, improve your communication with your team and with the public. Explain to the people why you do what you do, thus reducing the risk of division among them. Three, be wary of Beijing's tactics to economically annex Taiwan. Implement policies that will strengthen Taiwan's economy without being overly reliant on China. In closing, I wrote, "I shall continue to champion Taiwanese nationalism so that influential parties in Washington and the international community will understand the importance of upholding Taiwan's sovereignty." I hoped A-bian understood my underlying message—people who walk different paths cannot make plans together. He and I had different values.

When I submitted my resignation letter, I was relieved and disappointed at the same time. I had honestly hoped that my role as senior advisor would help the country. Even though that didn't happen, I was looking forward to making a difference in another capacity for Taiwan. I expected to hear back from A-bian with a standard reply that he regretted my departure and wished me luck on my next endeavor, but I never got a reply. Since there was no acknowledgment of my letter, I didn't know what to do. In my mind, I had resigned, so I stopped going to my office. All my paychecks were stacked on my desk, untouched. Finally, someone in the Presidential Office called and urged me to sit down with A-bian. I agreed, even though I didn't think there was anything left to say. But surprisingly, our meeting lasted two and a half hours.

I detailed all the ways in which A-bian had ignored my suggestions and advice. He listened politely but didn't say much. At the end of the meeting, he refused to accept my resignation, promising that things would change. A-bian asked me to join his council of economic advisors, a group that had absolutely no influence on policy whatsoever. In exasperation, I told him I wanted to make a difference for Taiwan. I didn't want to take another position where my contributions would be ignored. He clearly wasn't listening to me.

A-bian would not give up and pulled out more empty positions. Finally, his eyes lit up. He explained that his administration would soon undergo a reorganization and there would be a new position that suited me. Furthermore, I would be able to have a team of my choosing to help with whatever policies or issues interested me. I don't know how he changed my mind. Perhaps it was the glimmer of hope that I would be productive in the way I had originally envisioned. Perhaps it was how hard he was trying to get me to stay. Regardless, I agreed to stay on.

Taiwan's media outlets picked up on the news of my attempted resignation. The reporters wrote about how the president refused to allow me to step down because of our close friendship and his reliance on my advice. These stories were flattering, but the reporters obviously didn't have the full picture of the challenges I'd face. The relationship I had with A-bian was not ideal, but I was hopeful, once again, that things would improve.

Tension between A-bian and Lee Teng-hui

During A-bian's time in office, there were rumblings of discord between him and former President Lee Teng-hui. I'm not sure of the cause, but I witnessed the escalation of tensions between them following the meeting with James Soong.

In 2005 I helped President Lee plan a visit to the US. My old friend Frank Murkowski, who was governor of Alaska at the time, invited President Lee as an official, gubernatorial guest of Alaska. Frank would also personally accompany him when he traveled to the East Coast and Washington, D.C. After some coordination, we finalized President Lee's preliminary schedule for a visit in October.

During a routine US Department of State press briefing, a reporter raised questions about Lee's visit. The spokesperson, Sean McCormack, answered, "Mr. Lee Teng-hui is a former president and a civilian. He can visit the United States as long as he has all the valid travel documents." The reporter then asked, "Is he allowed to visit Washington?" McCormack tactfully dodged the question with the same reply. McCormack's evasiveness made Lee anxious, since it would be a huge embarrassment to him if his travel plans were curtailed in the middle of the trip. It took much back-and-forth, with Frank using his contacts with the State Department and the National Security Council, before we received confirmation indicating that the former president could visit Washington as planned.

But just as things were falling into place, A-bian coincidentally decided to visit Taiwan's diplomatic allies, which meant a transit in the States. Douglas Paal, director of the American Institute in Taiwan, asked President Lee to postpone his trip since it didn't make political sense to have two presidents of Taiwan visiting the US within the span of a few weeks. Taiwan's minister of foreign affairs, Mark Chen, also approached the former president with the same request. Despite all this, we decided to move ahead with our original plans because President Lee preferred not to travel in the winter. If he postponed, he would have to wait until late spring, which he felt was too much of a delay.

Then James C. F. Huang, deputy secretary-general to the president, also requested that Mr. Lee postpone his trip. Huang showed me an email written by the US State Department asking that the rivalry between Lee

Teng-hui and A-bian be handled internally. If this couldn't be resolved, the US would not block either visit but could refuse entrance to A-bian's retinue of aides. Huang asked me an interesting question, "Which president is more important, the one in office or the one who's left public service?" He pleaded with me to convince Frank to retract his invitation to President Lee, to which I emphatically refused. I wasn't about to call it off after all the work Frank had done.

When I brought Frank up to date on the situation, he was puzzled because he hadn't been aware of any restrictions placed on Lee or Chen. He called the US National Security Council for clarification and found out that there were no restrictions on A-bian or his aides. We suspected that someone in President Chen's administration had colluded with a low-ranking staff member of the National Security Council or State Department to create and distribute this misinformation, putting pressure on Lee to postpone his trip. I was thrilled it was not the US standing in the way of the simultaneous visits by two Taiwanese presidents. Yet the possibility of this deliberate petty tactic by A-bian's administration left me disappointed and angry.

Lee's Visit to the US

Since I helped organize the trip, President Lee asked me to travel with him to the US. I was hesitant because I'd rarely taken any leave since I took on the senior advisor position. But under the circumstances, I felt an obligation to make sure the trip went according to plan. I asked Yu Shyi-kun, secretary-general to the president, to put in the leave request for me. To my great surprise, A-bian turned it down. He said his administration had instructed all the consular offices to arrange for the highest-level reception of support for President Lee. There was no need for me to go. I had to laugh. This was the first time I actually felt needed by A-bian!

I wouldn't allow him to manipulate and use me, though. I turned to Frank once again for assistance. He sent President Chen a letter. "I am unable to offer President Lee Teng-hui a proper reception without Senior Advisor Wu present. This is because Mr. Wu is well connected with both Taiwanese and American officials. I ask that he be given special permission to take leave." If A-bian had followed protocol, he would have written a reciprocating memo with his approval or refusal. Instead, he showed his reluctance by writing his reply, "Very well," directly on Frank's official letter and asked an assistant to deliver that letter to me.

As planned, I accompanied President Lee to Alaska, where Frank, very much in his element, rolled out the red carpet for the former president as soon as he arrived at the airport. From there, my old friend gave us a tour of Anchorage's coastline on his luxury yacht. Even though it was only October, Alaska's famous Arctic chill proved too much for President Lee, who was trembling from the cold. Frank's aides came forward with blankets and a portable heater.

After Alaska, President Lee continued to the East Coast, while I flew to Los Angeles to oversee the planning of a formal luncheon and dinner banquet that he would attend in the latter half of his trip. The luncheon was hosted by the Formosa Foundation and connected Taiwan's former president with mainstream American political leaders and influencers. That evening's welcome banquet was an impressive production attended by numerous Taiwanese expats. President Lee was thrilled with the entire trip and the royal treatment he received, and I was honored to be able to help make it happen for him.

Organizing this trip opened my eyes to how complicated politics could be. Upholding the interests of Taiwan drives me in everything I do. I care very little for the pettiness that arises from rivalries and conflicts. When I agreed to be senior advisor to President Chen, my priority was to help Taiwan build stronger bridges with the US. Playing favorites is not my style. When A-bian, as a private citizen, chooses to make a trip to the US like President Lee, I hope I will have the chance to arrange a visit for him and provide the reception and fanfare he deserves too.

Chapter Forty-Four

FRUSTRATIONS

When I came on board as senior advisor, Lin Hsin-i had just taken over the post of convener for a group of economic advisors that A-bian created to provide direction on Taiwan's economic policies. It was composed of five or six people, most of whom were entrepreneurs or academics. This economic council was known for advocating with the slogan "Going West with Courage and Sureness," meaning establishing strong economic ties with the country to the west of Taiwan—China. I felt A-bian needed advisors with different perspectives, so I mentioned Huang Tian-lin, former president of First Commercial Bank, and encouraged A-bian to tap into his profound financial expertise. Mr. Huang was already posted as the president's national policy advisor, with an office in the presidential building. I also suggested that those with investment interests in China be excluded from the council because of conflicts of interest. A-bian appeared amenable to the suggestions and reiterated his plan to reorganize and have me sit on the council, possibly as convener. I wanted to believe that this was the fresh start I was looking for, but when I returned to my office that afternoon, there was a letter of appointment for me as economics advisor on my desk, nothing more.

Economics Advisor As Office Ornament

I plunged into my new role as economics advisor with the same fervor I brought to any other job I'd ever had. I convened many closed-door meetings, graced by some of the most prestigious economics and finance experts in Taiwan, to exchange views on ways to wean Taiwan's economy off China. The participants included Huang Tian-lin, Chen Po-chih (former minister of the Council for Economic Planning and Development), Wang To-far (an economics savant), and Peng Pai-hsien (former Nantou County magistrate), among others. We all agreed that it was absolutely imperative for A-bian's administration to think outside the box and find ways to slow the economic momentum toward China before it was too late. I also met with Chiou I-jen (secretary-general of the National Security Council), Wu Rong-i (vice premier), and Hu Sheng-cheng (the economist who led the Council for Economic Planning and Development).

Most of our ideas were simply Band-Aids and wouldn't do much to change what was already happening. As much as we tried to find unconventional approaches to this issue, turning back the tide was difficult simply because it was President Chen's administration that had opened the floodgates to economic ties with China in the first place. Many of Taiwan's entrepreneurs wanted to ride the China wave, and A-bian accommodated them. Key growth industries, like Taiwan's high-tech companies, started the exodus to China en masse, which in turn boosted China's competitiveness in technology. It was a foregone conclusion that all the economic growth that Taiwan initially enjoyed from this cross-strait relationship would slow down because China would eventually bite the hand that fed it.

When Lee Teng-hui was president, he was also pressured to establish strong economic ties with China. However, he instead adopted a "no haste, be patient" strategy. His administration implemented policies that prohibited Taiwan's high-tech industries and infrastructure services from moving to China. A-bian implemented a policy of "active opening up and effective management" at the beginning of his first term to accelerate Taiwan's investments in China. Even though Taiwan's export figures appeared impressive during this time, an overwhelming majority involved business orders being processed in Taiwan but manufactured in China. These types of exports were, in fact, hurting Taiwan's employment market and economic growth in the long run. In 2006, A-bian modified the language of the policy to "effective opening up and active management." It didn't matter what catchphrase was used. It would not change the course of Taiwan's progressively China-leaning economy.

A-bian attempted to make a slight course correction away from his China-leaning economic policy, but the corrective measures were only minimally effective. His administration eventually became hamstrung by its previous economic policy blunders and the various corruption scandals that dominated the end of his second term. Once the negative publicity took hold, any and all damaging stories were widely circulated. Everything that was wrong with his administration came to light, and his approval ratings dropped to a heartbreaking 18 percent. These challenges distracted A-bian so badly he couldn't focus on government affairs. As for me, the newly crowned economics advisor, I became nothing more than an office ornament.

The Removal of Senior Advisors

I agreed to stay on as senior advisor after submitting my resignation in March 2005 because of A-bian's insistence and my hope that I would somehow do good work for Taiwan. Despite everything I tried, it was all for naught. The main reason for our lack of achievement was that our economics council never had a common goal. I naïvely assumed all government officials would work toward the best interests of Taiwan. But like all things in politics, there are layers of agendas and egos which can get in the way of public service. Some cared more about their own investment interests rather than what was best for Taiwan's economy. Some cared about political power and looking good in front of their constituents. All would talk the talk, but few would walk the walk. The dysfunctionality of the group was embarrassing, but I continued to press forward as best I could, even though some members went as far as trying to sabotage my work. I recall a few instances when my reports or presentations were deliberately altered in order to satisfy somebody else's agenda. I could no longer ignore the reality—I was simply wasting my time.

Less than eight months after my first resignation attempt, I delivered my second resignation in writing on October 27, 2005. Once again, I wrote some farewell advice for A-bian, encouraging him to retain experts and specialists for the economics council who were capable and unbiased. This group needed to provide him with advice that would propel Taiwan's long-term interests. I also suggested that he divide his senior advisors and national policy advisors into expertise-based groups so that they could focus on specific action plans.

Just like last time, I received no response. It appeared A-bian still wanted to keep me on his advisor team. I was so determined to leave that I submitted two more resignation letters, the last asking him to simply let me go. I could have just left, but I respected the office of the president and the man who sat in that office. I wanted to end my time as senior advisor on mutually acceptable terms. I felt I owed A-bian that much. To this day, I'm not sure why he was so insistent on me staying.

By May 2006, the position of senior advisor had been eliminated from President Chen's administration altogether. In early 2006, pan-Blue legislators criticized him for giving senior advisor and national policy consultant positions as rewards for past political favors. The pan-Blue camp claimed these positions didn't add value to the government or Taiwan and were nothing more than a drain on Taiwan's taxpayers. A-bian caved to the pressure and eliminated these positions.

If he had explained there were budgetary constraints, I'm sure many of the salaried advisors, like myself, would have been perfectly fine performing our duties pro bono. Like much of my experience with this administration, what should have been done was very different from what was done. It was a frustrating and disappointing two years.

Delegation Head to the National Prayer Breakfast for Three Consecutive Years

Even though my plans for my time with the Chen administration didn't work out as I had hoped, when I look back on that period, there were a few moments when I felt I was doing some good for Taiwan. One such time was when A-bian asked me to lead the delegation from Taiwan to Washington, D.C. to attend the National Prayer Breakfast, an annual event held in late January or early February. It was hosted by members of Congress and attended by some 3,500 representatives from over one hundred countries. The president of the United States is usually one of the key speakers for its main event.

Taiwan's delegation would typically remain in Washington to meet with US politicians, officials from the Defense Department and National Security Council, and a range of think tank members and other policy experts. This was a rare opportunity to give Taiwan access to key American politicians and other policymakers while circumventing the usual State Department vetting that such meetings would require. Our delegation and the American political elite could even host press conferences, providing Taiwan with much-needed media exposure. I was fortunate and honored to lead Taiwan's delegation on three occasions.

These closed-door discussions between Taiwan and US officials inevitably touched upon very sensitive topics. On two occasions, I experienced firsthand the challenges inherent in US–Taiwan relations. The first occurred in 2005, when the topic of China's Anti-Secession Law was at the top of the agenda. I felt it was imperative for our delegation to voice our outrage to the US. In a meeting with American officials from the NSC, we lodged a strong protest. I raised my concern about the safety of Taiwanese living in China. Beijing could easily convict any one of them by citing this law. I urged the US to condemn China and do something about this.

Only then did the American officials answer that Washington was following a "silent diplomacy" protocol and had sent someone from the

NSC to address the issue with Beijing. I was far from satisfied with that answer. I asserted that Beijing would never admit to any wrongdoing without considerable international pressure. I emphasized that Washington's reticence on the matter would force Taiwan to be more aggressive in countering Beijing. This would lead to even more instability in the region. I also told them that I planned to urge every member of Congress I met that week to speak up for Taiwan. My goal was to have a formal resolution from the US censuring Beijing's military threat against Taiwan.

I believe the NSC officials were somewhat taken aback by my aggressiveness. Perhaps the past Taiwanese delegations were less accustomed to dealing with Americans and, as a result, more polite, but I found these types of situations fit me like a pair of well-worn shoes. The NSC knew that they could not stop me from speaking to members of Congress, nor could they control what Congress did.

When we met with members of Congress, many were willing to condemn Beijing behind closed doors, but I did my best to emphasize that public condemnation would lead to heightened international pressure, something China would like to avoid. I felt a sense of pride when Congress passed a resolution to condemn the Chinese Anti-Secession Law on March 16, 2005. All the work we did during that week paid off.

My second trip to Washington, D.C. for the National Prayer Breakfast was scheduled for January 29, 2006, around the same time as Lunar New Year. As soon as our flight took off for Washington, unknown to the delegation, President Chen announced that he was considering eliminating the National Unification Council and the Guidelines for National Unification. When A-bian considered becoming the head of this organization during his first term years earlier, the public outcry from his supporters, including me, was deafening. To consider eliminating this organization altogether created the same kind of outcry, this time from the pan-Blue camp and the international community. This unexpected announcement was regarded by the US as unilaterally changing the status quo with China, creating a headache for the US State Department.

As soon as we touched down in Washington, the delegation and I were immediately besieged by questions from the press. I was completely unaware that A-bian was even contemplating this, so we were obviously unprepared to field questions. The only statement I managed to scrounge up was that the Taiwanese government had never said anything about being unified with China, and therefore the status of the NUC was inconsequential. This seemed to placate the press and bought us some additional time to get ready for what would be an eventful few days in the US capital.

The press wasn't too difficult to fend off, but our encounters with Washington officials were a much greater challenge. During one of our meetings, an American politician bluntly said, "We don't care whether it's election rhetoric or otherwise—we take every one of his utterances very seriously." We entered each meeting faced with questions that were pointed and difficult to handle. There were times when they implied that we didn't believe the US stood up for Taiwan enough, hence the need for Taiwan to be the aggressor against China. The Americans also indicated President Chen's surprise announcement about the NUC was in direct violation of Chen's own Four Noes and One Without pledge given during his first-term inauguration and repeated when he met with James Soong in 2005. They complained, "China seeks unification, and you also seek unification. This makes things easy. Just let the National Unification Council be!"

Most of our delegation, which included noted reporter and columnist Chin Heng-wei and Steve Chan, a physician, weren't professional diplomats or government officials. They were prominent members of Taiwan's intelligentsia and had very little experience handling Washington's glaring political spotlight, but we knew we had to step up.

It was imperative that we rebut this thinking that unification was inevitable. I explained that the concept of unification with China was the core principle of the KMT era. The DPP pledged that unification with China was not the only option. They were not changing the status quo in the Taiwan Strait by attempting to circumvent the pledge of Four

Noes and One Without. President Chen's administration was simply allowing the functioning of the NUC to cease, not outright deactivating or abolishing it. In doing so, the DPP was considering the whole picture, returning to the Taiwanese people the right of self-determination yet honoring Taiwan's commitment to avoid provoking any confrontation with China per the Four Noes and One Without pledge. We respectfully asked the US to stop its barrage of rebukes to A-bian. When we put our position in these terms, the US officials had a new appreciation for our perspective. Our delegation was ultimately able to push forth our agenda.

My third visit to the National Prayer Breakfast had a similar tone to the previous one. A-bian's proposal of "One Country on Each Side," along with his other reform plans, appeared to Washington to have departed from his earlier pledge of Four Noes and One Without. For this particular breakfast, the US allowed Taiwan a delegation of only two people—Frank Hsieh, who had just left his post as premier, and me. Following a closed-door meeting with officials of the NSC, we, as was customary, hosted a press conference at the Twin Oaks estate arranged by TECO, Taiwan's diplomatic office. Since I was not a professional diplomat, I asked David Tawei Lee, the head of TECO in Washington, D.C., to confirm with the American officials if there was any particular topic to avoid or emphasize.

His answer left me speechless. "Senior Advisor Wu, you're the expert. You know what to do. You don't need me." We were at a press conference with the opportunity to show the health and strength of US–Taiwan relations, and this was the advice I was getting from our top diplomat? Was he being polite? Feeling helpless? Or was he apathetic to the plight of A-bian's administration? Lee's words drove home the feeling that there was still a tremendous amount of work that needed to be done, in both the US and Taiwan, in order for the US to support us in the way I hoped.

Overall, these three National Prayer Breakfasts presented opportunities and challenges. I believe our delegations handled things as best as we could and represented Taiwan as a proud and responsible member of the international community.

Parting Advice

My parting advice to A-bian when I left my position as senior advisor was to focus on the job at hand and ignore what could not be controlled. I repeated the counsel I gave previously, that he must commit Taiwan's diplomacy resources to Japan, South Korea, and other countries in Southeast Asia—countries whose geostrategic significance paralleled that of Taiwan. I again urged A-bian to strengthen Taiwan's economic, trade, and political exchange with European countries and those in North America rather than focusing on smaller nations in Africa, Latin America, and the South Pacific. Stronger economic ties with these more developed countries would encourage them to speak up on behalf of Taiwan.

I'm not sure I'll ever understand A-bian's thinking on many issues. Even though we technically worked side by side, it was not a deep relationship. In retrospect, A-bian may have felt my advice was too challenging and perhaps impractical. Since we didn't have much dialogue, I'll never fully understand the challenges he faced as president of Taiwan. To this day, I can't say for sure what A-bian thought of me. Perhaps he viewed this senior advisor position as a reward for my help during his presidential bid. Perhaps he felt I should be satisfied by simply having a fancy title, a salary, and a nice office. Perhaps the president felt I wasn't capable enough to be a senior advisor, which explained why he didn't involve me in key policymaking discussions. Perhaps A-bian hoped to be a president for everybody and avoided antagonizing opposing factions. I don't think I'll ever know the answer, but I am sure I went into this with the best of intentions and continue to hope for a bright and prosperous future for Taiwan.

Chapter Forty-Five

DOWNHILL

When A-bian was the mayor of Taipei, I could see why he was so well regarded among the pan-Green constituents. He was well spoken, respectful, and seemed to have a true calling for public service. He had enormous promise as a future leader within the DPP. As Mayor Chen, his administrative prowess was nothing short of stellar, and he quickly became one of the most popular politicians in Taiwan. Even though his reelection bid for mayor came up short, I was so impressed with his ability to bounce back and lead the DPP to presidential victory. Like many, I had high hopes that he would be the one to free the Taiwanese people from the KMT and establish an independent, sovereign nation called the Republic of Taiwan, free of threat and encroachment by China. I really thought A-bian would be the one to fulfill my lifelong dream. I didn't expect his undoing to come so quickly.

Land Mines

My direct experience as senior advisor to President Chen gave me a unique perspective on the man's character. While I admired him in many ways, I always thought A-bian's Achilles' heel was his inability to take decisive action as president. When he was the mayor, he was able to enact policies and make swift moves to implement them. As president, unfortunately, he seemed lost on the national and international stages. He appeared to try too hard to please instead of taking firm steps to enact his agenda.

But even though A-bian didn't fulfill all the aspirations we had for him, I have never, in all the years I've known the man, seen him compromise his integrity to serve his own greed. The alleged corruption scandal that embroiled A-bian's second presidential term was so out of character that I was highly suspicious of the merits of the accusations. Regardless of my personal beliefs, I do regret the lost opportunities that plagued Chen's presidency. He should have taken advantage of the team of advisors, including Dr. Peng and me, who were ready to help him.

I honestly don't know who President Chen turned to for counsel, but one thing was clear—those closest to him did not necessarily have his best interests at heart. From the onset, I was concerned that his wife, Wu Shu-chen, would be the president's undoing. Wu Shu-chen was tragically injured in a car accident in 1985, after which she used a wheelchair. There are still many unanswered questions about this accident. It occurred during a political event for A-bian in 1985, and many believe Wu Shu-chen was targeted by the KMT for political retribution. A-bian was unflinchingly loyal to his wife.

In a public setting, A-bian was usually sharp as a knife, confident and charismatic, but as soon as he stepped foot into his household, he turned into a different person. The polished politician became timid, deferring to Wu Shu-chen's every whim. Some people found this unwavering loyalty endearing and showed A-bian's good heart. But when rumors circulated early on in his presidency that the first lady was using her position for financial gain, I felt it was necessary to confront A-bian. I hated meddling in another man's marital affairs, but if it affected the president's ability to govern, then there was no choice.

When I expressed my concerns to A-bian, he said, "You must understand, she's paralyzed for life because of me, so I let her have her way." I understood A-bian's loyalty, but he needed to keep his house in order and maintain the credibility of the presidency. I explained that neither I nor anybody else had any interest in how Wu Shu-chen ran her household. What was important was how she conducted herself as first lady. I delicately conveyed that she appeared to be using her position for personal gain and didn't seem to understand the importance of a public image. I encouraged A-bian to keep her out of all public affairs. I also alluded to the stories of her using her position to contact financial advisors and other prominent business people to get information on stock trading. This was a clear abuse of authority and likely insider trading.

A-bian's defense of his wife was shocking and disappointing. "She's only investing a couple of million dollars. It's nothing more than a hobby!" I immediately thought of all the decades of unscrupulous corruption by the KMT, effectively stealing money from the Taiwanese people. Now that the KMT was no longer in power, it was our responsibility to show the public how a proper democracy should work. I didn't believe A-bian was personally involved in any of these scandals, but overlooking the wrongdoing can be just as bad as the wrongful act itself. I implored A-bian to think about the integrity of the office and the expectations of his supporters.

The inordinate coddling of Wu Shu-chen by President Chen was a continuous problem for his administration. The lines between official and private business constantly blurred where the first lady was concerned. It was a never-ending topic of discussion—what was Wu Shu-chen's latest transgression? We, the supporters of A-bian, would shake our heads in bewilderment upon hearing about Wu's excessive influence in the administration. None of us had any problems with a first lady who had influence on policies and legislative agendas. But in Wu Shu-chen's case, the problem was that her behavior disqualified her to advise on any topic. It gutted us to see the president, who symbolized new hope for Taiwan, being tarnished by the bad reputation of his spouse. Li Hong-hi, National Taiwan University emeritus professor, commented once, "She needs a private tutor to coach her on being the first lady." Unfortunately, no such person ever materialized.

Dissuading Annette Lu from Being A-bian's Deputy

I was also concerned about A-bian's running mate, Vice President Annette Lu. Within Taiwanese circles, beats of silence inevitably occur at the mention of Annette Lu, also known as the "disgruntled vice president in the bowels of the Presidential Office." Traditionally the vice presidency was seen as a supportive role to the president, with little formal political power. Annette Lu, however, was anything but traditional. She was extremely opinionated on a wide variety of topics, and there were times when she overshadowed the president by sheer virtue of her strong personality. Things became even more of a problem when she openly challenged or criticized certain policies that A-bian supported. The perception was that Vice President Lu was not working on behalf of A-bian but on her own agenda.

As President Chen's first term was coming to an end, there were constant discussions on reelection strategy. The idea that A-bian should choose a different running mate was one of the first topics brought up. There was no shortage of people close to the president who wanted to see Ms. Lu off the ticket, including me. There was a group of old-timer senior advisors, including Dr. Peng and Mr. Koo Kwang-ming, who strongly encouraged the president to pick a different VP candidate, but A-bian was adamant about keeping Ms. Lu.

Dr. Li Hong-hi confided in me that he had gone to A-bian's residence to discuss this matter. But before Dr. Li could even open his mouth, A-bian told him he had just gotten into an argument with the first lady because she was encouraging him to drop Ms. Lu, but he would not. A-bian even asked Dr. Li to try to smooth things over with A-bian's wife. Dr. Li realized that if the first lady couldn't make A-bian budge, then he had no chance. He left, defeated before he'd even said a word.

When I traveled with A-bian in October 2003 to visit the US and Central America, Dr. Li rang me up and asked me to convince A-bian to change running mates. My answer was an emphatic no. If none of the president's most senior and trusted advisors could convince him, how could I? Dr. Li was insistent, believing that I would succeed since I'd be spending a lot of time with A-bian. I reluctantly agreed to try.

Once I accepted this task, I was determined to succeed. I needed an approach that differed from the other advisors. I had to be creative in my approach, so I paid $5,000 out of my own pocket to commission a poll on who was the best running mate for President Chen in the 2004 presidential election. Several questions were included in the poll to dig into voter acceptance levels among various potential candidates, including Annette Lu. The poll results confirmed many of our fears and concerns, ranking Annette Lu at the bottom for every benchmark. Now that I was armed with tangible facts, I wrote a memo that I planned to use during the October trip. I included the poll findings in the report to emphasize the negative public perception of the vice president.

A-bian's trip to Panama was packed with public appearances and meetings, and I never found the right opportunity to bring up the topic. I felt it best to wait until the diplomatic mission was completed before approaching the president. The meetings in Panama went well, so everybody was in a celebratory mood as we boarded the return flight back to Taiwan. I decided this was the time to make my move.

After the delegation settled in for the long flight, I saw a vacant seat next to President Chen and asked if I could have a word. When he nodded, I sat and began my carefully crafted speech. "A lot of people have expressed concern about your choice of Annette Lu as your running mate. Since this will be your second term, I know you want to be extraordinarily bold and decisive as you move forward with your agenda. I think it will be difficult to implement that agenda if there is discord between you and your vice president. The people of Taiwan need a united voice from your administration. Annette Lu does not provide that unity." I presented the results of the poll comparing the prospective vice presidential candidates, highlighting Lu's ranking at the bottom of every category. Respondents also ranked Lin Yi-hsiung among the most favorable in the poll.

When A-bian replied, I felt a rush of relief at his words. "Senior Advisor, you're correct on all counts," he answered. "I'm aware of the issues where she's concerned." Then my relief turned to dismay as he continued. "But think about this. Would you rather have her on the ticket where we can control her somewhat or let her loose on her own? How will I ever have time to campaign if I'm too preoccupied putting out the fires she starts? It would be me against her, not me against the KMT candidates." I was surprised by how much he had thought this through. After all the preparations I'd made, A-bian's answer left me speechless.

Since I had no reply, I thought our discussion was done, but A-bian continued. He commented on Lin Yi-hsiung, my recommendation for his running mate. "Senior Advisor Wu, since you mentioned Lin Yi-hsiung, you deserve to hear my honest position on the matter. I also think it would be wonderful if Big Brother Lin wanted to run. But please ask him if he'd like to run for president. I would be honored to be his selection as vice president. It was Big Brother Lin who made my presidency possible in the first place, so I am eternally indebted to him. I have been president for one term, and I have no intention of hogging this position."

A-bian's oratorical flourishes and political cunning were a sight to see. He had easily put me in a corner from which he knew I could not escape. Speechless and defeated, I put my head back, closed my eyes, and slept all the way back to Taiwan.

Order of the Propitious Clouds with the Second-Class Cordon

A couple of months before President Chen's second term was to end, I received a call from the Presidential Office, informing me that I was to be awarded the Order of the Propitious Clouds, Second Class (Grand Cordon), an award presented by the president to civilians who made extraordinary contributions to the country. The liaison officer I spoke with wanted to schedule a ceremony at the Presidential Office to present the award. As with most presidents, A-bian was taking care of various administrative and honorific activities before his final term was completed, and this award was his way of showing his appreciation. My initial reaction was to politely decline. As a Taiwanese independence advocate, I was uncomfortable accepting a medal that had the words "Republic of China" etched on it. I asked who else would be receiving a medal. When the officer told me Chiou I-jen, the secretary-general of the National Security Council, that confirmed my decision. I apologized and said I would be in the US during that time.

Another call came from the Presidential Office as soon as I returned to Taiwan from the US. The officer was more persistent this time. "Senior Advisor Wu, the president insists that you come to accept the civilian order." He continued with a long-winded speech, and I waited for a pause so that I could once again decline. I had spent the last four years living in Taiwan, hoping to contribute in some way to the country's well-being, but it felt like wasted time, and I didn't feel I deserved this honor. But the liaison officer would not be deterred. He emphasized that this was the will of the president—declining was not an option. I reluctantly accepted and thought perhaps this would be a good way to close this chapter of my life.

The award ceremony was held in an impressive banquet room at the Presidential Office two weeks before A-bian was to leave office. Because of my mixed feelings, it was difficult to enjoy the moment. One after the other, the recipients went up to the podium to accept their award. Each followed the standard script of obligatory words of gratitude. When it was my turn, those mixed feelings again overwhelmed me, particularly when A-bian recited my "contribution" to the country. "Mr. Li-pei Wu has long dedicated himself to promoting greater ties between Taiwan and the United States."

What happened next was not planned. When I walked to the podium, I simply spoke from the heart. "It's difficult to describe my feelings about this occasion. I was hesitant about coming and said as much a couple of times. But Mr. President insisted, and his order carries much weight. I accept this civilian order with guilt and shame. All my life, I have wanted to overthrow the Republic of China, but instead of vanquishing it, I'm here shamefully accepting one of its orders." I looked down at the intricately designed medal. "I will, therefore, regard this order as a stern reminder that my lifelong goal is a long way off and that I must continue my fight to bring down the Republic of China." The room was dead silent following my speech. Everyone was frozen in place, their faces expressionless. I returned to my seat. Lai In-jaw, former president of the Judicial Yuan, clasped my shoulder and expressed how touched he was.

Regret

President Chen was by no means a stellar political leader. In many ways, he disappointed me and many of the supporters who had hoped for more from him. But I simply can't find it in my heart to be overly critical of him. During A-bian's eight years in office, the legislative branch was controlled by the pan-Blue majority, making it extremely difficult for him to enact any meaningful change. The KMT and its supporters, infuriated that somebody of A-bian's humble background could defeat them twice, made things difficult for him. He once said to me, "All they want is their pound of flesh! How can I get anything done?" My sympathy went out to him.

I look back at his presidency and recognize that the difficult political environment, the various missteps, and the lack of a strong inner circle should not be excuses for the mediocre performance. But I can't help but wonder if A-bian's ascendency was premature. Had he lost the presidential election in 2000, he would have had four more years to prepare and perhaps create a stronger vision of Taiwan's future. Would the end result have been better? One can wonder, but there is no turning back, only looking forward.

Chapter Forty-Six

A DESCENT INTO THE MAELSTROM

On February 2, 2008, President Chen asked me to come by his official residence to discuss a sensitive matter. I wasn't able to get there until the next morning, but my curiosity was piqued. I'd rarely heard such urgency in his voice, and this was only my second invitation to his residence. He got right to the point when I arrived. "Someone has made a donation for the purpose of improving Taiwan's standing in the international community. I want to authorize you to use the money to enhance Taiwan's diplomatic relationships. You have complete discretion."

I was taken aback and slightly amused because for years, he'd ignored my advice on Taiwan's diplomatic status. Now that he was only months away from leaving office, he was suddenly keen on strengthening Taiwan's foreign affairs? But I was touched that he'd thought of me, and this was exactly the kind of work I had hoped to do. Perhaps he wasn't as indifferent to my counsel as I'd thought. I told him that I believed the best plan was to lay the groundwork for the US to reestablish official diplomatic ties with Taiwan. A-bian concurred and gave me his blessing to move forward.

Two Million US Dollars from A-bian

My banker's instinct kicked in when A-bian told me the donation he received was in the amount of $2 million. I asked for more details, and he told me the funds were currently in Singapore and that the donor was based overseas. He'd been thinking about what he would do after he left office, and the donor suggested that he use the funds for diplomatic purposes. Since the funds did not need to be remitted from Taiwan, I didn't think there would be an issue. I did ask him why he waited so long to take on this initiative. His response was, "You've advised me on this issue for years. I was always committed to this cause, and we were on the same page, but I didn't think it was possible to make any progress during my presidency. Now that my term is nearly over, the two of us can make this happen!"

His words stirred something in me. I truly believed that we were on our way to seeing my lifelong dream of a Republic of Taiwan become a reality. I envisioned using this donation to expand Taiwan's relationships with the US, Japan, and Western Europe. We would work in a bottom-up fashion, beginning at the grassroots level to ultimately influence the president of the United States to abandon the One China policy. We needed to make this president reevaluate the US's laissez-faire approach to the Chinese Communist Party. I believed the US would eventually recognize the threat from China and realize the strategic value of Taiwan, not only as an economic ally but also as a key strategic partner in the Taiwan Strait.

As part of this grassroots effort, I suggested that we first set up a national organization called the Friends of Taiwan, which would have a network of chapters throughout the US, with local political leaders, scholars from think tanks, and media influencers as directors. Next, we would appoint someone who was internationally recognized and of extraordinary character to be the national organization's executive director. I would mobilize Taiwanese expats across the US to serve as administrators or volunteers and make Taiwan's voice heard. Furthermore, the Taiwanese community would not have to work alone. Our overseas friends would help create momentum, especially within mainstream America. These Friends of Taiwan chapters would voice their views when the US Congress moved to pass bills related to Taiwan. We would also sponsor research reports on China that would highlight its imminent threat to the American people and their prosperity. All these steps would shine a spotlight on the value of the US's partnership with Taiwan.

When I finished speaking, I could tell my words had reached A-bian. I had made similar suggestions in the past, but this time, I felt he was really listening. It was gratifying to think that after all the time I'd spent planning this strategy, something was finally going to be done.

I wanted to move as quickly as possible. I proposed we convince Washington, D.C. to establish a behind-the-scenes strategic planning committee made up of members of the US National Security Council, the CIA, the State Department, and other foreign service experts to explore one specific topic: What would Beijing's reaction be if the US recognized the Republic of Taiwan as a sovereign nation? How would the US counter China's reaction?

This was a radical idea that had never been implemented before. But if we could convince the US it was in the best interest of the American people, there was a chance it could happen. At a minimum, by researching this topic, Washington would recognize the vulnerability of the US, Japan, and South Korea to China's predatory tactics. Planting this seed would be an important first step.

No, A-bian Did Not Commit Graft

A-bian filled me with an optimism I hadn't felt for a long time. I believed in this opportunity, yet in the back of my mind, I was deeply worried about the constant rumors regarding A-bian and financial improprieties which had plagued his administration. I wanted to view these scandalous rumors as nothing more than fodder for a malicious press, but the overwhelming number of stories couldn't be ignored. They even began to crack A-bian's support base.

It all started back in 2006, when allegations were brought against the first family. Former DPP chairman Shih Ming-te orchestrated a mass rally called "Million Voices against Corruption—President Chen Must Go." These corruption scandals rocked A-bian's administration. There was little I could do to hold back the storm. Even though the constant rumors floating about were impossible to ignore, I never believed that A-bian was corrupt or taking bribes. In all the years I've known him, I have never once witnessed him use his office for monetary gain. In fact, I saw quite the opposite—there are numerous examples where he gave up personal financial gains for the greater good.

For example, in his first term as president, A-bian fulfilled his campaign promise to take a 50-percent pay cut, which ultimately saved the people of Taiwan almost $1.5 million over a period of eight years. A-bian's successor, Ma Ying-jeou, made the same promise, but he never honored it. A-bian also eliminated an off-the-books slush fund created by Chiang Kai-shek decades ago. This fund was allocated to Taiwan's National Security Council as an expense account and available at the sole discretion of the president. President Lee Teng-hui consolidated the money for easier accounting and placed it all in something called Project Fengtian Fund. When A-bian took office, Project Fengtian Fund had approximately $14 million. Since there was no legislative oversight, it would have been perfectly legal for A-bian to pocket the entire amount. Instead, he enacted a new rule to keep himself accountable. Eventually, Project Fengtian Fund was returned to the government coffers.

Another source of potential financial gain for A-bian was Taiwan's voter subsidy rule, which allocated money to presidential candidates based on votes attained. A-bian earned more than 11,440,000 votes total in the two presidential races. At a dollar per vote, A-bian was allocated approximately $11.5 million. This money was for his campaign, but it would have been perfectly legal for him to claim the funds for personal use. A-bian instead donated a lion's share of that money to the DPP headquarters to support fellow DPP candidates' campaign needs.

He used the rest to establish the Ketagalan Academy, an educational institution dedicated to teaching young Taiwanese people political and advocacy skills. He emphasized that the academy would not be affiliated with any party, interest group, business, or individual. A-bian asked Dr. Peng and me to serve on the board of directors. Initially I thought he wanted a donation, but that was not the case at all. He had already allocated $1 million from the surplus of his campaign funds to the academy and only wanted Dr. Peng and me to be involved in this worthwhile organization.

As A-bian was preparing for his 2004 reelection campaign, he told me he didn't need the North America Friends of A-bian to raise funds for him. The Taiwanese American community had shown great commitment to A-bian over the years, raising money for his 1998 mayoral reelection bid and his run for president in 2000. When was the last time you heard of a politician turning down donations? Since the 2004 election would be A-bian's last, the organization was dissolved. The funds already raised were rightfully A-bian's, and I handed him a check for $170,000. He refused it. "Please keep the money, and please don't disband North America Friends of A-bian. I plan on visiting the US from time to time. Use this money to cover whatever expenses are needed to make arrangements for these trips. This way you won't need to raise additional funds."

This was why it was so difficult for me to believe the rumors about A-bian's corruption. It just wasn't in his DNA to care about or hoard money that wasn't his. But regardless of my feelings, A-bian's reputation was irrevocably tarnished.

Quicksand

Nearly three weeks had gone by since I spoke to A-bian about our diplomatic mission. I received a call from my overseas bank confirming that a total of $1,918,000 was wired in from a Singaporean account titled Awento Limited. Since the amount wasn't exactly what we had discussed,

I phoned A-bian to inform him of the discrepancy. He confirmed the shortage and said to let it be for the time being.

I wanted to make sure our accounting was completely transparent, so I presented a simple, handwritten expense worksheet to him. He didn't even bother looking at it. "These funds are at your disposal. There's no need to report to me." I couldn't wait to get to work, but I felt it was important to keep good records. I insisted he sign off on the handwritten worksheet, which he did.

We both understood that this mission was extremely sensitive in nature, and we agreed that what we discussed and our activities would remain private, not for public knowledge. Our contacts in the US also wished to be discreet. It was well known that China had an extensive network of covert operatives in Taiwan and the US. If word leaked of our objectives, the number of obstacles that would be thrown our way could be insurmountable. We had to be as vigilant and careful as possible. Now that the funds were in place, I was ready to get to work.

But my euphoria didn't last long. Little did I know then that my excitement would soon give way to a nightmare that would entangle me in litigation for three years. The salacious stories claiming that the first lady filed fraudulent expense receipts for reimbursement for so-called state affairs, totaling more than $600,000, came to light around the same time I was to begin my diplomatic mission. The funds I received had come from an overseas account, so the scrutiny on Wu Shu-chen should have had absolutely nothing to do with my diplomatic work with A-bian. But once the press and the pan-Blue coalition smelled blood, facts and common sense no longer mattered. The scandal became a tsunami, and anybody having anything to do with the first family and money would be caught up in it, including me.

A-bian Voluntarily Tipped Off the Media

After A-bian left office in May 2008, he was immediately targeted in many investigations. In October 2008, he was subpoenaed as a witness in a case involving former Bureau of Investigation Director-General Yeh

Sheng-mao for leaking confidential information. During the trial, the judge asked A-bian about a particular account of his in Singapore. He answered: "I'm planning to promote unofficial diplomacy work, and those funds have been handed over to a stalwart in the pan-Green camp who is a veteran in international diplomacy affairs. I have the utmost trust in him." He told the reporters the same thing on leaving the courthouse.

That statement sent the media outlets into a guessing frenzy on the identity of the president's confidant. Reporters hunted down Dr. Peng and Dr. Chai Trong-rong, but they both denied any involvement. By process of elimination, anybody with half a brain would eventually figure out the identity of the "stalwart." When my phone started to ring off the hook, I knew our secret was out, but I didn't take any calls at first. I needed time to plan my response. Once A-bian let the cat out of the bag, there was no way we would be able to move forward with our mission. I felt it would be better to control the narrative instead of letting rumor and speculation dominate the news, so I agreed to an interview with Ching-wen Tsou, a veteran reporter of the *Liberty Times*, on October 10, 2008. I provided a thorough account of what happened, leaving no stone unturned. When the interview was released, it only took a couple of days for Taiwan's Supreme Prosecutors Office, Special Investigation Division (SID), to come knocking at my door. I was summoned by the SID team as a witness to testify that Chen Shui-bian had indeed remitted more than $1.91 million to my overseas accounts.

Chapter Forty-Seven

FROM WITNESS STAND TO DEFENDANT'S TABLE

That visit by the SID marked the beginning of my three-year battle with Taiwan's legal and political system. My case was one of many whereby any link, direct or indirect, to President Chen would be pursued regardless of merit. Throughout A-bian's presidency, the KMT used every means possible to delegitimize him and his agenda. A-bian's successor, President Ma Ying-jeou—along with the rest of the KMT—seemed intent on continuing this persecution. The day after A-bian left office, no longer shielded by executive privilege, he was arrested for corruption and abuse of power. To see our president named as a defendant in a criminal investigation was difficult for all who had supported him over the years. I chose to reserve judgment until the facts came forth. At that time, I wanted to believe Taiwan's legal system would provide a fair and thorough investigation. But the country was about to embark on a journey that would test the very fabric of our young democracy, and I was given an unwelcome front-row seat to the circus.

Stepping into the KMT's Trap

The turning point came when I was called as a witness on November 15, 2008, in the case of Yeh Sheng-mao. I had no link to Yeh whatsoever and didn't understand why I was being called to testify. It soon became clear that this subpoena was just a ruse by the prosecution to put me on the stand to talk about A-bian. The judge on this case, Lee Ying-hao, began the questioning by asking if I knew Yeh. When I said no, he immediately pivoted and began asking about A-bian's money transfers to my overseas account. His tone indicated to me that he believed I was guilty of some kind of wrongdoing. Lee continued to pepper me with questions that had nothing to do with the Yeh case.

On December 4, 2008, when Judge Lee ruled Yeh Sheng-mao guilty, he also accused me of money laundering. His reasoning was utterly absurd. Lee indicated that since I was a personal friend of A-bian's and a banker, it would naturally follow that I would launder money for the former president. The logic was so twisted, and I couldn't believe this was considered legitimate due process.

A few days after the Yeh trial, the SID requested that I wire the diplomatic funds from my account to an SID account at Bank of Taiwan. I didn't believe the Taiwan government had any right to those funds, but at this point I was willing to find a compromise. I suggested instead that I transfer the funds to another account in my name held at a Taiwan bank. This way, the SID could monitor the account's activity. The disposition of the funds would be decided after the legal proceedings were completed. They agreed to my proposal. As soon as I wired the money to the Taiwan account, the SID froze the account. This interaction was an indication of the kind of scrutiny I would be under for the foreseeable future.

Support from Friends

Being accused of money laundering by the Taiwan authorities was unimaginable. I was fortunate and grateful for so many of my friends around the world to come to my defense. On December 11, 2008, over seventy expat organizations in the US and Canada, along with many of my closest friends, bought a large ad in the *Liberty Times* vouching for my character and innocence. My former colleagues at General Bank also wrote a public statement detailing my integrity and rectitude. Dr.

Peng wrote a letter to the SID, corroborating that I had informed him of these funds and their purpose. My good friend Frank Murkowski also wrote to the SID expressing his willingness to travel to Taiwan to be my character witness. I'll never forget the kindness and support from my friends during one of the most challenging times in my life. It was comforting to know that so many good people were in my corner.

Testifying As a Witness at A-bian's Trials

Over the next few months, I was called as a witness in A-bian's corruption case, along with other members of his administration. In most instances, I had nothing to contribute, and in some, I hadn't even met the defendants. But the topic would inevitably revert to the diplomatic funds. I thought as long as I was consistent and truthful in my testimony, I would be fine.

When I was questioned as a witness for A-bian's corruption case, Tsai Shou-shun, the presiding judge, focused again on the $2 million diplomacy fund. His questions went on like a broken record for two hours. It was obvious his only strategy was to continue to ask the same questions over and over again in the hopes that I would stumble. This was never going to happen, because I had truth on my side. I did my best to state the facts clearly and objectively.

On September 11, 2009, Chen Shui-bian was found guilty of money laundering, forgery, embezzlement, taking bribes, and other charges and sentenced to life in prison. In the verdict, Judge Tsai also accused me of money laundering. He had the same passage that Judge Lee's statement had verbatim: "Chen Shui-bian falsely claimed to Wu Li-pei that there was an overseas donation, and Wu Li-pei was knowingly aware that the money came from government funds."

Their claim was completely illogical. If Chen Shui-bian had "falsely claimed" this, then how could I have been "knowingly aware"? These so-called officers of the court had clearly made up their minds from the get-go to frame me, and nothing I said in my testimony had made a difference.

Nightmare

From the moment the SID first contacted me, it was clear the prosecutors involved in A-bian's case had predetermined his guilt and were going after anyone associated with him. I would soon have a bull's-eye on me. I had entered a new phase in my dealings with the Taiwanese legal system. As a witness, I had testified truthfully and consistently, yet I was painted as being complicit in illegalities by the same two judges that presided over the cases. On November 30, 2009, the Taipei District Court that had tried Yeh Sheng-mao's case identified me as an accomplice in A-bian's money laundering and transferred my case to the prosecution office. I was then listed as a defendant and formally charged with money laundering. My nightmare was about to take a turn for the worse.

Prosecutorial Abuse

I asked the prosecutors to show me one shred of evidence to corroborate the charges against me. Their response was stunning. "We don't have any evidence. But certain judges want you to be a defendant, so that's what we are doing." How could civil servants with no moral compass or competence be appointed prosecutors of the SID, widely considered the elite members of the legal profession?

My disdain and outrage poured out. "So you can prosecute and indict people at will without any evidence. What will happen if Judges Tsai and Lee are assigned to preside over my case? There will be no need for a trial. Just move on to the execution!" The SID's silence spoke volumes. They were simply following what Lee and Tsai had claimed in their reports, with no regard for evidence or the lack thereof. The SID was not even pretending to put forth a modicum of integrity or professionalism.

My Star Witnesses

How does one fight against an entire legal system where the rules are made up by those in power? I vowed to fight this injustice with my last breath, but I needed a clear legal strategy. I knew I had the truth on my side, and the SID had essentially admitted they had no evidence. I was supposed to be innocent until proven guilty, but I realized with mounting fury that I was now assumed guilty until proven innocent.

I knew I needed a more proactive strategy, so I asked three witnesses to testify on my behalf. They verified my previous statements and also attested to my character. Two of the witnesses resided in California, Julie Lee (Chang Chu-hui) and Wendell K. Hu. Julie was very active in the Taiwanese American community and always extremely helpful on whatever projects I happened to be working on. Wendell was an attorney who had been my go-to for any kind of legal advice. Julie's testimony corroborated our preliminary work on the diplomatic project. The last person on my witness list was Dr. Peng.

Wendell and Julie traveled to Taiwan from California to appear in Taipei District Court on May 17, 2010. Julie Lee testified that I had asked her to be my point of contact in charge of all the necessary arrangements in the US. She confirmed that I met with American politicians and produced meeting minutes accordingly. She also verified that I met with approximately one hundred Taiwanese expats in the US and had mentioned that I had the funds on hand for this diplomacy work but I did not say anything about A-bian.

Wendell confirmed that I spoke with him after A-bian pledged the $2 million because I wanted his legal opinion to make sure the funds were handled appropriately. I was no longer a US citizen, so I needed to be discreet on this diplomatic mission. There was no way I was going to break the law. Wendell testified that we had memos for everything we discussed to confirm that I was going to use the funds for legal, yet informal, diplomacy missions. Wendell also confirmed that he did not know the funds came from A-bian.

My final witness was Dr. Peng. Having a witness of his stature and credibility was invaluable. He testified that I approached him immediately after A-bian and I first met and that we had spoken about the project and how best to deploy the funds. A-bian was not brought up in our discussions at all. This contemporaneous corroboration was a powerful piece of evidence, further showing that the purpose of the funds was exactly as I had originally explained.

After the testimony from my star witnesses, the judge turned to the prosecutor and asked if he had any follow-up questions. He merely shook his head.

The Verdict

As I stood ready to deliver my closing statement, I found myself face to face with the prosecutor who turned my life upside down. Rage boiled in me, and I put my written statement aside. Pulling up my courage, I said, "You have provided absolutely no proof to support the charges brought against me, yet you abused your power to prosecute me. You've wasted valuable public service resources, and most importantly, you trampled on my liberties and those of the people of Taiwan, who expect a fair and unprejudiced legal process. You've put me, a man close to eighty years old, and my family through years of living hell." The anger nearly overwhelmed me, but I fought back the tears and gritted my teeth. I turned toward His Honor to present my closing statement, rebutting the SID's charges and outlining the reasons that substantiated my innocence.

The presiding judge eventually found me not guilty on November 5, 2010. He refuted the prosecutors' charges against me one by one, calling them groundless and biased, with no proof to support their accusations. I was ecstatic, but it could not erase the ordeal I had gone through for something I should never have been charged with in the first place. The verdict did bring a tremendous amount of relief for me and my family. Our relief was short-lived, however, as the SID indicated they had not exhausted their options.

Seeing A-bian Again

The pan-Blue persecution and witch hunt of A-bian took a toll on his health, to the point where he needed to be hospitalized at Taipei Veterans General. When he was finally permitted to see guests, I asked Mark

Chen, a DPP legislator, to take me to see him. We met in a small lounge by the ward. A-bian's hands trembled, and he stammered badly. I briefed him on the status of the funds, which were still frozen by the SID and probably would be for a while. A-bian, still mentally alert, told me the funds were mine to use the way I saw fit, whenever they were released. Seeing him like that, thinking about all he had gone through in the last few years and hearing him confirm that he continued to trust me, left me profoundly sad.

He also apologized for dragging me into this mess. He would later write a book during his incarceration called *Crucified for Taiwan*. He spent one and a half pages apologizing to me and my family for pulling me into the maelstrom surrounding him. He had not known when he gave me the money for the diplomacy mission that I would be implicated and harassed for over three years.

Because of ongoing health issues, A-bian was granted medical parole in late 2014 and finally reunited with his family. In March 2020, he and his son came to my home for lunch, where he again apologized. I believe he suffered unimaginable mistreatment for this alleged money laundering litigation. I don't begrudge him at all, and I will never believe the pan-Blue coalition's malicious portrayal of him. It was difficult seeing A-bian in poor health. I look upon him now with some regret on what his presidency could have been, but even after everything we've been through, he still has my utmost respect because I know his heart was and always will be for Taiwan.

Chapter Forty-Eight

DEFENDING MY REPUTATION

My friends and family rejoiced at the not guilty verdict, yet the prosecutors moved forward with an appeal without submitting any new evidence. Perhaps I shouldn't have been surprised. Throughout this process, they showed absolutely no regard for the rule of law or due process. I had won the first skirmish, but the war wasn't over yet. The next battle would take place at Taiwan High Court.

Found Not Guilty Again

The High Court trial played out very much the same way as the previous one. As I made my closing statement, I once again found myself facing my enemy, and I couldn't help but address these "public servants" directly. They'd gone after me with no evidence and wasted taxpayers' money. They had failed to find me guilty before, and I told them that they wouldn't find me guilty now, or ever. My words went unheeded as my persecutors just glowered at me, unmoved and indifferent.

The judge of the High Court made his ruling fairly quickly. The decision was rendered on October 13, 2011, more than three years after I first spoke with A-bian about the diplomatic mission. The verdict was not guilty. The SID, as expected, found this decision unacceptable. But there would be no third trial. A recently enacted law, the Criminal

Speedy Trial Act, limited appeals to very specific circumstances, none of which applied in my case. In other words, my not guilty verdict was final. The roller-coaster ride I had endured for over three years was finally over. Although I came out victorious, the price was high. The years of persecution almost jeopardized the reputation that I had built over the span of my lifetime.

More Humiliation

Throughout my trials, I believe the SID intentionally leaked details to the news outlets in order to sensationalize the story. The media was more than willing to make up preposterous stories about me. The KMT spread rumors that I had managed and stashed the former first family's assets all over the world. There were claims on talk shows that the reason for the months of inactivity in the diplomatic account was because I was scouting for ideal spots to conceal the money. People bad-mouthed me on TV, wondering why a highly respected banker with a stellar career would stoop to thievery. Another declared that I was a white-collar criminal who broke financial laws in the US and was banished by the American government. There were those who wanted to convince the US to imprison me for life.

Fighting Back

Vindication by the High Court was satisfying, but my anger toward those who used Taiwan's legal system to malign me would not subside. I consulted my attorneys on whether I could sue these dishonorable prosecutors and judges for abusing their judicial authority. I wanted to file a civil suit and force the other side to pay for my attorneys' fees and litigation costs. Both my attorneys shook their heads and indicated that the odds were against me. One of my attorneys warned me that the civil court would likely refuse to hear the case. I told him it wasn't about money—my main goal was to finally confront these people and make them the accused for once. Even though I was almost eighty years old, I was determined to give it my all.

On March 19, 2013, accompanied by my attorneys, I filed lawsuits against the two judges, Tsai Shou-hsun and Lee Ying-hao, for false accusations and two SID prosecutors, Chen Yun-nan and Tsai Tsun-his, for prosecutorial abuse. The next day, I held a press conference where I publicly denounced the widespread depravity in Taiwan's judicial system.

I wish my lawsuit and tactics had borne fruit. I wish I could report that I was able to single-handedly rehabilitate Taiwan's legal system. I wish I'd had the chance to make my accusers suffer as I was forced to suffer for three years. I'd been found not guilty, but I never got what I really sought—true justice. My civil suit went nowhere because the judges and prosecutors never made an appearance. When they subpoenaed me, they had all the leverage in the world to force my appearance. But I had no such leverage. I couldn't fight my accusers, and I couldn't fight those in the media who had tainted my good name.

But then I realized the enemy was not necessarily a name or a face but the circumstances that allowed this atrocity to happen in the first place. This experience proved to me that when we let the immoral corrupt our system of justice, we let the invisible enemy win. Even though I had to endure this nightmare, I will always stand for what is right against that invisible enemy.

PART VI

THE PRESIDENT TSAI I KNOW

Chapter Forty-Nine

MY RELATIONSHIP WITH THREE PRESIDENTS OF TAIWAN

It has truly been an honor to have had the opportunity to work with three of the first four directly elected presidents of Taiwan: Lee Teng-Hui, Chen Shui-bian, and Tsai Ing-wen. Who would have thought a poor country boy from a small village would grow up to one day help fight for democracy and independence for Taiwan?

President Lee was the first Taiwanese president to be born in Taiwan. He was also the last to be indirectly elected and the first to be directly elected. While I never served President Lee in an official capacity, we shared the same values and vision for Taiwan's future. I couldn't bring myself to vote for him since he was affiliated with the KMT. But I was hopeful when he was elected in 1996 because it was the first time the Taiwanese people chose their own president. I saw firsthand President Lee's love of Taiwan and his vision for a brighter future. I am proud to have known Lee, whom many call Taiwan's "Father of Democracy," and cherish the memories we shared.

Although A-bian's time as president didn't yield the results that we were all so hopeful for when he was elected, he will always be remembered as the first non-KMT president, breaking the KMT's fifty-five-year rule of Taiwan. And while my time as senior advisor didn't pan out like I had hoped, I was still honored to serve alongside him in our mutual pursuit of an independent Taiwan. Most recently, I served as senior advisor to Tsai Ing-wen, the first female president of Taiwan.

Chapter Fifty

RISE OF PRESIDENT TSAI ING-WEN

Tsai Ing-wen, who was minister of the Mainland Affairs Council at the time, was scheduled to visit Washington, D.C. in the latter half of 2001. Her itinerary included a two-day stopover in Los Angeles. During her Los Angeles visit, she hoped to make a public speech and meet a few American friends. I was a member of the Pacific Council on International Policy at that time, so I arranged for Tsai to be the keynote speaker on "China–Taiwan Relations" for the September conference at City Hall.

A couple of days before the conference, I was at my son's home in the San Francisco Bay Area. My plan was to fly back to Los Angeles on the day of the conference. When I awoke on September 11 and turned on the news, I—like the rest of world—watched in horror as the devastation of the 9/11 attacks unfolded. At first, I thought I was watching special effects from a movie. But when it became clear that this was real, the thought that random acts of terrorism could afflict the most powerful country on the planet was horrifying.

I broke away from the television to make calls about the status of the conference for Tsai Ing-wen. When I couldn't reach anybody, I began to worry. My imagination ran wild, especially with the terrible images of New York and Washington, D.C., flashing across the TV. I needed to get back to Los Angeles as quickly as possible. All flights had been canceled, so my only option was to have my son drive me home.

Throughout the six-hour ride, I tried to contact anybody I could by phone, but to no avail. I called Tsai at her hotel, the Biltmore, but there was no connection. It wasn't until the skyline of downtown Los Angeles appeared on the horizon that I was able to speak with one of the organizers of the conference. All events had been canceled until further notice. I tried the Biltmore one more time and was finally able to speak with Tsai directly. With the conference canceled, she was free that evening, so we had dinner together. Our conversation was dominated by the events of the day. During that dinner, she struck me as someone very intelligent and shrewd, always knowing the right thing to say.

My New Sister

As Tsai's prominence in Taiwanese politics grew, I saw her from time to time. She was always willing to help whatever cause or project I was involved with. Each time I saw her, she was very polite and respectful and treated me like an elderly relative. More often than not, we would share a meal together, and I'd always order steak. She joked with my wife, Jenny, not to let me eat too much red meat. She also always found a way to pay the bill before I had a chance to reach for my wallet.

In 2004 I led a group of Taiwanese expats belonging to the North America Friends of A-bian to attend a campaign rally for A-bian's reelection race. During the rally, my nephew, Joseph Wu—currently the minister of foreign affairs in Tsai's administration—and I hung out in the backstage area of the Taipei Municipal Chungshan Baseball Field. Chen Chu, who would later become the mayor of Kaohsiung, was onstage rallying the crowd in her distinctive deep, throaty voice. Tsai appeared out of nowhere, put her hand on my shoulder, and said, "Can I be your sister?"

Startled, I turned to look at her and paused for moment. "Sister? I'm old enough to be your father!"

She turned to my nephew with a deadpan look. "Call me aunt!" I chuckled in amusement at Tsai's quirky sense of humor. I genuinely enjoyed her company.

Tsai's Rising Star

In 2008 Frank Hsieh, the DPP presidential candidate, lost to the KMT's Ma Ying-Jeou in a rout. Morale in the DPP was very low, and Tsai stepped up to the challenge and became the chairperson for the party. She rallied the party and got the DPP up and running again. Four years later, she became the DPP candidate for the 2012 presidential election, where she faced the incumbent, President Ma. She ultimately lost this election, but she demonstrated that she was a political force in Taiwanese politics. Tsai got a second chance in 2016. This time, all the momentum favored the DPP. President Ma was ending his second and final term with approval ratings approaching single digits. The pan-Blue camp's election strategy was in disarray. James Soong of the People First Party and Eric Chu of the KMT split the pan-Blue vote again, just like in 2000 when Soong ran as an independent.

On January 16, 2016, Taiwan elected its first female president. President-elect Tsai won over 56 percent of the popular vote. The DPP also captured an outright majority in the Legislative Yuan for the first time in Taiwan's history, winning 68 of 113 seats. With the DPP's victories, the new administration was in a position to aggressively pursue its economic and cross-Strait goals. I was so excited for President Tsai and the people of Taiwan. I couldn't wait to see her in action.

Chapter Fifty-One

SENIOR ADVISOR TO PRESIDENT TSAI

When President Tsai was elected in 2016, she invited me to be her senior advisor. I emphasized that I didn't want to be an advisor in name only; rather, I wanted my counsel to be heard and taken seriously. President Tsai promised that this would happen. Just like with A-bian, she was always polite, gracious, and ready to hear my suggestions. And just like with A-bian, I was hopeful I was finally in a position to help Taiwan in a meaningful way.

Critical Issues for the Future of Taiwan

Soon after my advisor appointment, I gave the president my thoughts for what I hoped to see happen during her presidency. First, I felt it was imperative that she use the name "Taiwan" when referring to our country so that the international community knew we were not the Republic of China. Taiwan needed to establish its own identity without the obsolete legacy of the ROC. We needed to educate the people on cultural identity and then persuade the international community to respect our choice. The fact that Taiwanese people could not choose our own name and didn't have the right to call ourselves whatever we wanted was ridiculous. I felt it was important that the leader of our country set this example. It might take years, but we needed our president to lead the way to our goal.

Second, we needed to end the systematic corruption in the government. In China, for thousands of years, every government project resulted in kickbacks at multiple levels. It became an accepted way of life. The KMT brought this horrible practice to Taiwan after WWII, and it continues to this day within the Taiwanese government. Taiwan wastes billions of US dollars in corrupt activity, and I wanted to figure out a way to end it. We needed to establish a new culture so that Taiwan could become a more advanced democracy. I suggested in detail how to establish reforms to stop the corruption from happening. Tsai agreed to everything I said, and while I understood that it would take years to implement the plan, I was disappointed because, as far as I know, Tsai didn't start the process on my suggestions.

Third, there have always been too many people in government and state-run enterprises who aren't productive. This inefficiency puts a strain on Taiwan's economy. We needed to streamline and restructure the workforce to run these entities more efficiently, similar to what I had done in my banking career. But I understood that in government, it's difficult to force the issue because no one wants to be the bad guy. Which is why I suggested President Tsai hire an internationally known consulting firm to help us figure out how we could improve. Recommendations from an outside consultant would make it easier for the government to make the necessary changes. Again, I did not see any actions taken as a result of my suggestion.

And fourth, since Taiwan doesn't have abundant natural resources such as oil or natural gas, we have to rely on other countries. It was critical for Taiwan to identify the countries with which it had long-term, friendly relationships that were also essential to its productivity. I suggested to President Tsai that Taiwan should collaborate with specific US states that were rich in natural resources, such as Alaska. I felt it was important to choose a nation with plenty of resources to form joint ventures so we could explore how to share these resources. This way, in the contract, we could state that Taiwan would have the first right of refusal for whatever natural resource we procured for our use. If there were any resources left over, we could then sell them to other countries. It is vital for Taiwan's security that we have a stable source of energy, particularly oil or natural gas. Tsai said she would talk to the economic ministry to get this going, but again, nothing happened.

In my opinion, these four points were critical to Taiwan's future. I know I was just one of her senior advisors and that she didn't have to agree with my point of view. But just like with A-bian, I felt my suggestions weren't being taken seriously. Once again, I found myself in a situation where I wasn't contributing anything as senior advisor. I submitted a letter of resignation in April 2017, six months after my appointment, but President Tsai refused to accept it.

My Fears for Taiwan

In 2018, only two years after President Tsai's overwhelming victory, the DPP was trounced in the local midterm elections. The KMT won thirteen jurisdictions, while the DPP only won six. Cities like Kaohsiung, which were DPP strongholds, shockingly voted for the KMT. One only needed to look at President Tsai's approval ratings leading up to the election to see that the people were extremely dissatisfied with her administration. Whether they disapproved of her handling of internal issues or her ambiguous policy toward China, the public clearly wanted change. I was in tears when I saw the results of the midterm election. President Tsai's approval ratings were in the teens, so low I didn't believe she had any hope of being reelected in 2020. There was no doubt in my mind that a pro-China KMT president would have no qualms dismantling all the democratic progress that Taiwan had achieved in the prior two decades.

I spoke to Dr. Peng about this, and he was in agreement with me. We came to the difficult conclusion that given President Tsai's untenable approval ratings, her chances for reelection were virtually zero. Something had to be done. We needed to convince her to forgo seeking reelection. We did not come to this decision lightly. We knew how difficult it would be for her to step aside in this way. Our concerns were never personal or an indictment on President Tsai; rather, we were solely worried about Taiwan's future. We had spent our lives advocating for democracy in Taiwan. We couldn't stand by and see that democracy threatened.

Obviously, the president would not acquiesce without some kind of pressure. Our first step was to draft an open letter expressly requesting the president not run for reelection. This was a draft only, not to be used unless absolutely necessary. Our hope was that through private conversations, we would be able to convince President Tsai that stepping aside after her current term was best for the DPP and Taiwan. After we completed the draft letter, we sought to add signatories who would bring more attention and significance to the document. We looked for like-minded people who met the following criteria: those known for their dedication to a democratic and independent Taiwan, with impeccable reputations, who were well respected by the people of Taiwan; those with no political affiliations and not currently DPP members, so there would be no real or perceived threat to President Tsai; and those old enough to have no long-term personal or political aspirations.

One of the people who immediately came to mind was Lee Yuan-tseh, a lifelong advocate and supporter of Taiwan. Dr. Lee, a chemist, became world renowned in 1986 as the first Taiwanese to win a Nobel Prize. Since he was not a professional politician, his endorsement to this mission would carry much weight. We asked a good friend of ours, Mr. Lu Shi-shiang, who was a consultant to the *Liberty Times*, to contact Dr. Lee for us and give him a draft of the letter. Dr. Lee signed the letter as soon as he read it, before he even spoke to us.

We then approached Kao Chun-ming, a minister of the Presbyterian Church in Taiwan. He was also very well respected and widely recognized as having devoted his life to the freedom and democracy of Taiwan. Kao was quite ill at the time, but he also signed the draft letter, even though we did not meet with him in person.

Once we had the letter and signatories in place, I met with President Tsai at her official residence near the end of 2018. I asked her to announce publicly that she would not seek reelection in 2020. It was a difficult conversation, but I did my best to assure her that my intentions were not personal. I and many others wanted only what was best for Taiwan's future. She still had more than one year as president, and I advised her to use that time to strengthen Taiwan against the ever-present threat of China. Also, given the results of the recent elections, if she demonstrated that she was willing to sacrifice her own political gains for the betterment of Taiwan, she would be looked upon as the savior of the DPP. Despite all my efforts, she resisted any notion of not participating in the 2020 election. She even went as far as saying she would run even if the DPP didn't back her.

Dr. Peng, Dr. Lee, and I met in person to discuss my meeting with the president. When I informed them of the president's response, Dr. Lee let us know that he'd had the exact same conversation with President Tsai and had also been unsuccessful.

The Open Letter

We decided to publish the letter in the *Liberty Times*, publicly imploring her not to seek reelection. We gave the letter to Mr. Lu and requested that it be published in the December 31, 2018, edition of the paper. We bought a half-page space to make sure it would be displayed prominently.

When the paper came out, our letter was nowhere to be seen. Unknown to us, the letter was somehow leaked to the Presidential Office and was not published until January 3, 2019. Those extra few days may have saved Tsai's presidency. In a stroke of fate, on January 2, 2019, the day before the *Liberty Times* ran our letter, the leader of China, Xi Jinping, delivered a New Year speech in which he said that Taiwan belonged to China, that there was no such thing as Taiwan. This stirred an outcry among the Taiwanese people, and President Tsai immediately jumped on the opportunity. She changed her tone against China. She announced unequivocally that she would stand up against China at all costs. Her declaration was just what was needed to swing confidence in her direction, so much so that her supporters nicknamed her "La Tai

Mei," basically saying she was on fire. Her assertiveness and vigor in her defense of Taiwan seemed to be just what the people needed at a time when public morale was so low. The momentum behind her grew, and her popularity rose again, all because of the well-timed speech of the Chinese president.

The timing of the publication of our open letter vis-à-vis President Tsai's newfound popularity was awkward, to say the least. While there were some who praised our courage in speaking our concerns, the backlash the four of us faced was intense. Many, including the media and political talk show hosts, scolded us for going up against her. Even though we'd planned to publish the letter days before any of this happened, it appeared that we were intentionally trying to create dissent during a time when many were rallying to President Tsai. I was the designated spokesperson, so I received most of the criticism. Given our age, many of our critics called us old and out of touch. I wasn't bothered by the negative reactions, because our reasoning for the letter was honorable. We only wanted to see a path that was best for Taiwan.

When we published the letter, we never endorsed or even mentioned any other candidate for president. It was not our intent to push President Tsai out with someone else waiting in the wings. We simply asked her not to run again so that the DPP could then find the best candidate for the 2020 presidential election.

Situation in Hong Kong

In early 2019 the dissatisfaction of the people of Hong Kong toward the Chinese government reached a tipping point. The principles of One Country, Two Systems were put to the test when China's authoritarian government unilaterally enacted laws which curtailed the fundamental rights of the citizens of Hong Kong. In February 2019, the Hong Kong city government proposed amendments to laws that would allow extradition to China. Many believed this proposal was yet another critical step perpetrated by China to weaken Hong Kong's democratic principles. Hundreds of thousands took to the streets in what was the largest demonstration in Hong Kong history in protest of these amendments. The protests lasted months and occurred in the middle of Taiwan's DPP primary and well into the campaign for the general election.

President Tsai publicly announced her strong support for Hong Kong and used the nightly images of protestors battling armed police as a backdrop to her campaign. She regularly invoked Hong Kong as a cautionary tale of Beijing's ambitions to tighten its grip on Taiwan. The slogan "Hong Kong today, Taiwan tomorrow" regularly appeared at her campaign rallies. This campaign strategy was very effective in galvanizing Taiwanese toward one common goal, pushing against closer ties with China.

Ex-Premier William Lai

The primary to select the 2020 DPP presidential candidate was to take place in April 2019. One highly regarded DPP politician, Lai Ching-te (William), announced his candidacy in March 2019. Lai was extremely popular and well regarded in Taiwan. He was twice elected mayor of Tainan, one of the largest cities in southern Taiwan, the second time by an overwhelming majority of the vote. He also served as premier during President Tsai's first term.

I had met William Lai from time to time in the previous few years, but I didn't know him particularly well. In early 2019 a friend from Tainan, Maysing Yang, ambassador-at-large, arranged a get-together between Lai, Dr. Peng, and me. The more I got to know Lai, the more I liked what I saw. His integrity was beyond reproach. His love of Taiwan was inspiring. I didn't know at the time if he had presidential aspirations, but I knew he was the type of leader that cared more about Taiwan than political ambition. When he called me out of the blue in March 2019 to say that he was on his way to register for the DPP presidential primary, I was elated. Throwing his hat in the ring and running for president against a fellow DPP incumbent was courageous. His popularity, experience, and reputation instantly made him a viable candidate to defeat President Tsai.

I and the other senior advocates discussed Lai's candidacy and decided we would lend our support to him.

Presidential Election

William Lai's bid to become the DPP presidential candidate failed. He lost the primary to President Tsai in June 2019. The primary election, originally scheduled to take place in April, was delayed multiple times by the DPP. Clearly, the party leadership sensed that President Tsai needed more time to shore up support and altered the rules to her advantage. The additional two months were critical because the constant drumbeat of news from Hong Kong added to President Tsai's momentum. The delays did not sit well with me. It seemed unfair and undemocratic for the rules to be changed in the middle of the primary. I had no qualms about making my feelings known. Newspapers quoted me saying: "Changing the rules during a game is a way of cheating. If President Tsai wants to be president forever, she should just declare martial law!"

Once President Tsai won the DPP nomination, attention turned to the general election, where she would face the KMT candidate, Han Kuo-yu. Han had made a splash in Taiwan politics by being elected mayor of Kaohsiung in 2018, a position that was held by the DPP for twenty years. A few short months after being elected, he declared his candidacy for president, which earned him the nickname "running away mayor." As a presidential candidate, his main platform was to restore closer relations with China, not knowing then that the situation in Hong Kong and the growing distrust of China by the Taiwanese would be his undoing. In addition, media coverage of his campaign demonstrated to many his inexperience and inability to articulate important policy issues. This raised serious doubts about his qualifications to become leader of the country. With such an unworthy opponent, on January 11, 2020, the Taiwanese people exercised their democratic freedom and reelected President Tsai in a landslide victory.

Going Forward

Naturally, we were ecstatic that the KMT was soundly defeated. During the general election, I struggled on how I would vote. On one hand, there was Tsai, who didn't achieve much during her first term and changed the rules to her advantage during the primary. On the other, there was the KMT candidate, who was in so many ways much worse than Tsai, partly because he abandoned Kaohsiung for his own aspirations, but most importantly because he was willing to sell off Taiwan to China. Ultimately, I voted as I always do—for the security and well-being of Taiwan and its people. I was among the 57 percent who voted for Tsai.

There are those who still harbor ill will toward the four of us who signed the open letter. As I've said over and over, I believed it was the right thing to do at the time. The one thing the 2020 presidential election demonstrated was that the democracy which took root in 1996 with the first direct presidential election in Taiwan history is alive and well. The people voted for democracy, free will, and human rights. They voted against authoritarianism and corruption. I hope President Tsai can use these last years in office to lead Taiwan toward a truly free, democratic, and independent country, which is my lifelong dream.

Chapter Fifty-Two

RECENT YEARS

The years have flown by, and I am no longer the idealistic, passionate fighter I once was. I still feel as strongly about Taiwanese independence as I ever have, but I don't have the same physical and mental stamina. But as I approach my eighty-eighth year, it's important to think about what has been gained rather than what has been lost. I am proud of all that I have accomplished and look back on my life as one well spent. I am not one to dwell on events of the past, especially when I can't do anything to change them now. Regardless of past outcomes, I don't regret my efforts or intentions.

I am happy to have returned to Taiwan and expect to live the rest of my life here in my beautiful first home country. I am comfortable, and I spend most of my time at home now. Occasionally I travel to the US to see my sons, grandchildren, and old friends. I also visit Frank and Nancy Murkowski at their vacation home in Palm Springs once in a while. But other than that, I find comfort in staying home. Sometimes I have visitors: A-bian and others that I know from the pan-Green camp and Dr. Peng, who I reminisce with about our days fighting for independence.

I am proud of once being a Taiwanese American and hope my story will inspire other Taiwanese Americans to understand their roots better and learn about the country that I hold so dear to my heart. In writing this, I hope my descendants will never forget where we came from and what the Wu family has gone through to get to this point. It's a new chapter for our family, and I can't wait to see what they will accomplish as proud Taiwanese Americans.

Taiwanese American Citizens League - Annual banquet, mid 1990s

Dr. Peng Ming-min for President, 1996

Taiwan Center fundraiser, 1998

Chen Shui-bian for President, 1999

Vacationing with my old friend and mentor - Dr. Peng, 2000

Campaigning to A-bian's historic victory, 2000

The Dalai Lama and Richard Gere, 2000

The establishment of the Formosa Foundation, 2002

Accompanying President Chen (left) to Latin America, 2003

Frank Murkowski and President Chen, 2004

International Committee for Fair Elections. Me, Frank Murkowksi,
and Dr. Peng, 2012

My Taiwanese American family - Three generations, 2022
(back row left to right) Serena - granddaughter, Justin - grandson, Alice -
daughter-in-law, George, A-Jin - niece, Gene, Donna - daughter-in-law
(front row left to right) Jenny, me, Lucca - grandson

SPECIAL THANKS

This book is not a direct translation of the book I published in Taiwan in 2015; rather, it is a rewritten account of my life. I could not have published this English version without the help of some key people.

First, I'd like to thank my old friend, Dr. Peng Ming-Min. I often refer to him as the true father of democracy because he was one of the first pioneers of the movement. Without his 100-percent dedication to advocating for Taiwanese independence, I would not have been as consistently motivated as I was in our fight. What he has done for Taiwanese democracy is immeasurable and has proven him to be an ultimate leader of Taiwan. Dr. Peng recently passed away peacefully, at almost a hundred years of age. I will miss my dear friend very much.

Thank you also to my friend Frank Murkowski, former US senator and governor of Alaska. I was fortunate to have met him early in my banking career. His friendship, support, and trust in me have been invaluable in achieving my professional goals and dreams. I appreciate and am deeply grateful for his support of not only me but also my beloved Taiwan, which Frank has helped in so many ways.

A big thank you to all the people I have mentioned in this book who have helped me along the way and become my friends and supporters in every aspect of my life. Your friendship means everything.

Made in the USA
Columbia, SC
27 June 2022

62272829R00196